# Fundamentalist-Evangelicals
# and Anti-Semitism

# Fundamentalist-Evangelicals
# and Anti-Semitism

David A. Rausch

Trinity Press International        Valley Forge

First Edition 1993

Trinity Press International
P.O. Box 851
Valley Forge, PA 19482

© 1993 David A. Rausch

Cover Design: Brian Preuss

Library of Congress Cataloging-in-Publication Data

Rausch, David A.
    Fundamentalist-evangelicals and anti-semitism / David
A. Rausch.—1st ed.
        p. cm.
    Includes bibliographical references and index.
    ISBN 1-56338-049-8
    1. Christianity and antisemitism.   2. Fundamentalism.
3. Judaism—Relations—Evangelicalism.   4. Evangelicalism—
Relations—Judaism.   5. Evangelicalism—United States—
History.   6. Antisemitism—United States—History.   I. Title.
BM535.R325   1993
261.2'6—dc20                                         93-3923
                                                         CIP

Quotations throughout marked NIV are from The Holy Bible, New International Version, copyright © 1978 by New York International Bible Society

Permission granted by World Wide Pictures to reprint excerpts from the film His Land.

Printed in the United States of America
92  93  94  95  96  97      6  5  4  3  2  1

DEDICATED TO MY COLLEAGUES WHO FOSTER
UNDERSTANDING BETWEEN CHRISTIANS AND JEWS

JANICE M. BOVILLE

AND

P. JAKE JACOBS

# Contents

# PREFACE

*Fundamentalist-Evangelicals and Anti-Semitism* is written as a companion volume to my 1991 book, *Communities in Conflict: Evangelicals and Jews* (also published by TPI). *Fundamentlist-Evangelicals and Anti-Semitism* focuses and expands upon the prophecy-oriented branch of evangelicalism that for the last century has had a phenomenal effect on Christendom and is, perhaps, the most controversial evangelical movement in the eyes of both Christians and Jews.

Through a detailed analysis of the tradition and thought of the adherents of fundamentalist-evangelicalism, I have labored to ascertain their views on the Jewish people and their relationship to anti-Semitism. Portions of addresses, sermons, books and articles rarely seen in print are available here in context in an effort to more accurately portray a complex fundamentalist-evangelical movement. It is hoped that this will better delineate between the potential dangers and positive values of these controversial Christians.

I must thank the Sassoon International Center for the Study of Antisemitism (SICSA) for supporting my research. A special thanks to Dr. Yehuda Bauer of the Hebrew University of Jerusalem (and SICSA) for his foresight in realizing the importance of this project. Harold Rast, director of Trinity Press International, has worked diligently to make this research available to the public. Laura Barrett, administrator of Trinity Press International, provided crucial technical assistance. The faculty and staff of my liberal arts institution, Ashland University, not only gave me much encouragement, but also provided joyful comradeship on a daily basis. Among them are my friends in Andrews Hall.

My students bring me lasting fulfillment as well. This book, in fact, is dedicated to two of the best of my students, Janice M. Boville and P. Jake Jacobs, long since graduated. Now they teach students of their own and have become colleagues as well as friends. Through their conferences, lectures and teaching of the Holocaust and related courses, Janice and Jake act as lights piercing the darkness in the bleak history of Christian-Jewish relations. I am proud of them.

# INTRODUCTION

Fundamentalist-evangelicals have garnered a good deal of attention from the news media and in academic circles in the past two decades. As a strong movement within conservative Protestantism, their attitudes toward Jews, Judaism, and Israel have caused both consternation and admiration. From evangelist Billy Graham to Moral Majority leader Jerry Falwell, the fundamentalist-evangelical movement has proved to be complicated and elusive. When in 1985 eminent scholar Franklin H. Littell criticized the "provisional" friendship of these Christians during the Study Circle on Diaspora Jewry under the auspices of the president of Israel, he also clearly recognized that they were the "motors propelling a politics of Christian Zionism." "When it concerns Israel, I trust a head of the Moral Majority a lot more than I trust the president of the National Council of Churches," Dr. Littell stated during his response near the end of the session, adding, "although I sit on committees of National Council of Churches, and have for thirty years, and belong to a denomination [Methodist] which is its chief financial supporter. You have to pick your friends and enemies according to the issue at hand."[1]

Four and a half years later, in June of 1989, Rev. Jerry Falwell announced that the Moral Majority would officially close its doors on August 31, proclaiming that "our mission is accomplished." Meanwhile, seventy-year-old Rev. Billy Graham was televising recent evangelistic "crusades" even as he was gearing up for overseas evangelism. Graham vowed to continue "preaching the gospel" until his health gave out or Jesus Christ came back to "rapture the saints." Falwell vowed to continue to speak out on moral and political issues even as he returned to concentrate on his beloved Liberty University, "Old Fashioned Gospel Hour," and Thomas Road Baptist Church. Although he admitted that the political activity had taken a toll on his religious work, Falwell declared that the decade of Moral Majority activity had been "the agent to train, mobilize and electrify the Religious Right" and had produced a "terrific maturing process on the right, Jerry Falwell included."[2]

Indeed, political analysts insisted that Moral Majority's disappearance would make little difference in fundamentalist influence and that "the religious conservatives in America are now in for the duration." As if to underscore that point, the presidency and political structure of the 14.8-million-member Southern Baptist Convention was again captured by such conservatives two days after Jerry Falwell addressed them and announced his decision. The denomination's new president, Rev. Jerry Vines of First Baptist Church in Jacksonville, Florida, proclaimed that "Southern Baptists believe that the Bible is the incorruptible word of God," urging his fellow Baptists to put past controversies behind them and concentrate on "winning souls" to and "building churches" for Jesus Christ.[3]

In light of the resiliency of fundamentalist and evangelical Protestantism, this study seeks to trace the complicated history of the American fundamentalist-evangelical movement from its roots in nineteenth-century evangelicalism to its present status, focusing on its relationship to anti-Semitism and garnering its attitudes toward the Jewish people. The response of an equally diverse Jewish community and other Christians to fundamentalist-evangelical theology and attitudes will also be analyzed throughout. Since many of the materials used (sermons, treatises, periodicals, lectures) are not readily available to scholars and laypersons, I have endeavored to convey the context and message of the movement in the words of the adherents through generous use of quotations. It is hoped that this not only will lead to further scholarship through the provision of primary materials, but also will add to the clarity and fair portrayal of fundamentalist-evangelical thought and logic. The attempt has been made to focus such quotations clearly on the crux of the point being discussed, while at the same time portraying the personality and attitudes of those who wrote or spoke such words. The following sections of this Introduction will provide the definition and context of nineteenth-century evangelicalism and Jewish response to these religious practitioners. Chapter 1 previews the rise of the prophetic theology that undergirds fundamentalist-evangelicalism and analyzes the movement into World War I; while chapter 2 builds on this mass of material, piercing to the heart of attitudes and anti-Semitism. Chapter 3, "From War to War" deals with fundamentalist-evangelical attitudes from World War I through the Great Depression and into World War II; while chapter 4 analyzes fundamentalist-evangelical susceptibility to conspiracy theories and anti-Jewish thought during the Holocaust years. Chapter 5 studies the post–World War II era of Cold War and the formation of the new State of Israel. My conclusion, "Toward Understanding," seeks to draw clear deductions from the past in order to alert to dangers for the future and, perhaps, alter the incipient course toward anti-Semitism, prejudice, scapegoating, and stereotyping. My hope is that such a study will be the base of future discussion and understanding, a constructive tool for building bridges of mutual respect between Jews and Christians.

This book serves as a companion to my *Communities in Conflict: Evangelicals and Jews* (Philadelphia: Trinity Press International, 1991). In the introduction to the present volume, as well as in chapters 1, 2, and 5, I have occasionally drawn upon *Communities in Conflict* – either by excerpting specific paragraphs or by paraphrasing several paragraphs – in order to place the current discussion into its appropriate historical and social context.

## THE CENTURY OF EVANGELICALISM

The word "evangelical" is derived from the Greek noun *euange-lion*, originally meaning in the ancient world "a reward for good news." Later it was applied to "glad tidings" or "good news." In the Christian Bible it came to specifically refer to God's good news, the gospel (see Rom. 1:1; 1 Cor. 15:1). The word *euangelion* appears in nearly every book of the Christian Testament, almost one hundred times, and from the Latin *evangelium* passed into modern language.

While the term "evangelical" was used in the Roman Catholic Church in the medieval period, it came into prominence during the Protestant Reformation in the sixteenth century. The Protestant movement affirmed the concepts of individual conscience and freedom of religion,[4] grace and faith, the authority of the Bible, and the priesthood of all believers. Martin Luther and his followers were described as "evangelicals" because of their assertion of such principles during the Protestant Reformation, and soon the term "evangelical" was commonly applied to all German Protestants, Lutheran and Reformed. In England, the term "evangelical" came to be applied to the Anglican "Low Church" party in contrast to "High Church" sacramentalism.

The nineteenth century was the century of modern evangelicalism. Protestantism was permeated by revivalism, and its adherents sought to spread the message of the gospel to every corner of the earth. In England the small minority of evangelicals had grown remarkably in spite of the opposition from High Church clergy. Cambridge University became the training center for evangelical clergymen, and gradually British middle classes were drawn to the movement. Building on the foundation provided by the Methodist revivals of John Wesley and George Whitefield, evangelicalism was the most vital religious force in England by the nineteenth century. Distinguished evangelical Anglicans, such as Lord Shaftesbury and William E. Gladstone, were leading political figures, and English evangelicals achieved their most notable successes in philanthropic endeavors and social reform.

In the United States during the 1800s, the mainline Protestant churches (Episcopalians, Methodists, Presbyterians, and Baptists) called themselves "evangelicals." Like the British, their enthusiasm to "spread the gospel" and "win precious souls to Christ" was fervent and aggressive. Their goals went far beyond revamping society. Indeed, nineteenth-century American evangelicals intended to remake the world. Their home and foreign missionary societies flourished, and most of these evangelicals believed that the Protestant Christian church would bring in "the millennium," a thousand-year period of peace and prosperity. Through the auspices of Protestantism, they believed the world would be "Christianized," would become progressively better, and would facilitate the return of the resurrected Jesus Christ to earth to reign over the world. This theological view was known as postmillennialism, and it dominated the evangelical culture of nineteenth-century America.[5]

In 1846 the Evangelical Alliance was formed in London to provide a worldwide fellowship "on the basis of great evangelical principles" and to present a united front. While declaring that the summary of beliefs it espoused should not be "regarded in any formal or ecclesiastical sense as a creed or confession," the Evangelical Alliance advocated the divine inspiration of the Bible, the Trinity of Persons within a unified Godhead, the atoning work of Jesus Christ and the justification of the sinner by faith in him, and the judgment of the world by Jesus Christ ("with the eternal blessedness of the righteous, and the eternal punishment of the wicked").[6] One century later, this very same Evangelical Alliance would sponsor the evangelistic crusades in England led by Billy Graham, in 1954–55 and in 1966–67.

## JEWISH RESPONSE

The response of the Jewish community to the evangelicalism of the nineteenth century is quite evident in the life, writing, and contacts of Isaac Mayer Wise (1819–1900). Rabbi Wise became an important leader in American Judaism during the latter half of the nineteenth century. A native of Steingrub, Bohemia, and the son of a poverty-stricken teacher, Wise was dramatically affected by the free religious atmosphere in America after he emigrated in 1846. As rabbi of Congregation Beth El in Albany, New York, he introduced reforms such as mixed seating, a choir of men and women, elimination of Hebrew prayers that included reference to the messiah, and confirmation for Jewish young people. In 1850 the congregation split, and Wise and his supporters organized Albany's first Reform synagogue. In 1853 Rabbi Wise was hired at Cincinnati's B'nai Jeshurun, where he spent the rest of his life as leader of Reform Judaism. His goal in the beginning was to unite all American synagogues into one organization, and in 1873 he established the Union of American Hebrew Congregations, the first nationwide cooperative organization of Jewish congregations.

Rabbi Isaac Mayer Wise planned that the Union of American Hebrew Congregations would be an umbrella organization for all of American Judaism, and this kept the organization from radical changes during the first decade of its existence. The Union grew from an initial twenty-eight congregations which included some traditional synagogues to almost two hundred synagogues by 1880. To Wise's delight, Hebrew Union College was founded in 1875 in Cincinnati, Ohio, the first institution of Jewish higher learning still extant in America. For nearly half a century, Rabbi Wise edited and published *The American Israelite* (until July 3, 1874, it was called *The Israelite*). The early years of the periodical reflect the attitudes of American Jews of all persuasions toward American Protestants. *The American Israelite* is a potpourri of articles, excerpts and speeches that reflect Jewish perceptions and ideas of the later nineteenth century.

Throughout the issues of *The American Israelite*, the Jewish reader was informed about the differences among Christians, even among Protestants. On October 24, 1873, under "New York News," a correspondent for *The Israelite*, Phil Point, sought to contrast the sessions of the conservative Evangelical Alliance with the sessions of the liberal Free Religious Association. It was clearly evident that both Wise and the correspondent favored the latter over the evangelicals. The Jewish correspondent related:

These two conferences, though they both assembled in the name of religion, were as widely separated as the poles. The [evangelicals] came here for the purpose of advancing the interests of Protestantism, and this was to be best accomplished by finding effective means to check the growing influence of science, skepticism, and Roman Catholicism—those three terrors of the evangelical Christian. Theologians of undoubted ability and learning, came here to attend the meetings, from all parts of the world.[7]

"While the [Evangelical] Alliance was in session," the correspondent continued, "the halls and churches where the different branches met were always filled by people whose enthusiasm was of a fervid kind, and akin to fanaticism." In contrast, an "intellectual tone" prevailed in the audience of the Free Religious Association, "which listened to the speeches and debates with cool interest and critical attention." Rabbi Wise chose to publish the report of the *New York Tribune*, including some remarks and speeches, on the Free Religious Association sessions, while ignoring the content of the meetings of the Evangelical Alliance.

In November, Rabbi Isaac Mayer Wise applauded the "liberal sentiments in religion" propounded by "the eloquent and generous President of the Free Religious Association, Rev. O. B. Frothingham," agreeing that the religion of the future generations of America would not be "Christian." And yet, Rabbi Wise exhibited some religious triumphalism of his own when he chided president Frothingham for not being able to name the future religion of America. In his editorial, "What the Religion of America Will Be," Rabbi Wise insisted that there "will never be a religion without a God, and the God of Israel is the loftiest conception of which the human mind is capable." He concluded:

But the world has not outgrown its prejudices against the Jew and Judaism; therefore not even Mr. Frothingham, as liberal a gentleman as there is one in this country or elsewhere, can tell us what the religion of America will be, and must stop short in telling us what it will not be. Every thinker in this country knows that the belief in the Christian story, miracles, and dogmas, evaporates rapidly; that science, philosophy, reason, and humanity demolish the bulwark of traditional faith; every rational mind can see that monarchical Christianity can not live much longer in democratic America.

The unsophisticated and unprejudiced can see no less clear that the rational and humane elements of Christianity will survive the revolution; but these elements are part and parcel of rational Judaism. Therefore we know what the Religion of America will be.[8]

Later, elaborating the principles of freedom, human dignity, the striving for goodness and perfection, equal opportunity, and so on, central to the Jewish faith, Rabbi Isaac Mayer Wise underscored his major thesis to a friendly questioner: "Therefore we declared Judaism, in its pure and denationalized form, as the religion of future generations—the religion of all free men."[9]

In a century that was absorbed in the upward progress of humankind, many Jews agreed with Rabbi Wise when he declared in the pages of *The Israelite* that "Christianity, in any of its known forms, can not maintain itself beyond the current phase of civilization, which is absolutistic in State and Church." Wise asserted:

Therefore, the perpetual warfare of the Church against the onward march of progressive and irresistible liberty in all parts of the civilized world, by the Pope and his prelates on the one hand, by the established churches of England and Prussia on the other, and by the fragments thereof in our own country. Make this country Catholic, Episcopalian, Presbyterian, or Evangelical in any sense, and free government is at an end. This is generally admitted.[10]

Because the nineteenth century was the century of evangelicalism, the Jewish community was certainly at odds with the permeating influence of evangelicals on the structures of politics and education. The pages of *The American Israelite* in the 1870s abound with actions and court cases attempting to prohibit the use of the Bible in public schools. The imposition of religion on secular institutions was feared and constantly combated by the Jewish community.

During Passover in the March 27, 1874, issue, *The Israelite* editorialized that "the attempts in our country, in behalf of the cross, to undermine and upset liberty, are frequent and violent" and that "the repeated attempt to change the Constitution of the United States into an instrument of evangelical sectarianism" excludes all citizens "who love freedom above church discipline, and

prefer blunt honesty to oiled hypocrisy." Even the women's
suffrage movement within evangelicalism was suspect, because
"the strength of all sectarian establishments in this country is in
the female members," and women were "led easily by preachers, deacons, and fanatics . . . made the tools of priestly cun-
ningness and dissimulation." Underscoring that "the very idea
of worshiping a prince of the house of David [Jesus] is anti-demo-
cratic" and that "the very idea of being exclusively right is the
mother of fanaticism, and the belief that all not believing as we
do are damned, arms fanaticism with poisonous daggers," *The
Israelite* asserted that "the Church must oppose the progress of
freedom as it does the progress of science," and therefore the editor called for freedom from this "Pharaoh," concluding that "liberty is not safe yet in this country, and it will never be here or
anywhere else as long as the symbol of the cross stands above the
symbol of freedom."[11]

The readers of *The Israelite*, however, were at the same time
made painfully aware, as was editor Wise, of anti-Jewish rhetoric
that infested the most liberal bastions of Christendom. For example, on November 7, 1873, Rabbi Wise added an excerpt from *The
Index* under the heading "An Outrage on the Jews." A liberal Uni-
versalist minister of Dumferline, Scotland, the Rev. James U.
Mitchell, had preached a sermon in Boston on Sunday, October
16, that labeled the "cursed" in Matthew 25:41 (a parable that
Jesus told about the judgment of the nations) as referring to the
Jews. Rev. Mitchell exclaimed:

> The curse which was then pronounced on that stiff-necked nation
> had clung to them to this day; they were once the favored people
> of God, and now they are outcasts, for they abused the privileges
> granted to them, and "to whom much is given much shall be
> required." What matters it that they are rich in this world's goods?
> What matters that a stroke of a Rothschild's pen can let loose the
> war-horse, and plunge nations in a deluge of blood? The race is a
> down-trodden one, and the name Jew is a synonym for cringing
> meanness: the stigma of that curse will remain forever. It has stuck
> to them upward of eighteen hundred years, and will hang over
> them, like a pall, as long as the race exists; and this is the everlast-
> ing fire to which they have been condemned. They were promised

an eternal priesthood in Melchisedec, but that did not last more than two centuries; and shall we hesitate to call that everlasting which has existed more than eighteen?[12]

Nevertheless, labeling such an interpretation "bigotry" deserving "to be lashed with a whip of scorpions" and the liberal minister as one who treated the biblical text "like a mad dog [who would] amputate its tail just behind the ears" in an effort to adapt it to dogma, the excerpt blamed such a view on "bibliolatry," a view that went to any ends "to save the reputation of an infallible Bible." Thus, the evangelical milieu with its belief in an infallible Bible was blamed for the liberal minister "doing his utmost to perpetuate a false, hateful, cruel, and damnable prejudice against the Jews!"

Jewish congregations, however, could be tenderly touched by evangelicals who felt that their Bible taught them to love and respect the Jewish people. Congregation Children of Israel in Athens, Georgia, forwarded to Isaac Mayer Wise a letter from the pastor of the Presbyterian church in the same city. He had been commended by the synagogue for procuring the pardon of Henry Leon, a Jew who was in prison sick and ill, "wasting away of Consumption." Rev. C. W. Lane had been in the habit of visiting convicts, and the evangelical minister immediately took pity on Henry Leon. He convinced Governor Smith that Leon had "satisfied the demands of justice" and that "humanity required his pardon." Thanking the Jewish congregants for their "very kind letter" of appreciation, Rev. Lane wrote:

> Allow me also to express through you, to the congregation you represent, my long felt interest in the Hebrew race. In preserving the Old Testament scriptures in their purity with religious care, from age to age, your race, though often wronged and ill-treated, have done a grander service to mankind than did all the nations together during the first forty centuries of the world's history. And no nation, ancient or modern, has surpassed the "children of Israel," in the greatness and splendor of its illustrious names.

> There is indeed an immense difference between your belief and mine as to the Messiah. You believe that he has not yet come, while I believe that Jesus of Nazareth is the Messiah, able to save to the

uttermost all that come unto him. Still, I do not forget that the Messiah in whom I trust, was, as to his human nature, a Hebrew of the house of David, of the tribe of Judah—that the great Paul and many of his co-laborers were Hebrews too, Israelites indeed as we believe, in whom there is no guile.[13]

"We Christians are indebted to the Hebrew race both for the Old Testament and the New," Rev. Lane noted. "As I look then at my Bible and consider my great indebtedness to your people for it, my heart warms toward the 'children of Israel.'"

M. I. Morris, an avid reader of *The Israelite* and secretary of Congregation Children of Israel (a congregation founded only eighteen months before with twelve Jewish families among a gentile population of five thousand), asked Rabbi Isaac Mayer Wise to publish the letter to show "the rapid success of your brother Israelites, in this, our romantic and beautiful mountain city Athens, Ga.," and "to prove to you and the world at large, how our brother Israelites are respected and honored, in the beautiful land of the sunny South." Isaac Mayer Wise published the letter without comment.

This in brief is the nineteenth-century context in which both modern American Judaism and American fundamentalist-evangelicalism originated and developed. As will be shown in the following chapters, the theologies, philosophies, and controversies of the latter decades of the nineteenth century and the early decades of the twentieth century molded the attitudes of each movement—some of which persist to this very day.

# I

# THE RISE OF FUNDAMENTALIST-EVANGELICALISM

The American Jews of the latter part of the nineteenth century understood much more about traditional Christian belief and practice than they often are given credit for knowing. And yet, many of their attitudes were couched in stereotypes and caricatures. To Rabbi Wise and many of his readers, evangelical Christianity was "monarchical" and obsolete, "absolutistic" and unsophisticated, antidemocratic and antiprogressive. Revivalism had turned seventeenth-century American Puritanism into nineteenth-century American evangelicalism. This "fanaticism" and "enthusiasm" was viewed by the Jewish community as barbaric and uncivilized, a threat to pure religion and liberty. Evangelists, using the "extreme measures" the apostle Paul had "adopted" to reach the heathen Roman masses, were only a further indication to Wise and other Jewish leaders that traditional Christianity would soon be (or would have to be) demolished. For many American Jews, fear of further evangelical control in America and dread of the advance of the Christian gospel message was intense.

## DWIGHT LYMAN MOODY AND REVIVALISM

This is clearly seen in the response of the Jewish community to the most popular evangelist of the day: Dwight Lyman Moody

(1837–1899). In August 1875, D. L. Moody docked in New York City after a two-year evangelistic tour to the British Isles. He had left his home in Chicago in relative obscurity, but his success and fame in England and Scotland made him an instant national figure upon his return. Teamed with his ever-loyal singing associate, Ira Sankey, Moody had an influence and message that remind one of Billy Graham and his singing associate in the 1950s, George Beverly Shea. Certainly D. L. Moody had much the same influence in the last quarter of the 1800s as Rev. Billy Graham has had in the latter half of the twentieth century.

Dwight L. Moody plunged into large urban evangelistic crusades upon his return to the United States. After a month-long evangelistic campaign at the invitation of the churches in Brooklyn, Moody held evangelistic services from November 1875 to January 1876 in Philadelphia. From these cities he moved on to Chicago, Boston, Nashville, St. Louis, and Kansas City. Organized through the efforts of a cross-section of evangelical churches, vast audiences attended these revivalistic meetings and evangelistic enterprises. The American Jewish community was not amused.

Jewish correspondents from the campaign cities wrote faithfully to *The American Israelite,* and letters poured in. Moody's Brooklyn crusade prompted this response from Washington, D.C.:

> Brooklyn, that great city of religious sensationalism, after having supplied the press and public with the famous, or rather infamous scandal of the last year [the accusation of adultery leveled on liberal minister, Henry Ward Beecher, pastor of Plymouth Congregational Church in Brooklyn], has now gone vigorously into the preaching business. The great revivalists, Moody and Sankey, are making their parades and ostentatious harangues in order to excite people to an open and public profession, of what is called religion. As one of the papers of the day irreverently states, Brooklyn is trying to run God Almighty in the high pressure circus style. People who remember the same sort of cant that prevailed in various parts of the United States about a year or two back, run by a moly of so-called crusaders, will recognize in the present forced excitement about the same sort of an affair. Van Pelt, the first convert of the crusaders, and their special apostle, soon fell from grace, and it may be of

course expected that the new fangled patent saints that are being gathered into the folds under the rink in the city of churches, will, when the tension is withdrawn, relapse to their old ways, this is the history of all such movements, when sudden impulses are appealed to and not convictions. The proceedings become almost ridiculous at times, and quite a farce when under excitement the crowd resolute as follows . . .[1]

The writer then related instances of "the familiar and profane manner in which sacred things are treated" in the revivalistic crusade.

A section entitled "Flippant Moodyisms" followed, mocking the revivalist's statements. Moody was accused of using revivals for his own personal monetary gain, and future editions of *The American Israelite* included sections entitled "More Moodyisms." "The revival still rages and will have its run all through the country, like base ball [fanaticism]," the November 26, 1875, edition announced. A letter sent by a Jewish man two days later to *The American Israelite* from Philadelphia began: "It is Thanksgiving Eve. I sit pondering over the events of the day . . . What makes me so pensive? Moody and Sankey are in our city."[2]

Such evangelistic crusades and revivals were believed by the Jewish community to be an attempt to make traditional Christianity the state religion of the country. In "That Brooklyn, N.Y., Harangue," an editorial in *The American Israelite* related:

The Rev. Dr. Talmadge last Sunday, at the Brooklyn Tabernacle, harangued an audience in the Plymouth-Rock- spread-eagle style, spiced with Moody fanaticism, to terrify all persons of weak nerves who think the Bible ought not to be kept in the public schools as a text-book of sectarianism on the one hand, and of hypocrisy to teachers and pupils on the other. The reverend gentleman, in his fierce anger—artificial or serious—denounced all sorts of persons who happen to differ with him in opinion, and up to the point of cursing and swearing did all in his power to convince the audience of his serious fanaticism. It will not work, however. Either the Plymouth Rockers must pay the taxes all alone in support of the public schools, and say to the rest of mankind, "Stay away if you do not like it"; or they must see the public schools secularized to suit all classes of taxpayers, who demand value for money paid. The New York and Brooklyn clergymen and Christian congregations will have to do as we Jews do—give every one a chance to read the Bible and receive religious instruction in the Sabbath-schools. If the Rev. Dr. Talmadge honestly believes that children must read the Bible, let him and his friends do it; let them spend a few thousand dollars a year on special Bible schools of their own. The public schools, however, belong to the public, and not to the Plymouth Rockers; they are State institutions, and not Church establishments. All the harangues and all the fanaticism can not change this fact. Our government is based upon the principle of equality, and stands above all religious sects, notwithstanding all aristocracy and revival furore.[3]

"Harangues like those of Mr. Talmadge go far to show that the influence of illiberal clergymen is destructive and revolutionary, hostile to the Republic and our form of government," the article concluded, "and that influence must be neutralized by patriots and progressive men. We say, put the Bible out of the public schools, and let each church do her duty at home. Let the clergymen work at home, and not impose upon the public."

While to most Jews, D. L. Moody was a huckster, a villain, "an illiterate charlatan, ignorant of the Bible, not being able to distinguish logic from logwood" (as one Jewish writer in *The American Israelite* insisted), Moody was also linked to anti-Semitism. During the Philadelphia crusade, the great evangelist was cited in the newspapers as having preached a "passion sermon" that declared that the Jews crucified Jesus. It was also claimed that Moody had declared in his sermon that a thousand Jews in Paris had recently stated that they were glad they had killed "the Christian God." Jewish letters and editorials concerning the incident poured in to *The American Israelite*. One correspondent labeled such anti-Semitism "the fruits of revival," and Rabbi Wise put the statement in bold print.[4]

Dwight L. Moody denied making such a statement, and when the account of Moody's disclaimer was finally published in the March 25, 1876, issue of Isaac Mayer Wise's periodical, it was treated as another of the "pious frauds sent forth by Mr. Moody." Moody's private conversation with a young Jewish man concerning the allegations was published in newspapers around the country and appeared in *The American Israelite* as follows:

"I do not blame the Jews, and I have never spoken against them,"
said Mr. Moody. "The statement in a Philadelphia newspaper, that
I did is untrue. I never see a Jew but I feel like taking off my hat to
him. In my opinion, your people are to be the great missionaries to
convert the world to Christ. What better agency could there be? You
are scattered throughout the earth, and speak all languages. I
believe you will all go back to Jerusalem one day, and be restored to
your old kingdom – don't you?"

"No, I do not," was the [Jewish man's] reply. "You never could
induce intelligent Jews to settle in such a miserable, sterile little
patch of land as Palestine, when they can sit in luxury in their
homes in London, Paris, Frankfort, and Berlin, and there control
the commerce of nations and the destinies of empires. Why should
they go back to Palestine? In all their ancient glory − which was not
very great after all–they were never as prosperous and as
power[ful] as they are now."[5]

"You will all go back to Jerusalem, and you will all be brought to
Christ at last," Moody responded to the young Jewish man,
insisting, "I tell you, it's bound to come."

Later in their conversation, the young man dared Moody to
"prove" to him "that Christianity is purer than Judaism," in
which case he would "become a Christian." Moody responded
that it was "not a matter of reason," but that "conversion must
come from the heart and not from the head." Nevertheless, the
great evangelist insisted, "It will come at last. You will all be
brought to Christ." As he rose to leave, the young Jewish man
asked Moody if he had made any Jewish converts. "Well, several
have stood up and professed Christ," Dwight L. Moody answered as he took the young man's outstretched hand. "But I can
not say that I put much faith in converted Jews."

Rabbi Isaac Mayer Wise was livid at the responses in this account, editorializing: "We never heard of any Jew placing much
confidence in Mr. Moody, in Christian dogmatism or the revival
furore. Nor do we think the Philadelphia papers misrepresented
Mr. M.'s speech." Mocking Moody's talk of the Holy Spirit's leading during his sermons, Wise ridiculed both the evangelist's relationship with God and his lack of education as he wrote that
Moody "is not responsible all the time for what he says, as the

Holy Ghost sometimes makes a fool of him, who speaks ungrammatical rigmarole. But we will give him credit for his disclaimer. It is what might be called a backing out. Let him pass."[6]

In spite of the distrust Dwight L. Moody would engender among American Jews, he was so respected by Protestants that he was later claimed by both fundamentalists and liberals as one of their own. In spite of *The American Israelite*'s allegations that he was wallowing in money, his colleagues and associates consistently portrayed him as selfless, humble in spirit, charitable (he died nearly penniless and his family often complained of his compulsion to give away anything he owned), and yet as a man of conviction with a passion "to save the lost." Much like twentieth-century evangelist Billy Graham, Moody combined both liberals and conservatives in his evangelistic crusades, and had a catholicity of spirit and love that impressed ministers of all sectors of the Protestant faith. Ironically, his son William Moody became a conservative evangelical while his son Paul Moody would lean toward liberalism.

In a collection of sermons published in 1877, D. L. Moody underscored his positive feelings toward the Jewish people. In his sermon entitled "Christ in the Old Testament," he elaborated on God's promise to Abraham in Genesis 22:17-18. He said:

> Now, let me ask you, hasn't that prophecy been fulfilled? Hasn't God made that a great and mighty nation? Where is there any nation that has ever produced such men as have come from the seed of Abraham? There is no nation that has or can produce such men. . . . That promise was made 4000 years ago, and even now you can see that the Jews are a separate and distinct nation, in their language, in their habits and in every respect. You can bring almost every nation here and in fifty years they will become extinct, merged into another; but bring a Jew here, and in fifty years, a hundred years, or a thousand years, he is still a Jew.[7]

"When I meet a Jew," Moody continued (as he often preached), "I can't help having a profound respect for them, for they are God's people."

Moody believed that it was his literal interpretation of the Bible that led him to a deep respect for the Jewish people and to acknowledge that God's promises to them were still in effect. He often complained about the liberal Protestant propensity to refer to such promises as being "figurative." Moody alluded to those who "just figure away everything," declaring, "I notice if a man goes to cut up the Bible . . . when he begins to doubt portions of the Word of God he soon doubts it all."

In his book *Pleasure and Profit in Bible Study* (1895), Moody termed this "clipping the Bible." "Now, if I have a right to cut out a certain portion of the Bible, I don't know why one of my friends has not a right to cut out another. . . . You would have a queer kind of Bible if everybody cut out what he wanted to." These thoughts would be echoed time and time again by members of the rising fundamentalist-evangelical movement.[8]

And yet, Dwight L. Moody deplored the rancor and division that were occurring within evangelical Protestantism, between liberals and conservatives, modernists and fundamentalists. In the preface of *Pleasure and Profit in Bible Study* he wrote: "I think I would rather preach about the Word of God than anything else except the Love of God; because I believe it [the Love of God] is the best thing in this world."

Moody was so busy that he refused to take time off from his evangelistic pursuits. He traveled to Palestine, however, when shipping magnate Peter Mackinnon and his wife insisted that Moody accompany them in 1892. Moody's son William recounted his father's humorous as well as his touching experiences in Palestine. He noted:

> His [D. L. Moody's] visit to the Holy Land remained a vivid, living memory. He constantly referred to it in private conversation and public discourse, regretting on the one hand the present mean condition of Palestine, which, however, he believed was in accord with prophecy, and on the other looking forward with joy to its restoration, when the feet of the Messiah shall once more stand on Olivet.[9]

Moody's emphasis on the soon "second coming of Christ" was indicative of the growing influence of the premillennial view of the future among conservative evangelicals. This view would become the backbone of the fundamentalist-evangelical movement and the heart of the evangelical Christian Zionist movement.

## PREMILLENNIALISM

Both liberalism and fundamentalism arose within the vast theological and social sea of nineteenth-century evangelical Protestantism. Biblical criticism and Darwin's theory of evolution would challenge the conservative tenets of mainstream evangelicalism, and Protestants would face a predicament. The Bible claimed to be authoritative, and yet some of the miraculous accounts defied a scientific understanding of the universe. Some evangelical Protestant academics questioned whether they could retain the Protestant emphasis on the centrality of the Bible and continue to be biblical scholars of integrity in their modern age. The choice of liberal evangelicals was to adapt and modify their biblical faith. Even theology professors who considered themselves "modernists" in the early twentieth century continued to refer to themselves as "evangelicals." That is why Dwight L. Moody could be claimed by both ends of the Protestant theological spectrum in the fundamentalist-modernist controversies of the 1920s.

In the face of the castigation of the theory of biblical inerrancy by scientific and theological critics of the nineteenth century and the rise of liberalism within the broad sea of evangelicalism, conservative evangelicals steadfastly proclaimed the divine inspiration of the Bible. They used the work of Swiss Reformed pastor François Samuel Robert Louis Gaussen (1790–1863), who in *Theopneustia: The Plenary Inspiration of the Holy Scriptures Deduced from Internal Evidence, and the Testimonies of Nature, History and Science* (1841) declared that "we believe [the critics] to be erroneous in themselves, and deplorable in their results. . . . Scripture is then from God; it is everywhere from God, and everywhere it is entirely from God."[10]

Princeton theologians, such as Charles Hodge (1797–1878), concurred. Hodge insisted that "all Protestants agree in teaching that 'the word of God, as contained in the Scriptures of the Old and New Testaments, is the only infallible rule of faith and practice.'"[11] He substantiated his claim by quoting Lutheran, Reformed, and Anglican confessions of faith, implying that Protestants who did not subscribe to this "Protestant Rule of Faith" were outside the confines of historical Christianity. His student Benjamin Breckinridge Warfield (1851–1921), a later professor at Princeton, would continue what became known as the Princeton theology by asserting that the words of the Bible were inspired "without error" in the "original autographs." This would become a standard hermeneutical argument of the fundamentalist-evangelical movement in the twentieth century.

Therefore, the first key to understanding the Protestant fundamentalist-evangelical movement which arose in the latter decades of the nineteenth century is to comprehend its defense of biblical literalism. The early fundamentalist believed that the Bible was the Word of God. Not that it "contained" merely the principles of God's message to humankind, but that it was and is God's message to humankind. The Tanach (their "Old Testament") was as important to them as the writings of Paul.

Of crucial significance in ascertaining fundamentalist attitudes toward the Jewish people is a second key: their premillennial view of the future. Fundamentalist-evangelicals questioned the prevalent nineteenth-century postmillennial evangelicalism which held to an unbroken Christian evolution toward an absolutely perfect kingdom of God. In contrast, the premillennial fundamentalists declared that the Christian church was not the "new Israel," and they deplored a covenant theology that would ascribe to the Christian church biblical blessings reserved for the Jewish people. Fundamentalist-evangelicals could not accept the view that Protestantism would usher in the millennium, and they doubted the ability of evangelicalism (or any other Christian movement) to "Christianize" the world and to make it progressively better. In their estimation, the world would actually become worse (not better), and only the return of Jesus Christ, the Messiah, would institute a millennium of peace and prosperity. Thus, the fundamentalist-evangelical movement challenged the optimistic, socially acceptable, postmillennial evangelicalism that dominated the culture of nineteenth-century America.[12]

There has been much misinterpretation concerning this premillennial view of the future and its relationship to anti-Semitism.

While attitudes of individual fundamentalist evangelicals are complicated and diverse, the movement on the whole engendered a Christian Zionism that was positive and affirming of the Jewish people. The key of biblical literalism combined with the key of premillennialism to produce a Protestant movement of philo-Semitism in the latter decades of the 1800s. The early fundamentalist-evangelical movement stood nearly alone in Christendom in its support of Jewish peoplehood.

For example, the Bible told fundamentalist-evangelicals that the Jews were God's "chosen people." They believed it. The Bible told fundamentalist-evangelicals that God would "never forsake" God's people, the Jews. They believed it. The Bible told fundamentalist-evangelicals that God had a "special plan" for the Jewish people. They believed it. The Bible told the fundamentalist-evangelicals that the Jewish people had an inherent right to possess the Holy Land. They believed it. Their strict interpretation of the Bible and their view of the future in interpreting "God's Holy Word" fostered a love and respect for the Jewish community and a defense of the Jewish heritage that was unique in Christendom during this era.

### First International Prophetic Conference, 1878

This relationship between premillennialism and concern for Jewish peoplehood can be seen in the First International Prophetic Conference held at the Church of the Holy Trinity in New York City from October 30 through November 1, 1878. Its object was to stress the premillennial advent of Jesus Christ and to gather those of like mind in discussions on related topics. The inspiration for this conference was an earlier conference in 1878 held in Mildmay Park, England, where the call for an international conference to be held in New York was signed by 122 bishops, professors, ministers, and "brethren." Some of those who signed the call were to become the backbone of the early fundamentalist movement.[13]

The international aspect of this conference was represented by one British speaker, Dr. William P. Mackay, the evangelical Earl of Shaftesbury and pastor of the Prospect Street Presbyterian

Church in Hull, England. Mackay had spoken at the earlier Mildmay Park conference in England and believed very strongly in premillennial eschatology and the future restoration of the Jewish people to Palestine. He delivered two addresses to the conference. In the first, "The Return of Christ and Foreign Missions," he explained that "signs, times and seasons, as we find in [the biblical book of] Daniel, are for the Jewish people," and herald their restoration to the Holy Land.[14] In his second address, "The Three Days' Feast with David's Son," Mackay lamented that "Jewish truth gets hopelessly mixed up with Gentile truth" in ordinary eschatology, the church often usurping God's promises for the Jewish people. Emphasizing that the Jewish people would be "gathered" and "united" in their rightful land, he also believed that the returning Messiah would convince them that he was indeed their Lord and Savior Jesus Christ.[15]

Other speakers, such as Dr. Charles K. Imbrie, pastor of the Presbyterian Church in Jersey City, New Jersey, concurred. He spent considerable time on Israel's place in prophecy in his address, "The Regeneration." He concluded that there were two instruments to convey God's salvation to the nations and to restore the world to God. One instrument was Jesus Christ and the other was the Jewish people. Declaring that the restoration of the Jewish people to the Holy Land would bring blessing to the gentile nations, Imbrie stated that this "blessing" would come only after the Jewish people converted to Christianity. He said that

> this Regeneration shall be attended by the national repentance and conversion of the Jewish people, their gathering to their own land, and their perpetual residence there, exalted as a people to be a blessing in all the earth. . . . So the prophets speak of Israel as being a gathered nation from generation to generation; "their seed and their seed's seed dwelling in the land forever." So they tell us of the nations ever rejoicing in Israel's joy. (Ezek. chap. 36, chap. 37; Isa. 61:9).[16]

Dr. Imbrie's view appears to be a holdover from early-nineteenth-century thought that insisted that the Jewish people would all be converted and then gathered into their promised land. And yet,

the central leadership of the fundamentalist-evangelical movement would actually teach that the Jewish people would return to
the Holy Land as Jews (not as Christians or converted Jews). The
Earl of Shaftesbury even chided in his lecture that the church had
failed to make universal evangelization rather than universal conversion its goal; it had sought triumphalistically to conquer rather
than to follow Jesus' simple command to spread the message.[17]

This is clearly viewed in the principal address of the conference
relating to the restoration of the Jewish people to Palestine. Entitled "The Gathering of Israel," this address was presented by
Bishop William R. Nicholson of the Reformed Episcopal Church
in Philadelphia. He began by explaining to the crowds assembled
that he found himself "in the midst of an embarrassment of
riches" when it came to proving from the Bible that the Jewish people would be restored to Palestine. Bishop Nicholson emphasized
that "the regathering of Israel" spoken of in passages such as Ezekiel 36:22–26 "can possibly refer only to the literal Israel, and to
their restoration to Palestine. . . . It is yet in the future."[18]

Nicholson noted that the "gathering of Israel" would be accomplished in two installments. Before the Messiah returned, many
of the Jewish people would "be gathered back in their unconverted state." They would rebuild the Temple and reestablish temple services. The Messiah, Jesus Christ, would return, Bishop
Nicholson claimed, and then the rest of the Jewish people would
accept their Lord and be restored to the land as well. He preached
that the Holy Land would be restored to its former beauty, and
universal peace and harmony would bless the world.[19]

Bishop Nicholson then launched into a vibrant tribute to the
Jewish people that became a trademark of the premillennialist
fundamentalist-evangelical movement. He exclaimed to the conference that the world had not seen anything like the miraculous
preservation of the Jewish people. Bishop Nicholson declared:

> Can the world show anything like it? Twice 1,800 years old, they
> saw the proud Egyptian perish in the waters of the Red Sea; they
> heard the fall of great Babylon's power; they witnessed the ruins of
> the Syro-Macedonian Caesars, and outlived the dark ages. They
> have been through all civilizations, shared in all convulsions, and

have kept pace with the entire progress of discovery and art. And here they [the Jewish people] stand to-day, as distinct as ever, occupying no country of their own, scattered through all countries, identical in their immemorial physiognomy, earth's men of destiny, before the venerableness of whose pedigree the proudest scutcheons of mankind are but as trifles of yesterday.[20]

Bishop Nicholson perceived a spark of hope of restoration through the nation of England when he interjected: "Even now we may almost speak of England's protectorate of the Holy Land. God's providence is moving apace, and evidently is rapidly nearing the crisis of Israel's first recovery." Recalling the sufferings of the Jewish people up to the year 1878, Nicholson pointed out that "if so literally have been fulfilled the prophecies which foretold their sufferings and their preservation, equally sure are the predicted grandeurs of their future."[21]

Such prophetic interpretation (in spite of the problems discussed in later sections) questioned the triumphalistic interpretation of the mainline postmillennial evangelicalism of the nineteenth century, which attributed the biblical curses to the Jewish people while assigning "Israel's" biblical blessings to the Christian church. Nathaniel West (1826–1906), one of the early fundamentalist-evangelical founding fathers and a catalyst in convening the First International Prophetic Conference, decried the prevalent views of the Christian church, claiming that they were in error. In his lecture to the conference entitled "History of the Pre-Millennial Doctrine," West insisted that the premillennial doctrine that upheld God's covenants with the Jewish people was crushed by the union of church and state under Constantine. The Roman Catholic Church then "spiritualized" the doctrine to apply to itself. He protested against a postmillennial evangelicalism which stated that the Christian church was promoting the kingdom of God in an unbroken evolution toward absolute perfection and inveighed against the "vapid idealism which volatilizes the perfect kingdom into a spiritual abstraction, apart from the regenesis of the earth."[22]

In 1880, Dr. West's *The Thousand Years in Both Testaments* would assert boldly in the preface:

It is not to be denied that a large part of the professing church, swayed by its teachers, is indifferent to these [prophetic] themes . . . and regard the word of prophecy as unprofitable, and its unfulfilled part as unintelligible. . . . A false spiritualizing, allegorizing, and idealizing, interpretation has contributed to rob the predictions concerning Israel of their realistic value, failing to discriminate between what is common to Jew and Gentile alike, in the one spiritual salvation which comes to all . . . and what is peculiar to literal Israel, as the people bringing salvation to the world, and ordained in the future, as in the past, to a distinguished place in the kingdom of God. As a result of this false lure, "blindness in part" has happened to the Gentiles until Israel is saved, a blindness that affects all eschatological questions, and has brought the Church, in many places, to regard the doctrine of the pre-millennial coming of Israel's Messiah as a "Jewish fable" not to be believed.[23]

"The Anti-Semitism of our modern times, with its hatred of the Jew," Nathaniel West warned, "a thing disgraceful to Christendom, and so unlike the Philo-Israelism of the apostolic days, . . . is due, in no small degree, to these false systems of interpretation."

West had emigrated from England as a boy and graduated from the University of Michigan in 1846. An ordained Presbyterian minister and theology professor at Danville Theological Seminary from 1869 to 1875, he was soon to hold the pastorate of the First Presbyterian Church in St. Paul, Minnesota. His 528-page edited monograph of the addresses of the First International Prophetic Conference, *Premillennial Essays*, had been published in 1879 and was widely publicized. His *The Thousand Years in Both Testaments* received a large readership as well.

### The 1886 Conference in Chicago

The Second International Prophetic Conference was held in Farwell Hall in Chicago, November 16–21, 1886. Many eminent fundamentalist-evangelical ministers and theologians attended. Dwight L. Moody was unable to be present because of "binding engagements," but like a few others sent a letter expressing "for the purpose of the conference the greatest sympathy." George C.

Needham, organizer and secretary of the conference, asserted that one of the major reasons for holding the conference was "to give prominence to neglected truth." "It is a universally acknowledged fact," he declared, "that unfulfilled prophecy has, for centuries, been relegated to the theologians grave."[24]

Professor Ernst F. Stroeter, of Wesleyan University, Warrenton, Missouri, in his address the first day concurred. In "Christ's Second Coming Premillennial," Stroeter gently castigated the commentators who "are very ready to simply spiritualize away all that is prophesied to the political Israel and to the geographical Palestine of restitution and rehabilitation . . . and to appropriate quietly to the Gentile church all there is predicted of BLESSING TO ISRAEL." Dr. Stroeter intimated that anti-Semitism was linked to this spiritualization of the word "Israel" in the Bible to mean the "Christian church." "Without the equally literal fulfillment of this aspect of Israel's hope—to which Jesus himself and His disciples likewise stand committed—Israel's glory among the nations is lost forever . . . the name of Israel will continue a reproach forever among the nations."[25]

Three days later, Dr. Nathaniel West delivered a major address on the topic: "Prophecy and Israel." Concerning the Jewish people, West began by emphasizing that Israel was the focal point of God's plan. He preached: "The fortunes of the chosen people decides the fortunes of the world. History itself is Messianic."

West explained that Israel was comparable to the Messiah. He stated: "Israel and Messiah, though historically separated now, are indissolvably united, as mediators and bringers of salvation to the world; the one nationally, the other personally, alike in their humiliation and glory." As Israel brought salvation to the gentiles during the "first" coming of Jesus Christ, so Israel would bring salvation at the "second" coming of Christ. Nathaniel West added that "Israel" meant the Jewish people and must not be substituted symbolically with the Christian church as theologians had attempted over the centuries.[26]

He cited Paul's epistle to the Romans (chapters 9–11) as evidence for Israel's temporary rejection by God nationally, but subsequent future restoration and approval by God in the land of Palestine. The Presbyterian pastor and author paraphrased Paul's argument in Romans 11:25–32, explaining to fellow gentiles:

> For the same crimes for which Jerusalem was struck you may be stricken too when the mountain-stone shall SMITE YOUR CHRISTIAN "TOES." If, at Messiah's first coming, the Holy City was "trodden down of the gentiles," and Rome arose the central seat of gentile Christendom, it may happen that, when He [Jesus] comes again, Rome shall go down, and Jerusalem "arise and shine," a "crown of glory in the hand of the Lord, and a royal diadem in the hand of her God!"[27]

Dr. West proclaimed that Paul meant that the Jewish nation would finally accept their Messiah, Jesus Christ, whom they rejected the first time and the nations of the world would receive the message of salvation through God's chosen people. Israel would be resurrected to "life," just as Jesus was resurrected.

It is important to note that Nathaniel West, like most evangelicals, preached that the Jewish people would accept Jesus Christ through the proclamation of the Christian church, and thus it was the duty of the Christians gathered at the conference to realize first of all "the debt" they owed the Jewish people, and secondly (because of that "debt") to tell the Jewish people that Jesus was indeed their Messiah. Dr. West stated emphatically, "WE ARE DEBTORS TO THAT PEOPLE in the deepest sense, and our imperative duty, to give them the gospel, is designed to hasten the coming of the Lord."[28] In this manner, premillennialists answered the charge from other evangelicals that they had forsaken the missionary enterprise.

In like manner, these premillennialist Bible teachers who spoke at the conference continued to speak of the "hardness of heart" of the Jewish people toward the gospel message through the centuries. For example, W. J. Erdman criticized the "conceit" of Christians who claim that Israel has "as a nation no future of SPECIAL BLESSING and pre-eminence." He noted that even John Calvin erred in this interpretation and that it was high time that such an error was brought to light. Nevertheless, Erdman stressed "that in due time Israel, though now as a people smitten with judicious hardness of heart, shall again be restored to the favor and bless-ing of God." Rev. Henry M. Parsons (like other speakers) openly declared that "the Jews are to be the missionaries to the nations in the opening of the next age, and have pre-eminence among them as God's earthly people."[29]

The speakers at the Second International Prophetic Confer-ence in 1886 were clearly confident that the Jewish people would one day be restored to the Holy Land. Their denunciation of Christendom's spiritualizing techniques and their emphasis on the literal interpretation of biblical prophecy would influence generations of fundamentalist-evangelicals. Ernst Stroeter de-clared that anti-Semitism accompanied such spiritualizing of "Israel" to mean the "Christian Church." Erdman asserted only Christian "conceit" could support such a view. Parsons and West believed that the Jewish people would become more important as an instrument of God and, ultimately, would carry God's mes-sage to the world.

These nineteenth-century fundamentalist-evangelicals held to a strongly divergent biblical hermeneutic in comparison to other Christian theologians of their day. *The Princeton Review* attempted to warn Presbyterian ministers not to be swayed by premillennial doctrine, while the Dutch Reformed *Christian Intelligencer* ob-served that very few Dutch Reformed ministers could accept this view of the Bible. At times, the *Christian Observor* (the voice of the evangelical party in the Church of England) seemed confused over the doctrine and ridiculed belief in the Jewish restoration to Palestine. The *Catholic World* was much more blunt, stressing that rather than the Jewish people being restored, the Jews would eventually accept the true faith [Catholicism] and only then could "the captivity of Judah and the captivity of Jerusalem" be ended.[30] The fundamentalist-evangelical espousal of Zionism not only was disdained in Christian circles, but was ridiculed by many Reform Jews of the day.

## ZIONISM

Classical Reform Judaism opposed the idea of the restoration of
the Jewish people to Palestine as much as the general consensus
of Christendom did. At the Pittsburgh Conference of American
Rabbis in 1885, the Union of American Hebrew Congregations
(founded in 1873 by Rabbi Isaac Mayer Wise) adopted an eight-
point program that would guide Reform Judaism for the next half
century, dashing all hope for reunion with traditional Judaism.
Article five of the Pittsburgh Platform of 1885 read: "We are no
longer a nation, but a 'religious community,' and we no longer
expect to return to Palestine or a Jewish state or offer sacrifices in
a Temple." *The American Israelite* in 1891 noted of the Sultan and
the Zionists' "merely romantic without any practical idea at the
bottom" plans:

> The Sultan is not opposed to the immigration of Russian Jews any-
> where in his empire except in Palestine, where he is not in favor of
> a large immigration for two reasons, the first of which is the increase
> of paupers of which Palestine always had a super-abundance
> depending on Jewish charity the world over. The second is the
> noise of the romantic nationalists among the Eastern Jews espe-
> cially, whose object seems to be to restore the Jewish nationality in
> Palestine. This, of course, the Sultan can not favor, as the indepen-
> dence of Palestine is closely connected with that nationalism. The
> Sultan and his immediate advisors do not know, of course, that all
> that national enthusiasm among Jews is merely romantic without
> any practical idea at the bottom; and is tolerated by rational men
> only to the end of turning those enthusiasts to agricultural employ-
> ment, the only salvation of the race.[31]

*The American Israelite* consistently ridiculed Jewish Zionists as
well as the growing Christian Zionist movement.

In a note (November 19, 1891), Wise mocked the great Orthodox Zionist leader, Dr. H. Pereira Mendes (1852–1937) of New
York, for being "a foreigner, who, by reason of education and idio-
syncracies, is unable to enter into the hopes and desires of the
patriotic Jewish-American, or even to understand them." Rabbi
Wise also derided Rabbi Mendes as representing "that portion of

Israel which sees no happiness, save in a visionary hope for the restoration to Palestine, and is a stranger to the Jew who has resolutely turned his back upon past sorrows and sees in the future hope for all that man holds dear, here in this broad country, under the best institutions the world ever saw." Dr. Mendes was born in Birmingham, England, and was educated in London. This "foreigner" received his medical degree at the University of the City of New York. Many leaders within the Reform movement, however, could not tolerate such devotion to a restored Israel. As Rabbi Isaac Mayer Wise concluded in the note on Mendes: "We need no monument of stone."[32]

### William E. Blackstone

Among Christian Zionists was a Methodist layman, William E. Blackstone (1841–1935). Born in Adams, New York, Blackstone joined the Methodist Church at the age of eleven and became active in its programs. He did not attend college, but during the Civil War directed the U.S. Christian Commission work at General Ulysses S. Grant's headquarters. After the war, he married and settled in Oak Park, Illinois (a suburb of Chicago), becoming a successful businessman in insurance, real estate, and construction. Continuing to be actively involved in his denomination, Blackstone even took charge of a small congregation for nearly a year.[33]

William E. Blackstone was attracted to the premillennialist movement, directing his studies toward the Bible's emphasis on prophecy and the return of Jesus Christ to the earth. He was appalled that he could find no tract on the subject and asked various Christian leaders to write one. When he approached James Brookes (1830–97), the pastor of Walnut Street Presbyterian Church in St. Louis and a prominent fundamentalist-evangelical, to write such a tract for lay people, Brookes startled him by insisting, "Oh no—you write it and I will publish it." As the editor of *The Truth or Testimony for Christ* from 1875 until his death, Brookes was highly respected in fundamentalist-evangelical circles and would also promote the Zionist cause. He was on the committee of eight men who initially planned the First International Prophetic Conference in 1878 and would mold many future leaders in the movement.

Certainly his encouragement of Blackstone was a lasting impetus to the political efforts of Christian Zionists. Although uneasy about his theological qualifications, William Blackstone wrote two tracts on the subject and distributed them among Christians. In 1878 a combination of those tracts was published as a ninety-six-page book, *Jesus Is Coming*.[34] In this treatise, Blackstone maintained that the Jewish people were "God's sundial" and that they not only had an ancient right to the land of Palestine, but also would be restored to the land, never to be expelled again. To Blackstone, all the biblical prophetic promises to the Jewish people would be fulfilled, and he believed that the "signs" of the times were pointing toward that restoration. By 1898, *Jesus Is Coming* had been expanded to nearly two hundred pages and was an extremely popular book among conservative Christians. To underscore the spread of premillennialist thought, the third edition, published in 1908, was distributed around the world and by 1927, 843,000 copies of *Jesus Is Coming* had been printed in thirty-six different languages (over a million by Blackstone's death).[35]

In the spring of 1888, Blackstone traveled through Europe to Palestine. Being in the "Holy Land" made a profound impression on him, for he spent a year in travel. Upon returning, he organized one of the first modern conferences between Christians and Jews. The conference members met in the First Methodist Church of Chicago, and the meetings were chaired by William Blackstone himself. The rabbis who participated were exclusively from the Reform movement, and Blackstone was shocked to hear Rabbi Emil G. Hirsch exclaim: "We modern Jews do not wish to be restored to Palestine . . . the country wherein we live is our Palestine. . . . We will not go back . . . to form again a nationality of our own." The Christian clergymen and Reform rabbis at Blackstone's interfaith conference did, however, pass "resolutions of sympathy" for the oppressed Jews of Russia, and copies were sent to the czar and other rulers.[36]

Nevertheless, Blackstone believed that these resolutions were inadequate, and he put together a petition that has been referred to as the Blackstone Memorial of 1891. It urged the President of the United States, Benjamin Harrison, to influence European governments "to secure the holding, at an early date, of an international conference to consider the condition of the Israelites and their claims to Palestine as their ancient home, and to promote in all other just and proper ways the alleviation of their suffering condition."

The petition's opening sentence is bold, asking the question: "What shall be done for the Russian Jews?" It answers: "Why not give Palestine back to them again? According to God's distribution of nations, it is their home, an inalienable possession, from which they were expelled by force. . . . Let us now restore them to the land of which they were so cruelly despoiled by our Roman ancestors." Through Blackstone's tireless efforts, the Memorial was signed by 413 influential Christian and Jewish leaders, including William McKinley, congressman from Ohio and future U.S. President; Melville W. Fuller, Chief Justice of the United States Supreme Court; Thomas B. Reed, Speaker of the House of Representatives; business leaders Cyrus H. McCormick, J. P. Morgan, and John D. Rockefeller; newspaper editors, bankers, and clergymen. William E. Blackstone presented President Harrison the petition on March 5, 1891, in the company of Secretary of State James G. Blaine. Blackstone hoped that Harrison would become a modern-day Cyrus, and the Washington correspondent of *The American Israelite* reported that "the President listened attentively to Mr. Blackstone's remarks, and promised to give the subject serious consideration."[37]

Unfortunately, the Blackstone Memorial reached the State Department while Selah Merrill (1837–1909) was U.S. consul in Jerusalem. A former army chaplain for the Union forces during the Civil War and an ordained Congregationalist minister, Merrill had no sympathy for Christian eschatological dreams or Jewish hopes of restoration to the Promised Land. Assistant Secretary of State and head of the professional diplomatic service

Alvey A. Adee agreed. The Blackstone Memorial of 1891, a petition that President Harrison had promised to give "serious consideration" in March 1891, was scuttled by the end of the year.

In his section on "News Items" in the April 16, 1891, issue of *The American Israelite,* Rabbi Isaac Mayer Wise wrote under the heading of "Our Fool Friends": "The Lord save us from our friends. Here are two examples of what they are doing to make us ridiculous in the eyes of the world." In his view, the Blackstone Memorial and its Zionism was one blatant example of "ridiculous" enterprises. He let an article from *The Independent* in New York (March 26, 1891) speak for him:

> It is amusing to see the facility with which some of our contemporaries have fallen into Mr. William E. Blackstone's net, and have endorsed in their editorial columns his appeal to the President to use his influence with Turkey and Russia and other countries to secure the territory of Palestine for the Jews. It is one of the most preposterous propositions ever offered to the public. The Jews do not want Palestine. It is only certain Christians that want to get the Jews there to accommodate either their prejudices or their interpretations of prophecy. The Jews could not be persuaded to go there. The American Jews are American citizens, and prefer to live in America. It is a better country to live in than Palestine is. The Jews who are in Palestine are the lowest of their class, as a rule; bodies of paupers sustained by gifts, unable otherwise to survive, and the most unfavorable reports have been made on their condition by Jewish commissions, of which we remember one that Mr. Samuel Montague, M.P., of London, was connected with and which was so unfavorable that it sent Sir Moses Montefiore in a hurry to Palestine, when nearly a hundred years old, to investigate the matter anew, to the terror of Mr. Montague and the commission, who were afraid they were murdering the good old man. This proposition of Mr. Blackstone's is pure child's play not worth a moment's serious consideration.[38]

Both the Jewish and Christian opposition to the restoration of the Jewish people to Palestine and the prejudice toward Jews settling the land is clearly evident in this excerpt. Most important for our consideration is the fact that the prophetic interpretation has been noted and attacked, as well as the mention that some Christians might want the Jews to go to Palestine because of "their prejudices." Blackstone was maligned throughout.

However, William E. Blackstone did not give up. He realized that anti-Semites within Christendom and a large percentage of Reform rabbis opposed Zionism. But, as a dispensational premillennialist, he also was fascinated with the organized Zionist movements (religious and political), insisting that Zionism was a definite "sign" of the end of the age and an indication that the Messiah's return was imminent. In a 1898 edition of *Jesus Is Coming*, Blackstone wrote a section on Zionism as one of the signs of the return of Jesus Christ and kept it in his subsequent revisions. He emphasized that "Zionism is now the subject of the most acrimonious debate among the Jews." He noted that "many of the orthodox criticise it as an attempt to seize the prerogatives of their God . . . while others say that God will not work miracles to accomplish that which they can do themselves." He divided the Jewish community into "three great sections" that had developed in the latter half of the nineteenth century: the orthodox, the status quo, and the "reformed."

While he praised the orthodox who "hold to the Old Testament Scriptures, as interpreted by the Talmud, as the literal Word of God" and believe that "some day they shall return to Palestine and become permanently settled as a holy and happy nation, under the sovereignty of their coming Messiah," Blackstone had little regard for the "reformed" [*sic*]. He wrote:

> The Reformed Jews or Neologists have rapidly thrown away their faith in the inspiration of the Scriptures. They have flung to the wind all national and Messianic hopes. Their Rabbis preach rapturously about the mission of Judaism, while joining with the most radical higher critics in the destruction of its very basis, the inspiration of the Word of God. Some have gone clear over into agnosticism. . . . They have no desire to return to Palestine. They are like the man in Kansas, who, in a revival meeting said he did not want to go to heaven, nor did he wish to go to hell but he said he wanted to stay right there in Kansas. Just so these reformed Jews are content to renounce all the prophesied glory of a Messianic kingdom in the land of their ancestors, preferring the palatial homes and gathered riches which they have acquired in Western Europe and the United States.[39]

"They coolly advise their persecuted brethren, in Russia, Rou-
mania, Persia and North Africa, to patiently endure their griev-
ous persecutions until anti-semitism shall die out," Blackstone
criticized, adding that those persecuted brethren "retort that
their prudent advisers would think differently if they lived in
Morocco or Russia, and that even in Western Europe anti-semitism instead of dying out, is rather on the increase."
    Believing as he did that the end of the nineteenth century had
many "signs" that indicated the soon second coming of Jesus
Christ to the earth (signs such as the prevalence of travel and
knowledge, perilous times, religious apostasy, accumulation of
riches, God's "sun-dial" Israel), William E. Blackstone's interest
in foreign missions increased, and he became one of the most
knowledgeable evangelical experts on mission work and missionary fields. He began speaking all over the United States on behalf
of the Christian missionary enterprise and painstakingly worked
on large up-to-date maps that detailed the condition of missions
around the world. When his wife died in 1908, he became a missionary to China, publishing and distributing evangelistic literature in Chinese. He spent five years in China, financed by Milton
Stewart of the Union Oil Company of California. When Blackstone returned, he was appointed trustee of the Milton Stewart
Trust Fund and distributed more than six million dollars for general evangelistic work around the world.[40]
    Nevertheless, the Jewish people and the Zionist movement
were never far from William E. Blackstone's heart and mind. He
would not give up his crusade on behalf of the Jewish homeland
and in 1918 garnered support for a new memorial to be presented
to President Wilson. In 1918 he wrote of "a rather strenuous but
very successful trip East" in June and July, "resulting in the new
Memorial to President Wilson in behalf of the Jews." He had
spoken to thousands of Jews and fundamentalist-evangelicals
across the United States, and his Christian Zionism was recognized by both communities. Elisha M. Friedman, secretary of the
University Zionist Society of New York, stated the same year: "A
well known Christian layman, William E. Blackstone, antedated

Theodor Herzl by five years in his advocacy of the re-establishment of a Jewish state."[41]

Blackstone was involved in the Zionist Congress held in Philadelphia in 1918, and he was deeply touched by the kindness showed to him by the Zionists. "I shall never cease to praise God for the cordial reception which I had from the Jews at the Zionist Congress in Philadelphia," he exclaimed. "The enthusiasm manifested by the delegates . . . gave me new inspiration concerning the future . . . for God's people Israel, who are dear unto Him as the 'apple of His eye.'"[42]

And yet, William E. Blackstone was a fervent and disciplined fundamentalist-evangelical. He was a dedicated Christian who loved his Bible and believed that Jesus Christ died for the salvation of every man and woman on earth. As a premillennialist, he insisted that Jesus would come back a second time for those who loved him and would initiate his kingdom on the earth. As a dispensationalist, he divided history into separate eras or dispensations, in which God worked the redemptive plan for humankind in differing manners, progressively revealing his will.

Blackstone viewed the world as a household administered by God, where men and women were responsible to respond to the revelation God had given them during their particular era. He insisted that God's program for the church was separate from God's program for "Old Testament Israel." He taught that the Christian church could not claim the promises made to the Jewish people or usurp their status as the "chosen people." To the surprise of many Jews, this biblical literalism coupled with prophetic fervor strengthened Blackstone in his love for the Jewish people and his advocation of their restoration to the Holy Land. While the First World War raged, Blackstone addressed a Zionist mass rally in Los Angeles on January 27, 1918. His remarks were indicative of his theology and also his innermost attitudes toward Jewish people.

After expressing his pleasure at the large audience of both gentiles and Jews, he excitedly spoke of the Balfour Declaration and the thrilling events transpiring in Palestine. "I wish all of you

Gentiles were true Israelites in your religious life, and I wish all of you Jews were true Christians," Blackstone shared with the assembled Zionists, continuing, "I am and for over thirty years have been an ardent advocate of Zionism. This is because I believe that true Zionism is founded on the plan, purpose, and fiat of the everlasting and omnipotent God, as prophetically recorded in His Holy Word, the Bible."

Blackstone explained to the large audience that there were only three options open to every Jew. The first was to become a "true" Christian, accepting Jesus Christ as Lord and Savior. He quickly added that few Jews would accept this option. The second option was to become a "true" Zionist and "thus hold fast to the ancient hopes of the fathers, and the assured deliverance of Israel, through the coming of their Messiah, and complete national restoration and permanent settlement in the land which God has given them." The third option was to be an "assimilant." He explained that assimilants were "Jews who will not be either Christians or Zionists. They wish to remain in various nations enjoying their social, political and commercial advantages."

The seventy-seven-year-old Blackstone then personally charged the Jews assembled at the Zionist rally:

> Oh, my Jewish friends, which of these paths shall be yours? We are living in tragic times. The most momentous events of all human history are impending. God says you are dear unto Him and that "He that toucheth you toucheth the apple of his eye" Zech. 2:8. He has put an overwhelming love in my heart for you all, and therefore I have spoken thus plainly."[43]

"Study this wonderful Word of God," William E. Blackstone concluded, "and see how plainly God Himself has revealed Israel's pathway unto the perfect day."

### The 1918 Prophecy Conferences

By 1918 liberal Christianity had begun a total warfare on the premillennialism and biblical literalism of fundamentalist-evangelicalism. Professor Kemper Fullerton of Oberlin College concluded in the *Harvard Theological Review* : "Is not Zionism, attractive as it is, really an anachronism, as the Reform Jews assert? Reform Judaism would seem to be on a far sounder basis when it seeks to solve the problem of Judaism by reinterpreting it in terms of modern life." *The Christian Century* in December 1917 had warned against the "Second Coming propaganda" of the premillennialists.[44]

Shailer Mathews (1863–1941) and Shirley Jackson Case (1872–1947) of the University of Chicago Divinity School disdained Zionism and scathingly attacked the premillennialist Christian Zionists. A postmillennialist, Case viewed the restoration of the Jewish people to Palestine as a picture painted by "afflicted Israelites." The professor of early church history and New Testament interpretation wrote in his *The Millennial Hope* (1918) that "one may well admire their [Jewish] unbounded confidence in God, even though they misjudged his intentions for the future and were slow to learn from the signs of the times that his purposes in history were to be worked out in a much less spectacular manner than they had frequently imagined."[45]

Case argued that apocalyptic movements, such as premillennialism, grew dramatically in times of political and economic crisis, and he portrayed premillennial fundamentalist-evangelicals as "pessimists" with a theology of "fairy stories." In his article published in Mathews's journal *The Biblical World*, Case declared that World War I was a "gigantic effort to make the world safe for democracy" and defended his view of the upward progress of the Christian world. He accused premillennialist teaching of being "fundamentally antagonistic to our present national ideal" and "a serious menace to our democracy."[46]

The fundamentalist-evangelicals were not to be deterred by anti-Zionist liberal Protestants. The Philadelphia Prophetic Conference was held May 28–30, 1918, in the Academy of Music of the City of Brotherly Love. The effect that World War I was having on a renewed interest in the prophetic passages of the Bible was evident in the success of the meeting. The seating capacity of the Academy was 3300, and it was filled. An eight-article statement of faith was adopted for the conference. The fifth article asserted:

"We believe that there will be a gathering of Israel to her land in unbelief, and she will be afterward converted by the appearance of Christ on her behalf."[47]

This article was affirmed and reaffirmed by speakers at the conference who recognized the special role of the Jewish people in prophecy. William L. Pettingill, dean of the Philadelphia School of the Bible and pastor of the North Church in Wilmington, Delaware, asserted that the "future of the world depends upon God's promises to Israel, for it has pleased God to promise to bring the universal blessing to this race through the despised and dispersed people called the Jews." In a later address, Pettingill declared: "I cannot, for the life of me, see how a Christian can do otherwise than love the Jew, when he remembers that everything he has in the world worthwhile came to him through the Jews."[48]

P. W. Philpott, the pastor of the Gospel Tabernacle of Hamilton, Ontario, emphasized that Dr. Weizmann's gift of a formula worth millions to the British government if they "would favor the reestablishment of his people in the land of Palestine" was the supreme sacrifice of a Russian Jew. To Rev. Philpott, God's blessing on the Jewish people and their love for the land were some of the greatest "signs of the times." He preached:

> Since I have been in my present pastorate, the first national council of the Jewish nation has been held. Think of it—for 2500 years without a king or leader, and for nearly 2000 years without a country, scattered and peeled, hated of all nations, and yet, they have survived and thrived, they have never been swallowed up by any nation. If any nation attempted it, it soon followed the example of Jonah's whale. Since the founding of the Zionist Society in 1896 the Jewish nation had made its presence felt in a manner that is nothing short of marvelous. If I had the time, I could show that as legislators, educators, and financiers, they are represented out of all proportion to their numbers.[49]

"We hear a great deal about patriotism these days, but I do not think that there is any patriotism equal to that of the orthodox Jew," Philpott insisted. "For nineteen centuries they have been out of their land, but ever longing for home." During the 1920s

Rev. Philpott would become pastor of the famed Moody Memorial Church, a few blocks down the street from Moody Bible Institute in Chicago.

One of the prominent speakers at the conference was well acquainted with the environment of early-twentieth-century Palestine. Rev. A. E. Thompson, pastor of the American Church in Jerusalem, had been driven from the Holy Land by the Turks at the outbreak of World War I. A Canadian and prominent premillennial fundamentalist-evangelical, Thompson was at the time of the conference the field secretary for the American Committee for Armenian and Syrian Relief. He became very emotional as he shared his experiences about the Turks in his discourse "The Capture of Jerusalem," and anti-Muslim rhetoric was interspersed throughout his lecture. "As we hurried down the street, I looked up to the tower of David," Rev. Thompson related to a spellbound audience, "and there I saw this [Turkish] flag. Look at it! What a flag! A blood-red field with 'the horned moon and one lone star within its nether tip.' Emblem of death! Emblem of night!"[50]

Thompson declared that the capture of Jerusalem by Great Britain was an event toward which those who studied prophecy had looked forward for many years. But far beyond this, Thompson found the capture of Jerusalem to be "a pivot in prophecy" and the beginning of a prophetic era. Until this period, Jerusalem had been under Muslim rule (with the exception of a few decades under the Christian Crusaders), and Thompson told those in the great hall of the Academy of Music that the Muslim rule was one of intense oppression. He stressed that Jerusalem "has lain under Mohammedan oppression, an oppression that no one can comprehend unless he has lived under it and tried to preach the gospel of Jesus Christ." He noted that the capture of Jerusalem was the beginning of the defeat of this tyranny.[51]

Although Thompson admitted that the ease with which the British captured Jerusalem was a surprise, it was no surprise to God who had appointed the hour. Furthermore, the former Jerusalem pastor stressed that Jerusalem's capture was the beginning of great things for the "Promised Land" and for the Jewish people. The forty Jewish colonies were "turning the wilderness into a very garden of the Lord" and soon more money and Jews would "pour" into the land with the blessing of the Allies. To Thompson, this meant that the "times of the Gentiles" was nearing an end, and Jerusalem would be "trodden down of the Gentiles" no more (he cited Luke 21:24). Rebuilding of the Holy Land under God's chosen people, the Jews, had been prophesied just as surely as their dispersion.[52] "The proof of the regathering of Israel is embarrassing in its riches," James M. Gray added in the address following Thompson's, subsequently proclaiming: "Zionism is only one of the many agencies for bringing her back."[53]

Later in 1918, Gray would participate in a second important prophetic conference. The New York Prophetic Conference was held in Carnegie Hall during the Thanksgiving holiday. Some had doubted that such a hall could be filled in New York, but every seat was taken the first evening and several hundred were turned away to an overflow hall in the Church of Strangers. Comparable excitement by the speakers and participants over the "prophetic events" concerning General Allenby's capture of Jerusalem and the regathering of the Jewish people to their historic homeland was recorded. William B. Riley, pastor of the First Baptist Church in Minneapolis, proclaimed: "Jerusalem now attracts the attention of the world; the land of Palestine is now promised by all belligerents to the Jew. History runs into the mould of prophecy and the day may be nigh at hand."[54] Arno C. Gaebelein, one of the most prolific writers and prophecy teachers of the early twentieth century, spoke on "The Capture of Jerusalem and the Great Future of That City."

Nevertheless, in future years Riley and Gaebelein (like most fundamentalist-evangelicals) were thought by many Jewish and gentile scholars to be basically anti-Semitic. Others insisted that, in spite of their pro-Zionist rhetoric, many fundamentalist-evangelicals were ambivalent or deceptive in their attitudes toward Jewish people. Therefore it is important to analyze the attitudes of this early movement toward Jews in an effort to better understand their later kin.

# 2

## ATTITUDES AND ANTI-SEMITISM

Anti-Semitism is usually defined as dislike or hatred for Jews, an extreme prejudice against Jews or Jewish customs. Actions and policies reflecting these attitudes, from social discrimination to physical persecution, have manifested themselves in hostility toward the Jewish people throughout history. While scholars debate today what actually constitutes anti-Semitism,[1] this study must contend with the question: Were the early fundamentalist-evangelicals anti-Semitic?

Those premillennialists who have been studied in the preceding chapter certainly believed that every man and woman had to accept Jesus Christ as the Messiah and Lord to be "saved." This belief included the need of each Jewish man and woman to "accept Jesus" as well. Thus the Christian emphasis on evangelism, of taking the gospel message to all people, continued to be an intrinsic part of the early fundamentalist-evangelicals' theological system. Since they believed that men and women were doomed to hell who did not acknowledge Jesus as the only Savior given by God as a sacrifice for the sins of humankind, they encouraged one another to be bold in taking this "message of life" to all people— including the Jewish community.

Certainly such evangelism was as repugnant to the Jews of the nineteenth and early twentieth centuries as it is today. Did it, however, constitute anti-Semitism? Jews throughout history had faced hostility of Christians who wanted to force them to convert to Christianity or who despised them for not converting. And yet, the belief in Jesus as the only Messiah of humankind was intrinsic to early Christian belief as well as historical Christian belief. Anti-Semitism actually preceded Christianity, and it seems to be rash to assume that the Christian belief system is necessarily anti-Semitic—that dogmatism on some theological particulars that are repugnant to Jews is anti-Semitic.

It appears that fundamentalist-evangelicals, with their unique view of the future and conception of the Jewish people, were in fact more positive toward the Jewish community than other Christians. As has been shown, their premillennialist eschatology contradicted the postmillennial triumphalism of their age. Premillennialists insisted that the Bible did not teach that the whole world would be converted to Christianity through the church. In fact, they were convinced that the world could not be converted to Christianity before the second coming of Jesus Christ. While the gospel message should be preached, in their estimation a virtual life preserver for the "unsaved," they knew that all would not accept the message.

In addition, no one should be coerced or forced to accept the fundamentalist-evangelical understanding of God's message. At his return, Jesus would convince the Jewish people and all others that he was indeed the Messiah, very God, the savior of the world. One Jewish woman of the latter nineteenth century responded to the evangelistic presentation of a fundamentalist-evangelical with this answer: "I don't know whether or not the Messiah was here the first time, but when he comes he will tell me if he was here before." How could the evangelist argue with such a response?

Again, the fundamentalist-evangelical's theology may have been distasteful or ridiculous to the vast majority of the Jews in the world, but was it anti-Semitic? The preaching of the fundamentalist-evangelicals did not single out the Jewish people as being under the wrath of God, but rather insisted that all human beings needed God's special provision in Jesus Christ. Dispensational premillennialists, such as James H. Brookes, William E. Blackstone, James M. Gray, Arno C. Gaebelein, and Cyrus I. Scofield (editor of the famed *Scofield Reference Bible* which had such a dispensationalist impact on the movement), even concluded that God only required men and women throughout history to respond to the revelation God had given during particular eras or dispensations. Thus, the patriarchs of the Jewish faith recorded in the "old testament" had responded to God's revelation—Abraham, Isaac, Jacob, David, and the rest had all been "saved" and would be in heaven. They had "looked forward" to the sacrifice and resurrection of "God's Son," Jesus Christ. The fundamentalist-evangelical had to acknowledge as well that God would be the final judge, who would separate the "wheat from the tares" and in justice judge the hearts and actions of humankind.

Jesus himself had called into question whether mere words were sufficient for salvation when he declared in his Sermon on the Mount:

> "Not everyone who says to me, 'Lord, Lord,' will enter the kingdom of heaven, but only he who does the will of my Father who is in heaven. Many will say to me on that [Judgment] day, 'Lord, Lord, did we not prophesy in your name, and in your name drive out demons and perform many miracles?' Then I will tell them plainly, 'I never knew you. Away from me, you evildoers!'" (Matt. 7:21-23, NIV)

Fundamentalist-evangelicals were well aware of these verses, and their ministers and evangelists preached messages on this passage, a passage where Jesus began by warning, "Watch out for false prophets. They come to you in sheep's clothing, but inwardly they are ferocious wolves" (Matt. 7:15, NIV). Historically, the fundamentalist-evangelical of the nineteenth century knew that this could refer to some professing Christian Bible teachers or evangelists. In the modern period, it could extend to televangelists and the electronic church.

## CHOSEN PEOPLE?

In contrast to many Catholics and Protestants of their day, fundamentalist-evangelicals viewed the Jewish community as the chosen people of God. Arno C. Gaebelein in his book *Hath God Cast
Away His People?* (1905) explained that "God had foreknown His
people [the Jews] and called them to a distinctive and peculiar
place in the earth and for the government of the earth." Gaebelein taught that throughout the Bible God declared that the Jewish people "should never cease to be a nation before Him and
that they shall be at last that in the earth, as a nation, for which
He called them." Quoting from such Jewish scriptures as Jeremiah 30:11 and 31:35–37, Gaebelein assured his Christian readers that "numerous other passages could be quoted in which
God assures His people that He will never abandon them forever."[2]

"But what of the Jews' rejection of Jesus?" Christians asked the
fundamentalist-evangelical movement. To Gaebelein (as to others
in the movement), God's relationship with his chosen people in
the ancient period underscored his devotion to the nation in the
modern period. This analysis of the Jewish people of the ancient
world differed little from traditional Jewish interpretation.
"Again and again God's firstborn Son, Israel, (Exodus 4:22) had
been disobedient, a stiffnecked people," Gaebelein continued.
"They were punished and led into captivity, their city plundered
and razed, their temple burned and land laid waste, and still
God's infinite mercy hovers over the people and the land and He
never saith that He hath cast them away."

As for the sensitive area of rejection of Jesus, Arno Gaebelein
acknowledged that "a part of the nation, the Jews, had rejected
their Messiah and King, who had come to His own; they had
cried their awful 'Away with Him!' 'Crucify Him!' 'His blood be
upon us and upon our children!'" For Gaebelein, each individual Jewish person of his day had to make the choice to accept
Jesus or reject Jesus. This would form his categories of "believing
Jew" and "unbelieving Jew." Nevertheless, Gaebelein disputed
the Christ-killer theme, reminding Christians that from that same

cross "there came that wonderful prayer [from Jesus], 'Father, for-
give them for they know not what they do.' " God had not rejected
or cast away the Jewish people.

Gaebelein emphasized that the fundamentalist-evangelical's
"literal" interpretation of the Bible was quite a contrast to general
Christendom's approach. He wrote:

> What a different answer Christendom has to this question. If the
> Jew asks of Christendom the question about his national future,
> the promises of blessing and glory, he receives a strange answer. Or
> if he turns to the great [Christian] commentators on the Bible he
> finds teachings altogether opposite to the plain national promises,
> which belong still to his people. He is told that God hath cast them
> away and that there is nothing left for an earthly people. He hears
> that the church is Israel and all the promises given to the original
> Israel find now a spiritual fulfillment in the church.[3]

"But the intelligent, orthodox Hebrew refuses to accept this spiritualizing mode of interpretation," Arno Gaebelein related, "nor
does he find anywhere throughout Christendom that his national
promises and national glories are now fulfilled in a spiritual way
in the church." Fundamentalist-evangelicals found themselves
in much clearer agreement with Orthodox Rabbi H. Pereira
Mendes than with the classical reformist Rabbi Isaac Mayer Wise.

Such views are underscored as one reads the statements fundamentalist-evangelicals made about the Jewish people in the
preceding chapter. Gaebelein would become a foremost inter-
preter of these prophetic views in the early twentieth century
and would be a main contributor to the famed *Scofield Reference
Bible*.[4] It is extremely important, therefore, to understand that
like other fundamentalist-evangelicals, Gaebelein tied his entire
belief in God's faithfulness and an inspired Bible to God's treatment of the Jewish people. He insisted:

> If all this wrong and confusing [mainline Christian] interpretation
> of the Word of God, which does not distinguish between Israel
> and the church, were true, and if it were true that God hath cast
> away totally and finally Israel, then we certainly would have to give
> up the belief in a verbally inspired Bible. It would be true what
> higher criticism is constantly claiming, that the Jewish prophets

were patriots and dreamers and not inspired by God. Furthermore, God's gifts and calling would be not without repentance; God would have gone back upon His own word, and in consequence of this we as sinners of the Gentiles would have no assurance of our own salvation.[5]

If God had not been faithful to his promises and blessings for the Jewish people, Arno Gaebelein would have lamented, "Will He not do the same with us?" "For who can assure us that God really means what He hath said about us in Ephesians if He hath cast away Israel and is not keeping His promises?" Gaebelein concluded.

Arno C. Gaebelein and the early fundamentalist-evangelical movement, however, had no doubt that God still loved the Jewish people and had a wonderful future for them. William E. Blackstone cautioned Christians who would "spiritualize away" God's promises to the Jewish people: "Think a moment. Do you condemn the Jews for rejecting Christ, when He came in such literal fulfillment of prophecy, and yet reject the same literalness about his second coming? This is not consistent."[6]

Unlike many Christians and Jews of their day, fundamentalist-evangelicals believed that the Jewish people continued to be a "nation" rather than merely a religious "sect." Soon after the First International Prophetic Conference, James Brookes's periodical, *The Truth*, featured an article by Rev. A. C. Tris entitled, "Is Israel a Nation? Or a Sect?" Tris, who was from Lincoln, Nebraska, reaffirmed the belief of fundamentalist-evangelicals that this was a very important question, because "if Israel is a nation its restoration to the land of their fathers may be expected; but, if it is a sect, it has ceased to exist as a nation, and can only claim a temporal existence among other religious sects on the globe."[7] Through illustrations from the Bible, the Hebrew language, and the historical separation of Jewish people within the nations because of their religion, Rev. Tris emphasized that the Jewish people could only be considered "a scattered nation."

Rev. A. C. Tris concluded with statements that revealed his deep respect for the Jewish people:

We challenge any one acquainted with that wonderful people to prove, that as a nation they have relinquished their language and nationality and have acknowledged themselves to be a sect among the nations. The truth is, that the Jews pray every year, and many of them every day, for their restoration as a nation, to the land of their fathers. Israel scattered over the world, is like a spider's web mysteriously inter-woven with the nations by golden threads, and closely identified with the very sentiments of our own hearts. As a sect—Israel's people is a misnomer in the world; but, as a nation they are like the obelisks of former grandeur and future glory.[8]

The fundamentalist-evangelicals mocked other Christians who claimed that the Jews would be converted one by one and gradually absorbed into the Christian church. James Brookes chided: "It must be admitted that for eighteen hundred years, the work of conversion [of the Jews] has been amazingly slow, and there is no immediate prospect of its speedier accomplishment in the future."[9]

The early fundamentalist-evangelical movement believed that God was pro-Jewish and that those who hurt the Jewish people would be punished directly by God. They took seriously Genesis 12:3, where God promised Abram:

"I will bless those who bless you,
      and whoever curses you I will curse;
and all peoples on earth
      will be blessed through you." (NIV)

They affirmed Zechariah 2:8, which claimed that whoever touches God's Jewish people has touched "the apple of his eye." To the prophecy-minded fundamentalist-evangelical, anti-Semitism was a serious offense against God, which would incur grave consequences, and these premillennialists took to task a Christendom that maligned God's "chosen people."

## OPPOSITION TO ANTI-SEMITISM

James Brookes once remarked of the penchant of Christian theologians to appropriate the blessings of the Bible for themselves while relegating the curses of the Bible to the Jews: "Let not a Gentile talk anymore after this of the meanness of a Jew." In his book *I Am Coming,* Rev. Brookes bemoaned the fact that most Christians "do not see that God must have preserved this extraordinary people for some wonderful purpose." Of the anti-Semitism of the world empires he wrote:

> For 2500 years the four great world empires, and the kingdoms of Christendom, have sought to crush [the Jews], and at this day the most gigantic despotism of earth [Czarist Russia] is trying to grind them to powder. But all of this is but the outworking of Jehovah's plans, "till He make Jerusalem a praise in the earth," Isaiah 62:7, when "ten men shall take hold, out of all languages of the nations, even shall take hold of the skirt of him that is a Jew, saying We will go with you; for we have heard that God is with you," Zechariah 8:23.[10]

Before his death in 1897, Brookes would look fondly on the work of a young German Methodist minister, Arno C. Gaebelein, who had been converted to a premillennial and prophetic belief. Gaebelein would provide a commentary on the anti-Semitism of the Christian church in the next few decades. For example, in his book, *The Jewish Question* (1912), Gaebelein insisted that the Christian church had done all in its power to thwart God's plan for the Jewish people by afflicting them. Rev. Gaebelein had no doubt that God was going to punish Christendom for such actions against God's chosen people. Arno Gaebelein wrote about anti-Semitism:

> So it has been for centuries; so it is in the twentieth century. Instead of provoking the Jews to jealousy [by Christian good deeds and a life of love], that some of them might be saved, the Gentiles have hated and bitterly persecuted the Jews, and by their unchristian, yea inhuman, cruel and wicked treatment of the Jews, the Jews instead of being moved to jealousy, have become more hardened and their afflictions have been increased. The sin against Israel is the sin of the Gentiles, it will be the sin for which they will be judged by Him, who is not only King of kings, but also King of the Jews (Matt. 25:31; Joel 3:1-3).[11]

Gaebelein's journal, *Our Hope,* would be viewed by many fundamentalist-evangelicals as the successor to Brookes's journal, *The*

*Truth.* As will be seen in subsequent chapters, this important periodical not only brought to the attention of Christians dangerous anti-Semitic movements, but also clearly railed against prejudice against Jews, believing that anti-Jewish movements and attitudes were directly linked to the gates of hell and Satan himself. *Our Hope* would cross denominational barriers, and its readers represented a broad section of theologically conservative Christians from a wide variety of vocational and educational backgrounds.

At the Third International Prophetic Conference held in Allegheny, Pennsylvania, from December 3 through 6, 1895, Dr. Ernst F. Stroeter, the early editor of *Our Hope,* was an example of the constant criticism of Christian anti-Semitism by the early fundamentalist-evangelical movement. And he blamed Christendom for any Jewish hostility toward Jesus. "Fifteen centuries of Christian history, during which the professed followers of Jesus have shed more Jewish blood alone than Titus and Epiphanes combined, accentuate the Jew's objection," Stroeter declared, later underscoring that "it is as good as forgotten, that Christianity is the legitimate daughter of Biblical Judaism; that in all the essentials of a supernatural, revealed religion the orthodox Jew is our elder brother, not a heathen who imagines vain things and worships devils."[12]

Dr. Stroeter had reminded those scholars and laypersons at the conference that "Israel's history is unique. No other people on earth ever did or ever will stand as Israel does in covenant relation with the God of heaven and earth." He spoke of a basically triumphalistic Christendom that had dominated the century of evangelicalism, noting that "Greek and Roman, American and Chinaman, may in Christ Jesus, approach that same God and call Him Abba Father; but God has never undertaken to be the God of Americans or of the Chinese as He has to be the God of Israel."

Ernst Stroeter insisted that "anti-Semitism and Jew-hatred" was not "a thing of the past in Christendom." In addition, he believed that the Bible taught that the "greatest and most awful foe and destroyer of that wonderful people [the Jews] is still to arise." Premillennialists believed that the Bible taught of a Great

Tribulation period that would occur in the future and an Antichrist led by Satan who would try to destroy God's chosen people, the Jews. "The time of Jacob's greatest trouble is still to come," Professor Stroeter stated. Nevertheless, he believed that the Jewish people would be delivered from such a calamity, and God would bless the nations through Israel. Stroeter was glad that some Christian believers were "awakening to a deeper sense of their obligation and responsibility toward the long despised and neglected Jew."

He himself could not escape such feelings of obligation, although he was aware of the boisterous triumphalism among some members of the Jewish community. Ernst F. Stroeter preached:

> But here he is, the imperishable, ubiquitous, irrepressible Jew, the most conspicuous and emphatic figure of all history. The Jew, without a king or a government of his own, has seen the mightiest empires rise and has attended their funeral. An exile from his own land, he has witnessed every civilized country of the Old World change ownership over and over. No nation has ever prospered in his land, the land that flowed with milk and honey while he dwelt there; he has prospered in every land, under every clime. He receives no hearty welcome, no legislative favors, no social advantages anywhere, hardly justice; but in the race for wealth, for success and for honors in art and science and literature he leads everywhere. He has been branded with infamy, loaded with unutterable contempt; behold him, the cringing, crouching, unresisting object of pity!
>
> But a few brief hours of genial sunshine, a few decades of emancipation and equal rights, and behold the unbearably proud, and loud and obnoxious modern Jew, whose race-pride will yet fan the slumbering embers of inbred Gentile anti-Semitism into furious flame.[13]

"Talk of Egyptian Sphynxes and of Gordian knots," the former professor at Denver University exclaimed, "the greatest riddle, the one unsolvable mystery of all the ages, is the Jew. His very existence and preservation is an unanswerable challenge to the human mind for a rational explanation. No philosophy [is] yet equal to the task."

The same year Stroeter addressed this conference, Arno C. Gaebelein traveled to Russia to get a firsthand impression of Jewish conditions there. He also journeyed to Germany, Poland, Romania, Galicia, and England. Upon arriving at his destination, he often would head for the nearest synagogue and, because of his full beard, would immediately be categorized as a fellow Jew. Once he had established that he was actually a Christian, his sensitive spirit and his Zionistic zeal would endear him to the local Jewish community. For example, in Warsaw, Poland, an Orthodox rabbi invited him to address the local Chovevei Zion society "on his belief in the restoration of Israel and the Messiah."[14] Gaebelein returned to New York in November 1895, and Stroeter sailed for Europe in May of 1896.

Both Gaebelein and Stroeter were German in background and were appalled at the rise of anti-Semitism in their homeland. While in his former hometown in Germany, Gaebelein was asked by "one of the best Christians" in the town to lecture to the local Anti-Semitic Society. He responded immediately by giving the man a stern lecture on bigotry, which he noted "seemed to have a good effect." Writing home, Arno Gaebelein sadly noted: "It is only too true that Protestant Germany is Jew-hating, and we fear, from what we have seen and heard, that sooner or later there will be another disgraceful outbreak [of anti-Semitism]."[15]

Stroeter also referred to the intense and growing European anti-Semitism. During his second trip in 1897, he traveled to Palestine and then to Europe, deciding to stay in Germany and fight the anti-Semitic waves there. He also campaigned to convince Reform Jews to return to their traditional roots. He remarked in his first 1897 correspondence about Reform Jews in Germany with whom he had had detailed discussions:

And when I upbraided them for their "reform," i.e., their rationalizing and unbelieving Judaism, they took it in excellent grace, and acknowledged quite readily, that underneath the garb of assimilation and reform, the genuine, national Jew was still very much alive. They were frank enough to admit that the influence of "reform" was, after all, not very strong over the Jewish mind and heart. The Jew is stronger than the "reformer." So, when the question of

Zionism was up, they at first were very shy in committing themselves either for or against the movement. But when they saw my
earnest conviction of the providential character of this remarkable
sign of our times, and my deep interest in the awakening of Jewish
national consciousness, it did not take them long to discover that
they all were, in the depths of their hearts, real Zionists.[16]

On the whole, fundamentalist-evangelicals had little regard for
the rationalistic Reform Judaism advocated by Rabbi Isaac Mayer
Wise. They found the attitudes of traditional Judaism toward the
Bible and the Holy Land much more palatable.

Orthodox Jews, such as Rabbi H. Pereira Mendes, concurred.
Rabbi Mendes wrote a strong letter to the editor of the *New York
Sun* which insisted that the Bible was a central key to national
restoration. "True Zionism is founded on the Bible," Mendes asserted. "Any idea at variance with the teachings, direct or indi-
rect, of the Bible, will ever be rejected by the vast majority of
Hebrews as not being true Zionism." Rabbi Mendes also insisted,
"If there are Jews who do not live up to high ideas, they are no
more Jews than the convicts at Sing Sing are Christians," and "If
there are Hebrews who reject the Bible as an authority and who
oppose any idea of a Jewish state, even as a religious influence,
they may be born in the race, but they are not inspired by the
spirit which moved our prophets to preach, our psalmists to
sing, our poets and philosophers to write, and our martyrs to
die."[17]

Fundamentalist-evangelical periodicals spoke out against anti-
Semitism around the world and anti-Semitic acts in the United
States during the latter decades of the nineteenth century and
the early decades of the twentieth century.[18] And early fundamentalist-evangelicals were convinced that those who persecuted the Jewish people would be punished by God (both in this
life and in the next). C. I. Scofield, the famed editor of the *Scofield
Reference Bible,* a standard in dispensational fundamentalist-evangelical circles during most of the twentieth century, wrote in 1902
that the promises of God to the Jewish people in Genesis 12:1–3
were as valid as the day in which they were written. He declared:

Can you point to me a passage in this Bible which revokes that last promise ["I will bless those who bless you, and whoever curses you I will curse"]? Can you bring me one single illustration from history of a nation that has persecuted the Jew and escaped chastisement? If I had no other proof that this Bible is inspired the literal fulfillment in human history of that last promise would be to me the convincing, unanswerable demonstration that this book is from God. Never, never, has that statement been revoked. No nation ever persecuted the Jew and escaped national retribution. Hamen is always hanged ultimately on the gallows prepared for Mordecai.[19]

Scofield added that "the Scriptures account for the Jew, and that the Jew, in turn, is the ever-lasting, everywhere-present, verification of the Scriptures."

## THE PROPHETIC SCENARIO

Some modern scholars have questioned such philo-Semitism as self-serving, arrogant, and ambivalent. They point out that these fundamentalist-evangelicals believed that a horrible time of tribulation awaited the Jewish people and that a battle of Armageddon would be fought in the Holy Land. Others have insisted that the fundamentalist-evangelicals were trying to get the Jewish people back in the land to get them all converted and hasten the second coming of Jesus Christ.

In 1982 William Martin, sociologist at Rice University, wrote an article in *The Atlantic Monthly* castigating premillennial theology and explaining how it could "manifest itself in the activities of the Christian New Right, many of whose members accept its tenets." He cited Secretary of the Interior James Watt's statement to a House Interior Committee that he did "not know how many future generations we can count on before the Lord returns" as an implication of Watt's lack of concern for long-range conservation efforts of natural resources (Watt denied that charge). Dr. Martin then voiced great concern over premillennialists in key foreign policy posts:

Similarly, if a President were to appoint one or more premillennialists to key foreign-policy posts (who at the confirmation hearings would think to probe for beliefs about the Second Coming?), what incentive would they have to work for lasting peace in the Middle East, since they would regard a Russian-led attack on Israel as a necessary precursor of the Millennium? What stance would they assume toward the Trilateral Commission and the Council on Foreign Relations, both of which are viewed as major engines of the one-world Antichrist conspiracy? And if the nuclear destruction of Russia is foreordained, as in some pre-millennial schemes, might not a fundamentalist politician or general regard his finger on the button as an instrument of God's eternal purpose.[20]

As we have seen in the works of Shailer Mathews and Shirley Jackson Case in the early twentieth century, such fears have been expressed before. Although chapter 4 will underscore the fact that conspiracy theory may consume some of those who hold a premillennial view of the future, it is also evident that there has been much misunderstanding concerning the fundamentalist-evangelical belief system.

In all fairness to these prophetically minded Protestants we have studied, they believed that one should never try to force God's program on the world. In their thinking that would be an exercise in futility. The Second Coming would occur at precisely the time God had chosen and not one minute before. And only God knew that time. Fundamentalist-evangelicals could only look for the "signs of the times" and go about their business trying to pattern their life after their Savior, Jesus. Certainly, they often failed in both cases—to discern the signs and to love their neighbors as themselves—but the latter failing was part and parcel of all segments of Christendom (and, indeed, of the human race). The researcher must treat these men and women as human beings and beware of misunderstanding their motives and intentions.

In regard to politics, the fundamentalist-evangelical was often apolitical. For much of the twentieth century, "political fundamentalism" would have seemed an anomaly to the fundamentalist-evangelical, an exercise in futility. Contrary to the postmillennial evangelicals of the nineteenth century, these premillennialists believed that Satan was constantly trying to totally control the world system and only God's Holy Spirit kept him in check. In addition, they believed an Antichrist would arise and that the Bible told them that famines, plagues, and persecutions would intensify—in short, things were going to get worse, not better. One can imagine how the First World War horrified men and women around the globe and won many a convert to the pre-millennial fold. While politicians and theologians were claiming that a peaceful world was at hand during the early twentieth century, the prophetically minded fundamentalist-evangelical teachers had preached that persecutions and atrocities would come.

Because the Bible was a "Jewish" book and God continued to be concerned about the Jewish people as God's people, the events prophesied in the Hebrew scriptures and the Christian Testament were believed to be directly connected to the Jewish people. A popular story told at least once in most prophecy conferences and in premillennial books of this early period recounted that when Frederick the Great, king of Prussia, asked the court chaplain for an argument that the Bible was an inspired book, he answered, "Your Majesty, the Jews." After relating this story, the fundamentalist-evangelical prophecy teacher would declare that the oracles of God were given to the Jewish people, that a large number of biblical predictions concerned their own Jewish history and nation, and that "Salvation is of the Jews!"[21] With the increased immigration of Jews into Palestine, the promulgation of the Balfour Declaration, and the British capture of Jerusalem, the events prophesied in the Bible appeared to be right on cue.

In October 1916, the Moody Bible Institute of Chicago (named after the great evangelist who helped establish it) commissioned a special presentation edition of William Blackstone's *Jesus Is Coming* and sent copies to ministers, missionaries, and theological students, circulating it well into the 1920s. The prophetic scenario detailed in this volume is indicative of the dispensational premillennialist interpretation that had such impact on fundamentalist-evangelicals within the mainline denominations and within independent congregations scattered across the United States.

Using proof texts from the Bible, *Jesus Is Coming* insisted that Jesus was prophesied to be king of the Jewish people (Isa. 9:6),

was born king of the Jews (Matt. 2:2), declared himself to be king
of the Jews (Matt. 27:11), and was crucified as "King of the Jews"
(Matt. 27:37). However, Jesus "came unto His own, and His own
received Him not" (John 1:11). Blackstone believed that Jesus
would have set up his kingdom in the first century C.E. if his fellow Jews had accepted him as Messiah, but his rejection and crucifixion delayed the kingdom from being instituted. God raised
Jesus from the dead and sent the Holy Spirit to the earth to
preach the "good news" of the kingdom (Acts 2, for example). At
first the message went out only to the Jewish people, but when
it was rejected by most, the disciples carried the message to the
gentiles as well (Acts 13:46). Thus, Blackstone and other dispensational fundamentalist-evangelicals believed that a "church
age" had intervened—an age when God called out a body of
believers in Jesus (both Jew and gentile) to be a mystical body of
Christ, a church of true believers, a bride of Jesus (see Eph. 3:3–6,
5:23–32; Col. 1:24–27).[22]

Before a "tribulation period," Blackstone taught that Jesus
would return for his "saints," the true Christian believers, to take
them to a great marriage feast. Translated like Enoch of old, they
would be "caught up to meet Christ in the air" (see 1 Thess.
4:16–17). This event is called the "Rapture," a "catching up or a
catching away." According to this popular pretribulation premillennial interpretation, the church would therefore escape the full
brunt of persecution (cf. Luke 21:36; 2 Peter 2:9; Rev. 3:10).

The rest of the world, however, would enter a seven-year
period of unequaled tribulation (Dan. 12:1; Matt. 24:21; Luke
21:25–26). Since the church in the Rapture had been taken out of
the world, God would begin to deal exclusively with his chosen
people, the Jews, once again (Acts 15:13–17; Ps. 51:18, 102:16). At
this time, the Jewish people would be finally and totally restored
to their own land (Isa. 11:11; 60; Jer. 30:3; 31; 32:36–44; Amos
9:15; Zech. 8:7–8; Rom. 11).

The next event was considered to be one of the most solemn
and foreboding subjects in the Bible. An Antichrist, one who
is absolutely opposed to Jesus Christ and his teaching, would
finally reveal himself. According to 2 Thessalonians 2, he is a

"man of sin," "the son of perdition," "the lawless one." Funda-mentalist-evangelicals believed that just as Jesus was the express image of God, the Antichrist will be the culminating manifesta-tion of Satan. While the church was present on the earth, the Holy Spirit of God had hindered Satan's power. Now, with the rapture of the believers in Christ, the deceptive powers and unrighteous fury of Satan could be unleashed in full force during the Tribulation. The Antichrist would deceive the Jewish people early in the tribulation period by helping them to rebuild their ancient Temple and by making a treaty with them. Unknown to the Jewish community on earth at that time, this would be "a covenant with death and an agreement with hell." Blackstone cor-related Isaiah 28:14–18 with Daniel 11:36 and Revelation 13:11–18 to document this biblical interpretation.[23]

This Antichrist will exalt himself above all that is called God, insist on being worshiped, and blaspheme by sitting in the rebuilt Temple of God in Jerusalem. Turning against the Jewish people, he will persecute them immensely. The early fundamental-ist-evangelicals believed that, sometime during this period, the Jewish people would accept Jesus Christ as their Messiah (Zech. 12:10–14; 13:6), and God once again would protect God's people from total annihilation (Matt. 24:34; Ps. 22:30).

While the Rapture was believed by most early fundamentalist-evangelicals to occur at the beginning of the tribulation period (the pretribulation premillennial view), the actual second com-ing of Jesus Christ to earth was expected to occur at the end of the seven-year tribulation period. According to this early fundamen-talist-evangelical prophetic scenario, Jesus will return to the earth with his saints, the church, and reveal himself as Lord and King during this Second Coming. He will execute judgment on the earth. Delivering his chosen people, the Jews, he will destroy the Antichrist and conquer the rebellious nations. Although some have termed this the battle of Armageddon (from Rev. 16:16), Blackstone in *Jesus Is Coming* does not use the term, nor does he refer to the particular verse in the Christian Testament in which the term appears.

After Christ's victory (this view taught) Satan is bound and chained in the abyss, kept from deceiving the nations for a thousand years (Rev. 20:1–3). The millennium, a thousand-year period of peace and prosperity under Jesus Christ's "glorious reign," now occurs (Rev. 20:4). At the end of this period, Satan is loosed once again to show that he is indeed the great deceiver. Nevertheless, he is destroyed and the "great white throne" Judgment occurs, where God judges all of the remaining dead (Rev. 20:11–15). Death and hell are then destroyed; and a new heaven, a new earth, and a new Jerusalem appear. William Blackstone delighted in quoting Rev. 21:1–4, which reads in the *King James Version:*

> Then I saw a new heaven and a new earth, for the first heaven and the first earth had passed away, and there was no longer any sea. I saw the Holy City, the new Jerusalem, coming down out of heaven from God, prepared as a bride beautifully dressed for her husband. And I heard a loud voice from the throne saying, "Now the dwelling of God is with men, and he will live with them. They will be his people, and God himself will be with them and be their God. He will wipe every tear from their eyes. There will be no more death or mourning or crying or pain, for the old order of things has passed away."

The "ages of ages," Eternity, a continual unfolding manifestation of God to God's followers throughout the ages to come, is finally bestowed (Rev. 21–22).[24]

## ATTITUDES

What becomes clearly evident as one analyzes this complicated prophetic scenario is that the early fundamentalist-evangelicals did not believe that they could hasten the Second Coming through any political actions – a fundamentalist-evangelical could only "watch and pray." Nor were these Protestants delighted that a Great Tribulation would terrorize the Jewish people who had returned to their ancient land. Like the Jewish prophets of old, the fundamentalist-evangelicals could only relate the message they felt God had given them in the Bible and warn the world of the wrath to come. In addition, it was made clear that "a time of trouble [was] not limited to Judea, but [was] as extensive as the inhabited earth."[25]

One also must question why scholars who do not give credence to this belief system should insist that it is detrimental to the Jewish community. Surely if the Rapture was to occur before the tribulation, the fundamentalist-evangelicals did not dare to try to bring about the conditions for tribulation (even if their belief system permitted it). Professor William Martin's claim, "Might not a fundamentalist politician or general regard his finger on the button [of nuclear missiles] as an instrument of God's eternal purpose?" is patently absurd: he would push the button no sooner than a Jewish general upset at Russian persecution of Jews or an atheist general who saw no future for the world. Actually, his premillennial eschatology should prevent him from doing so.

Fundamentalist-evangelicals have historically admitted that they do not see every detail of the future "clearly" – that while they try to discern the "signs of the times," God requires them to watch patiently and wait expectantly for the glorious unfolding of God's plan. Trying to "rush" or "force" God's Plan would be futile and foolish (in fact, downright sinful) in their estimation. Finally, Blackstone and other prophetically minded fundamentalist-evangelicals clearly stated: "There is no prophesied event which has to be fulfilled before His [Jesus'] coming in the air to receive the Church." The Rapture did not need any "help" – it could occur at any time![26]

It will be evident in subsequent chapters that a belief in the future rise of an Antichrist and tribulation period helped the fundamentalist-evangelical recognize the dangers both fascism and communism posed to the Jewish community and to the world. The belief in the rise of a deceptive and decadent false prophet would sensitize fundamentalist-evangelicals to the necessity of the separation of church and state and the inherent dangers in forcing one's belief system upon others. Their belief in the futility of Christian conversion of the whole world and their belief in the return of the unconverted Jewish community to the Holy Land would pit the fundamentalist-evangelical movement against a Calvinist covenant theology that would emphasize the church's conquering of the social and political institutions of the world. It would also help them to stand against an ecumenical "progressive" Christian civilization that would annihilate Judaism.

And yet, did not the fundamentalist-evangelical believe that even the Jewish people would ultimately accept Jesus as their Savior? Indisputably they did. There appears to be a vast difference, however, between the church's conquering of Judaism through Christian civilization and conversion, and the fundamentalist-evangelical belief in a Jewish Jesus coming back as his people's Messiah, freely accepted by them. The first view allows for forced conversion and attitudes of triumphalism, while the fundamentalist-evangelical view allows more respect for God's continual dealings with God's chosen people, the Jews. And, most importantly, the events would have to occur as the prophetic scenario dictates. Many Jewish scholars are not too worried about those events taking place.

In a day and age when the Catholic pontiff was considered the forerunner of the Antichrist and the Roman Catholic Church was felt to be the "harlot" mentioned in Revelation 17, fundamentalist-evangelical attitudes toward Jews are much more positive than their attitudes toward other religious movements. In fact, they appear to be biased toward the Jewish people. Their ridicule of liberal or non-Jewish Jews certainly was in keeping with the traditional Jewish views about those respective movements and, as we shall see in the next chapter, was part and parcel of the fundamentalist-modernist controversy.

One should not classify these theological battles as being anti-Semitic, but one can understand well why the Jewish community was not attracted to the fundamentalist-evangelical's "fervid belief" (to quote *The American Israelite*). Revivalism terrified the Jewish community, and evangelism was felt to be a cruel imposition, in the light of history. Blackstone, Stroeter, and Gaebelein all worked with missionary enterprises aimed at Jews at one time or another during their lives, and the fundamentalist-evangelical movement supported such "Jewish missions." Although deceptive evangelism was opposed and although at times their particular Jewish missions helped feed and clothe the poor immigrant

Jews of New York and Chicago in the latter part of the nineteenth century, Blackstone and Gaebelein would be opposed by both liberal and traditional Jews.[27] If comfortable with any Christian, the Jewish community of the late nineteenth century and early twentieth century chose the more liberal and "freethinking" Christian. It was felt that the liberal Christian belief system could be controlled to some extent.

In addition, early fundamentalist-evangelicals were in part products of their culture—throwbacks to the "century of evangelicalism." Even a respected Christian Zionist such as William E. Blackstone, a man who like all fundamentalist-evangelicals believed that he was personally responsible for the crucifixion of Jesus and that Jesus died personally for him, used statements in *Jesus Is Coming* that could promote further the Christ-killer theme that was prominent in both liberal and conservative Christianity. For example, in his discussion of the church and the millennial kingdom, Blackstone wrote:

> But the Jews rejected it and slew their King. They were not willing to have this man [Jesus] reign over them, and therefore the Kingdom did not "immediately appear." It became like a nobleman which "went into a far country, to receive for himself a kingdom and to return." See Luke 19:11–27. By this parable Jesus distinctly taught that the Kingdom was in the future.[28]

As in most Christian theology, Jews are viewed as being in theological darkness. Blackstone quotes Paul's words in Romans 10:1–4 about the Jew's zealousness for God but lack of divine knowledge. He affirms Paul's cry that his "heart's desire and prayer to God for the Israelites is that [the Jews] may be saved" (NIV). He hastens, however, to affirm Paul's later words in Romans 11:1: "I ask then, Did God reject his people? By no means!" (NIV).

As has been seen, early fundamentalist-evangelicals could succumb also to the caricature and stereotypes that their culture attributed to Jewish people. Nevertheless, they often stood up against Christendom in defense of Jews. To a fellow evangelical who reminded him that the Jews must go "through terrible judgments and tribulations" before the Second Coming, editor Ernst F. Stroeter asserted in 1894 that *Our Hope* was not "written for

Jewish readers," but that its "mission is to the Christian churches. It aims to bring before the believers from among the Gentiles the special claims which Israel has upon their prayers, their sympathies and their labor of love." Emphasizing that the Jew's position in God's plan of salvation needs to be set forth, Professor Stroeter related: "The apathy, and even antipathy, toward the Jew, into which the church has fallen, must be removed, and a better feeling awakened in her toward God's age-lasting people. . . . In Our Hope we preach to the Gentile church in behalf of the Jew."[29]

Such feelings based on the premillennial belief system are difficult to comprehend and constitute some of the most delicate interpretations of the primary materials. Definitely, these attitudes of the early fundamentalist-evangelical movement are not anti-Semitic. Surprisingly, in many cases they constitute a philo-Semitism. The modern fundamentalist-evangelical movement based its beliefs on these early precursors. From Dwight L. Moody through Billy Graham, from Ernst F. Stroeter through G. Douglas Young, the enigma of biblical literalism, Christian Zionism, and prophetic belief will face us at every turn.

The complexity of the fundamentalist-evangelical's penchant for prophetic interpretation of the Jewish people is clearly evident in the addresses delivered at the World Conference on Christian Fundamentals held in Philadelphia in 1919. Attended by six thousand people who had just gone through a grueling world war, the conference spawned a series of regional meetings throughout the United States and Canada. In fact, those in attendance represented forty-two of the forty-eight states in the United States and nearly every Canadian province. Notably, the premillennial eschatology of the speakers was coupled to a fundamentalist interpretation of the Bible that would lay a battle strategy against the forces of Christian liberalism—a strategy that would be used for decades.

In his message, "Prophecy—Why Study It?" William L. Pettingill, dean of the Philadelphia School of the Bible and prominent fundamentalist-evangelical, explained to the large crowd of Christians before him:

What a pity that the church of God is so generally and willingly ignorant of God's purpose concerning the Jews! Twenty-five or thirty years ago when I began reading the Word of God to folks – reading what God said with reference to His purpose concerning the Jewish people – when I read to folks that God was going to bring His people back to their own land, well, folks used to touch their foreheads significantly. The idea of the Jew going back to his own land! The idea of Palestine ever again being occupied by the Jew! Back in those days no Jews were permitted to enter into that land except for a very brief visit and then they had to promise to leave it within three months or they could not get a passport to go through the borders at all. It had been shut to them centuries upon centuries. Folks would say, "Do you mean to tell us, us –?" No, I did not mean to tell them anything; I was reading to them out of the Word of God; but they did not know anything about it, except the little bunch [of fundamentalist-evangelicals] here and there. God bless that little bunch! You will find them everywhere.[30]

"I am saying to you," Pettingill urged, "we ought to study the Word of prophecy in order to be delivered from inexcusable ignorance."

# 3

## FROM WAR TO WAR

"Chiliasm [the doctrine that Christ will return to reign on earth for a millennium] is a kind of religious disease," asserted Lutheran scholar and Concordia Seminary professor Theodore Graebner, in *War in the Light of Prophecy* (1941). "'Crack-brained' is what one is tempted to call their way of reasoning on the war in its relation to the 'days' of prophecy," he continued.[1]

That Dr. Graebner was able to republish material from his World War I treatise, *Prophecy and the War* (1918), in this World War II book underscores the stability and persistence of the premillennial view of the future between the wars. Originally, Professor Graebner had been upset by prophetic predictions concerning the First World War and horrified that articles, pamphlets, and books had "flooded" the Protestant denominations. "In the *Christian Herald*, Dr. Gray of Moody [Bible] Institute has written a series of articles on the Thousand-year Reign of Christ and its relation to the War," Professor Graebner complained on December 2, 1917. "The publisher now announces a second series, because so much interest was aroused by the first that the office of the paper was 'deluged with letters.'" "This seems to be a live subject," the theologian surmised in his first edition of *Prophecy and the War*. "Let us investigate it in the light of Scripture, history, and common sense." Ironically, Theodore Graebner's book was soon sold out itself within eight weeks and was published in a second edition as well.[2]

It was, thus, with a sense of chagrin that Graebner in 1941 looked back at the earlier period. "Within the Protestant churches," he reminisced, "many teachers of prominence within their denominations found new support for their millennialism in the grouping of the nations involved in the [First World War] conflict and in the effect of the fortunes of war especially on the Jewish people." The conservative Lutheran theologian and amillennial evangelical pastor lamented that "throughout the interval between the First and Second World Wars chiliasts [premillennialists] have been at work urging their interpretations upon the Christian world." He wrote:

> The pity of it is that again men who are known as Fundamentalists and as firm believers in the verbal inspiration of the Bible have identified themselves with the chiliasm of the most extreme type. Such magazines as Our Hope, Destiny, Revelation, The Sunday-school Times, *The Prophecy Monthly,* have with greater or less emphasis stressed the millennial scheme. Prophecy Monthly is the official publication of the American Prophetic League, Inc., an organization devoted to the distribution of millennialistic doctrine. The issue for February, 1941, lists twelve new books promoting the dispensationalist eschatology. The League distributes "rare material" in monthly releases to its membership in order to supply it with "information of vital import along prophetic lines."[3]

"Well, we Lutherans are largely amillennialists [no millennium], and as I proceed, I shall try to make clear the reason why," Theodore Graebner continued in the introduction of his 1941 treatise. "At the same time I shall endeavor to show that World War II as little as its predecessor of twenty-five years ago has any specific relation to the prophecies whose fulfillment is so confidently asserted by most Fundamentalists of today."

There is no doubt that this evangelical professor had little regard for the prophetic interpretations of the premillennialists. In the broad sea of evangelicalism, the premillennial fundamentalist-evangelical appeared to be an anomaly. And yet, Lutheran seminary professor Theodore Graebner had some questionable beliefs himself. He insisted: "Antichrist is so clearly described, for instance, in verses 36–39 of Daniel 11 and also Daniel 7:25;

9:27; 12:7,11; 2 Thessalonians 2:3,4; 1 Timothy 4:1–3; Revelation 11:2,3; 12:6,14, that we may with great assurance identify him with the Pope." In addition, Professor Graebner asserted that this Roman Catholic "Antichrist" pope met his downfall "through the [Lutheran] Reformation." "And now there is no longer any new development to which we are to look forward in the history of the Church on earth," Rev. Graebner declared confidently. "This is but a season of waiting for the return of Christ in glory." To this Lutheran scholar, the "Christian Church fought her last decisive battle in Luther's day," and World War II (as World War I) was "as punishment for the rejection of the Gospel in all Christian lands." Earlier in this book, Graebner criticized dispensationalists for rejecting the idea that the pope was the Antichrist and mocked them for their interest in the Zionist movement.[4]

Even Professor Graebner had to admit, however, that "in the war now raging [the Second World War] there are issues at stake, in Stalinism, Fascism, and Nazism, which the church recognizes as inimical to her program and to the lives of her members." While the church was not at a "physical Armageddon," Graebner believed it did face spiritual wars, including foes "in the field of false philosophy without and in apostate Modernism within, a condition which prevails in all lands."[5] As a conservative theologian with a belief that the Bible was the inspired Word of God, Theodore Graebner was aware of the "battle for the Bible" that had transpired the past few decades. He was indicative of numerous conservative Protestant pastors and laypersons who believed in the inerrancy of the Bible and fought against "modernism" — battling furiously against modern biblical criticism from World War I to World War II, without considering themselves premillennial "fundamentalists."

## THE FUNDAMENTALIST-MODERNIST CONTROVERSY

While the premillennialist view of the future had won the hearts of millions of Protestant Americans throughout the United States after the First World War, the battle for control of the academic centers of Protestantism was lost to fundamentalist-evangelicals between the world wars. Not only was their eschatology rejected, but biblical inerrancy was often abandoned in mainline seminaries and denominational headquarters throughout the country. Although the 1920s would be a basically conservative period of American history, theological liberalism prevailed in the higher echelons of denominational and intellectual circles. Theological "modernists" attempted to use evolution, biblical criticism, and social method to understand the world that surrounded them and to meet the needs of Christians. The cleavage in Christianity was akin to that between traditional Judaism and classical Reform Judaism at the turn of the twentieth century.

Seminaries such as Union, Harvard, Yale, Boston University, and Crozer took up the gauntlet of liberalism. When John D. Rockefeller (1839–1937) generously funded the University of Chicago Divinity School (Baptist), hiring an accomplished faculty, it became one of the country's strongest centers of Protestant liberalism before the First World War. In addition, Congregationalist, Protestant Episcopal, Methodist, Baptist, and Presbyterian churches were heavily affected by theological liberalism and its modernist application. As denominational seminaries graduated liberally oriented ministers, this "new theology" progressively penetrated the grass roots of Protestantism.

Nevertheless, the fundamentalist-evangelical movement continued to spread, founding its own Bible institutes and Bible colleges as theological training centers. Between the wars, some of these would become Christian liberal arts colleges. Wheaton College in Illinois became a center of the fundamentalist-evangelical movement under its president, Charles Blanchard (tenure 1882–1925), son of the nineteenth century postmillennial founder Jonathan Blanchard. Charles had been converted to dispensational premillennialism in the mid-1880s, and he would draft the doctrinal statement of the World's Christian Fundamentals Association in 1919.

Wheaton College would work closely with its Chicago neighbor, Moody Bible Institute, during this period. In the 1930s Wheaton was one of the fastest-growing liberal arts colleges in the nation. Billy Graham graduated from Wheaton College in 1943, pastored a Baptist church in Western Springs, Illinois, for sixteen months, became a key evangelist for Youth for Christ, and accepted the part-time presidency of separatist fundamentalist William B. Riley's Northwestern Schools in Minneapolis from 1947 to 1951. Rev. Graham would become the D. L. Moody of the latter half of the twentieth century.

### "FUNDAMENTALS"

During the First World War, the expressions "fundamentals," "returning to the fundamentals," "holding forth the fundamentals of the faith," and so on, had been commonly expressed in premillennial circles and churches. *The Fundamentals*, a series of twelve books intended to reaffirm the "fundamentals" of Christianity, were published from 1910 to 1915. William B. Riley founded a paper entitled *Christian Fundamentals in School and Church* in 1918, and the World's Christian Fundamentals Association was founded at a Bible conference in 1919. Curtis Lee Laws, the editor of the conservative Baptist journal *The Watchman-Examiner*, used the word "Fundamentalist" to describe the movement in an editorial July 1, 1920.[6]

Thus the setting for the fundamentalist-modernist controversy of the 1920s was actually evident years before. Contrary to high school and college textbooks that portray American fundamentalism as a "redneck" agrarian phenomenon of the rural South and point to the 1925 Scopes trial in Dayton, Tennessee, about the teaching of evolution in public schools, as an example of the fundamentalist mentality and anti-intellectualism, the fundamentalist-evangelical movement was in fact the product of highly educated northerners from an urban environment. Bible and prophecy conferences as well as prolific publication efforts had molded the movement before 1920. Modernists were well aware of the prophetic orientation of the fundamentalist-evangelicals. During the First World War, *The Christian Century* ran a twenty-one-article series that attacked the fundamentalist-evangelicals' premillennialism, and we have seen that Shailer Mathews and

Shirley Jackson Case of the University of Chicago Divinity School spared no hostile invective in their castigation of the premillennial movement.[7]

The Christian Century's series on millennialists is quite significant, for the periodical was closely linked to the University of Chicago Divinity School subsidized by John D. Rockefeller. In fact, Rockefeller wrote articles for the religious periodical from time to time. Advertisements for professor Herbert L. Willett's extensive series on premillennialism began early in 1918, and preparatory editorials flourished in the first two months. A January 1918 editorial entitled "The Millennial Hallucination" underscored the steady spread of premillennialism and the concern it engendered in liberal Protestant circles.[8] The editorial began by declaring, "It is really astonishing to what an extent the idea of a Millennium has obtruded itself upon Christian thinking and literature . . . ," and using the intense war hysteria explained:

> The present outburst of agitation regarding this entire subject is due to persistent agitation on the part of some people who appear to believe that the coming of the Lord and the end of the world are at hand. It would not be difficult to show that whether or not there are any insidious influences at work from German sources to promote this propaganda, it is the very thing that would most of all assist the enterprise of the Central Powers [Germany et al.]. . . . The thesis of the millennarians is the immediate and visible coming of Christ to overthrow the forces of evil and inaugurate the millennial period of good. If then this change is so speedily coming, what is the value of any effort either to win the war or promote democracy and human welfare? In fact, on this hypothesis such efforts are useless and contrary to the divine will.

"The difficulty with this doctrine is that it is not only unscriptural and in the deepest sense pessimistic," The Christian Century concluded, "but it is unpatriotic and subversive of every interest now being urged by the national spirit." One notes that the University of Chicago modernists of the World War I era not only could sound like conservative "fundamentalists" when they ascertained what was "unscriptural," but also were far from "liberal" in their defense of the war effort and their use of unbridled invective.

It must be mentioned that some critics of the premillennial view saw value in the movement and testified in more than a backhanded way to the energy exhibited by the fundamentalist-evangelicals. In *The Promise of His Coming: A Historical Interpretation and Revaluation of the Idea of the Second Advent* (1921), a critical analysis of premillennialism, Chester Charlton McCown, professor of New Testament literature at Pacific School of Religion, insisted: "We need the driving power of Premillennialism. The comparatively small group of Premillennialists in the orthodox and Adventist churches is probably as vigorous and zealous as any corresponding number of their opponents." He continued:

> It may be objected that their zeal is not according to knowledge, and in fact that it seems to require a sort of fanaticism in one's make-up to prepare him to swallow the manifest absurdities of parts of the premillennial scheme. It is possibly true that the same extreme temper that opens his mind to his peculiar doctrine makes him zealous both as a propagandist and as a Christian. At the same time the fact must not be overlooked, nor by any partisanship obscured, that the premillennial view has contributed tremendously to Christian energy and activity along its chosen lines. Particularly is it to be noted that Premillennialism is the doctrine of many outstanding evangelists, such as "Billy" Sunday, J. Wilbur Chapman, R. A. Torrey, D. W. Potter, L. W. Munhall, A. J. Gordon and Dwight L. Moody.

Urging his liberal colleagues to abandon postmillennialism, Professor McCown stressed that "Postmillennialism entirely lacks this driving power [of premillennialism]." He explained that postmillennialism's "name and the doctrine, therefore, should be abandoned, not only for scientific, but also for practical reasons." The popular eschatology of the nineteenth century was no longer sufficient for a twentieth-century world in McCown's view, because "it lays emphasis on the negative side of the doctrine of Christ's coming, and, accordingly falls far below the positive doctrine preached by the Premillennialist." "We need the tension of apocalypticism," McCown concluded, and in a footnote below the text added: "The Premillennialist rightly claims to walk in most excellent company, with Luther, Melanchthon,

Milton, Burnett, Isaac Newton, Watts, Charles Wesley, Toplady, and a host of others."[9]

In the early decades of the twentieth century, fundamentalist-evangelical periodicals were also filled with articles and editorials against their opponents—the University of Chicago and other Protestant liberalizing institutions. They condemned higher criticism of the Bible, they ridiculed evolutionary theory, and they castigated postmillennial triumphalism. On the brink of the 1920s, Arno C. Gaebelein wrote "The Most Dangerous Infidelity." He summed up the attitudes that would clash in the 1920s as never before:

> That the modern criticism of the Bible, so-called and falsely called "higher criticism," is the most subtle and dangerous infidelity aiming at the foundation of our faith, has often been demonstrated. This wicked criticism is denying most of the facts of God's revelation in His own Word. Well has it been said, "Criticism, this child of the spirit, that always negates, takes everything from us, but gives us nothing." Revelation? No. Inspiration of the Bible? No. Miracles? No. Prophecy? No. Christ, God? No. Resurrection and judgment? No. What do all these negations profit me? What shall I do with them? It causes one to stand on the path of life like a freezing wanderer, totally bereft, clad only in a thin shirt of morality, and not knowing whither to direct his steps. Instead of the "it is written" with which our Lord and Master [Jesus Christ] conquered the mightiest opponent, we ask: Is it written? Where? Who wrote it? Is the passage genuine? Who will prove it? The foundations under us totter, and from bogs and swamps there rise up mists that hide from us the view of the eternal peaks, clad in radiant white. A malarial atmosphere of doubts and uncertainty envelops our spiritual life, forces its way into our schools, churches and poisons our Christian literature; we and our children breathe it wherever we are, and it makes us wavering and defenseless outwardly, and sick and languid inwardly.[10]

"Some of these critics may not have reached yet the complete denial of the faith," Rev. Gaebelein conceded. "However, any man who rejects part of the Holy Scriptures has done the first step on a road which ultimately leads to the denial of the Lord who bought us and into ultimate darkness."

Gaebelein related a number of excerpts from proponents of

higher criticism. He quoted George Adam Smith of Glasgow as stating:

> Whether the ultimate source of the materials employed in Genesis i–xi be Babylonian or not, there is agreement amongst scholars that they are drawn from early Semitic folk-lore—for the contents of which "myth and legend" are in our language the most proper terms. In such stories early peoples expressed their intellectual conceptions of the creation of the world and of its divine government.

Arno C. Gaebelein retorted that G. A. Smith's statement that there is agreement among scholars on higher criticism was a "downright falsehood" and that "there are numerous scholars of greater ability than these critics, who declare the very opposite."

Gaebelein also informed his readers that Smith insisted that scholars were "ignorant of the time at which the Hebrews received these stories," that Abraham "may not have existed," that "the story of Jonah is not true," that there was uncertainty "whether any written law has reached us from Moses himself," and that "present criticism has tended to confirm the impossibility of proving any given psalm in our psalter to have been by David." Gaebelein reminded his readers that Jesus himself declared: "David in the psalms saith." At the spread of European biblical criticism to the religious bastions of the United States, Gaebelein was horrified. "In fact the leading theological institutions like Boston, Union Theological Seminary in New York, Chicago University, and scores of others teach this infidelity," editor Gaebelein wrote, declaring: "It is a dangerous thing to follow such men or to recommend their books, which must destroy the faith in an infallible Bible. We must warn against them and especially caution young believers to beware of such hidden poison."[11]

## EDUCATION AND THE BATTLE FOR THE BIBLE

The problem of obtaining an advanced theological education for "young believers" in an institution that revered the Bible and was devoid of higher critical analysis and evolutionary theory became increasingly difficult after the First World War. Nineteenth-century fundamentalist-evangelicals had depended on conservative evangelical Ivy League institutions, and a moderate evangelical Calvinism dominated most Protestant seminaries during the 1800s. Early fundamentalist-evangelicals valued such education and intellectual stimulation. For example, Moody Bible Institute's first graduate, William Evans (1870–1950, diploma 1892), graduated from Chicago Lutheran Theological Seminary in 1896. He completed their postgraduate program for a B.D. in 1900. He then entered the Ph.D. program at the Chicago Theological Seminary (later renamed the University of Chicago Divinity School), receiving his Ph.D. in 1906. He obtained a Doctor of Divinity (D.D.) degree from Wheaton College the same year.

Theological liberalism, however, had radically changed such possibilities by the 1920s. Lewis Sperry Chafer, a noted Bible teacher, shared his burden for a dispensational premillennial seminary with other members of the fundamentalist-evangelical movement as early as 1921. In 1923, Chafer spoke at the First Presbyterian Church in Dallas, Texas, enlisting the support of William M. Anderson, pastor of the church. Together with other scholars in the movement, they formed a temporary board of directors in 1924 and held classes. February 16, 1925, the seminary was incorporated by the state of Texas under the name Evangelical Theological College. The name of the school was changed to Dallas Theological Seminary in 1936, and Lewis Sperry Chafer remained its president until 1952. It has been a bastion of dispensational premillennialism ever since, turning out thousands of pastors and professors for the fundamentalist-evangelical movement. Prophetic interpretation also has been stressed. Hal Lindsey, author of the best-seller *The Late Great Planet Earth* (1970), was a graduate of Dallas Theological Seminary, and it is said that the basis of his book was actually his seminary class notes.

It is interesting that "Evangelical" was in the incorporated seminary name in 1925. For a time in the 1920s both conservative and liberal Protestants used the term to express themselves. In his book *The Faith of Modernism* (1924), Shailer Mathews as dean of the University of Chicago Divinity School asserted: "Modernists as a class are evangelical Christians. That is, they accept Jesus

Christ as the revelation of a Savior God." Gradually, terms such as "liberalism" and "modernism" were accepted solely by Mathews and others to categorize their theological base. With the downfall of the postmillennial optimism amid the rubble of the First World War, liberal Protestants used the term "evangelical" less and less to express their roots.

The term "fundamentalism" was used for a time by most premillennialists, while their conservative colleagues of differing eschatologies preferred either to be labeled "evangelicals" or to be labeled by their theological orientation (Lutheran or Reformed, for example). These groups linked forces in a conservative Protestant alliance that continued between the wars. Most liberal Protestants called them "fundamentalists," and the battle lines between liberal and conservative Protestants were drawn during the 1920s. In 1922, Harry Emerson Fosdick (1878-1969), one of the most influential liberal American clergymen of the period, preached the sermon "Shall the Fundamentalists Win?" He was determined they would not. His message was later published in *The Christian Century* (June 8, 1922) and distributed in pamphlets.

Clarence E. Macartney (1879-1957), conservative pastor of Arch Street Presbyterian Church in Philadelphia, responded with an article in *The Presbyterian*, "Shall Unbelief Win: An Answer to Dr. Fosdick," accusing Fosdick of diverging from traditional Christianity. In the subsequent battle, the Baptist Fosdick was forced out of his pulpit at First Presbyterian Church in New York City. John D. Rockefeller built him the multimillion-dollar Park Street Baptist Church in New York; and Fosdick not only preached there, but also taught homiletics at Union Theological Seminary and later had a nationwide "National Vespers" radio program on NBC.

As the battle for the Bible continued, other Presbyterians took up the gauntlet of defending "the fundamentals," and J. Gresham Machen's *Christianity and Liberalism* (1923) became a classic defense of traditional Christianity. Machen was professor of New Testament at Princeton Theological Seminary, and neither he nor Macartney in the Calvinist Reformed tradition felt comfortable with being classified as fundamentalists. They did not subscribe to the widespread fundamentalist-evangelical premillennialism. Nevertheless, their war was against "unchristian" liberalism and modernism, and they fought as allies with the growing fundamentalist-evangelical movement. Machen would later feel forced to leave an ever "liberalizing" Princeton.

Unfortunately for the moderate fundamentalist-evangelical, the period between the world wars witnessed the rise of a more militant separatist Protestant fundamentalism which seized the name "fundamentalist" with a vengeance. The negative publicity over the John T. Scopes "Monkey" trial in 1925 seemed to change the original meaning of the word "fundamentalist," and more moderate fundamentalist-evangelicals felt the need to free themselves from the connotations of narrow, divisive, bigoted, redneck, anti-intellectual, uncaring, unloving, and antisocial associated with the word by liberal Protestants and a news-hungry press. In the 1930s they began to call themselves simply "evangelicals," joining once again the broad sea of conservative Protestants from the nineteenth century. The label "evangelical" seemed more appropriate, since those within American Protestant liberalism no longer used the term to identify themselves, and the massive immigration at the turn of the century had made the nation much more pluralistic. The twentieth century was not to be the century of evangelicalism.

In 1942 the National Association of Evangelicals (NAE) was formed. Although the NAE incorporated evangelicals from many religious traditions, the organization at its inception contained an extremely high percentage of premillennialist Protestants. The premillennial fundamentalist-evangelical movement of the nineteenth century had had an important impact on American Protestantism both in numbers and in attitude formation. The controversy in Protestantism between theological liberals and theological conservatives did not subside and, as in the nineteenth century, the American Jewish community felt more comfortable with more liberally oriented Protestants. Jews accepted liberal Protestant labels when it came to defining "Fundamentalists."

## JEWS AND FUNDAMENTALISTS

"Camouflage the matter as they may the fact remains that the Scopes trial in Dayton, Tenn., is neither more or less than a test of the power of the Protestant Evangelical churches to fasten a state religion on the people of this country," *The American Israelite* (July 16, 1925) proclaimed. "Whether in fear of the Roman Catholic Church, or an acknowledgment of the failure of Evangelical Christian religio-political organizations to hold the masses within the authority of the churches, the result is the same so far as the public is concerned."[12] A following article described the Ku Klux Klan and its growth, informing readers that "recently the Ohio Klan succeeded in enacting compulsory Bible reading for the State of Ohio, the Bill having been vetoed thereafter by the Governor." While the periodical asserted the "vanishing influence" of the Klan, there was no doubt in Jewish minds that fundamentalism and anti-Semitism walked hand in hand.

Readers of the prestigious Reform periodical had been bombarded with articles about religious test cases in the summer of 1925. In New York State, the Mount Vernon Board of Education was being taken to court by the Freethinkers Society for allowing parents to take their children out of school for religious training forty-five minutes each week. Clarence Darrow, the famed trial attorney involved in the John T. Scopes trial, wrote to the Society's president, Joseph Lewis, offering his services if the case was carried to the higher courts. "I can see that your case is as important as the evolution case in Tennessee," Darrow's letter stated in part. "Still I haven't the time to arrange matters so I can go into it next week. . . . I feel sure that you will win. I am glad that you are taking the fight."

The editors of *The American Israelite* gave the Mount Vernon case headlines. In "Is Fanaticism in Last Ditch?" a July 2, 1925, article commenced:

> It begins to look as if the unblushing attempt to fasten a state religion on the United States is about to come to grief, through the lately aroused anger of the masses suffering under the daily growing despotism of the religious and moral organizations.

The carefully prepared but clumsily executed plan to "spring" in the various states simultaneously the long list of measures to regulate and limit by law the religious, personal and civic liberty of the people, came to grief in most of the State Legislatures, and it is not likely a similar attempt will be made again in the near future.[13]

A sermon by Rabbi Samuel Schulman of Temple Beth-El in New York was cited, in which he stated that religion in some form was "an indispensable element in education," but that the public school was not the place in which religion could be taught, considering the American tradition of the separation of church and state. *The American Israelite* exulted that liberal associations and teachers' organizations also opposed "an actual movement to make religious training a part of the public school curriculum in New York City."

From the very beginning, the Mount Vernon test case was linked to the Scopes "Monkey" trial in the pages of *The American Israelite.* "The true significance of the Scopes case lies in the fact that it has become a matter of national importance," the "Fanaticism" article concluded, "for upon the final decisions by the highest courts, which it certainly will reach, depends the victory of the bitterly contested struggle between the forces of reaction and progress." Proudly the periodical noted:

Protestant Orthodoxy is hard pressed as it is, with prohibition, Sunday observance, religion in the public schools, and general supervision of the morals and habits of all mankind. It takes a long time to break a camel's back by piling straws, one at a time, on it. But Darrow, Colby, Malone and company use bricks and seem to have an unlimited supply of ammunition.[14]

"There is no room for doubt that the liberal organizations, representing the real attitude of ninety per cent of the people of this country, have gone into the fight to stay to the end," the article closed. "Fanaticism, as multiform as the Asmodeus of Bagdad, is fighting in the last ditch."[15]

Ironically, the decade of the 1920s was a very conservative era, and even the Federal Council of Churches and mainline Protestant denominations supported the Prohibition Amendment to the Constitution. Some fundamentalist-evangelicals, such as

German-born Arno C. Gaebelein, opposed prohibition. Liberal Protestants had spurred the Interchurch World Movement, a cooperative ecumenical effort to unite every benevolent and missionary agency in American Protestantism. Their April 1920 bulletin described "the biggest business of the biggest man in the world":

> Christ was big, was He not? None ever bigger. Christ was busy, was He not? None ever busier. He was always about His Father's business. Christ needs big men for big business.

A conservative theology of success so inundated the most "liberal" of Protestants that they wallowed in success-oriented clichés and endeavors.

President [John] Calvin Coolidge (1923–1929) declared, "America's business is business," and a number of books on Jesus as the "successful businessman" were published in the 1920s. Advertising executive Bruce Barton's *The Man Nobody Knows: A Discovery of the Real Jesus* (1924) depicted Jesus not only as "the founder of modern business," but also as an advertising specialist, a socialite, and an executive. The *New York Times Book Review* called his treatment "reverent," and Barton's following work on the Bible was entitled *The Book Nobody Knows* (1925). Multimillion-dollar churches were built, and Protestant pews were filled as a smug superiority settled over the nation.[16]

That *The American Israelite* could conclude that this was a liberal era indicates either wishful thinking or a gross misjudgment of the times. Still, the editors held the Vatican responsible for Polish crimes in the 1920s against the Jews, in spite of "expressions of friendliness toward the Jews which have hitherto come from the Vatican." The Vatican's official statements are portrayed in the respected journal as "mere platitudes."[17]

Statements of the Federal Council of Churches were questioned as well. For example, when James Myers, Industrial and Field Secretary of the Federal Council of Churches in New York, sent a brochure entitled "Labor Sunday Message," the editor of *The American Israelite* balked at the closing statements about "what the Christian spirit dictates," that "industry has a right to look to the churches for the creation and the encouragement of the co-operative spirit," and "the mission and function of the Christian church, as defined by Jesus Christ and taught in the New Testament." The *American Israelite* editorial (July 30, 1925) stated:

> Since the authors of this and similar documents ask the co-operation and the opinion of the Jewish press and people in the matter, it is proper to state that no one of any faith whatever, or no faith, can or would object to the church doing all in its power to bring about a closer relationship between the moral and religious forces and the people whom it is sought to reach. The trouble is that in all these movements the religious thought is not only uppermost, but is kept in the foreground, with the result that the Jews, however well inclined they may be toward a project, feel that they are not being solicited or accepted on an equal footing with their Christian neighbors. Why everything that is common property and of ancient origin should be made Christian and sectarian is beyond the comprehension of the ordinary Jew.[18]

That the professors of liberal Protestantism's Union Theological Seminary would not cross the street to fraternize with the professors of the Jewish Theological Seminary in New York City in the 1920s perhaps heightened concerns over the "narrowness of Christianity," either liberal or conservative.

Nevertheless, the perceptions of fundamentalists struck home. The lessons of the Scopes trial were immediately applied in this July 30, 1925, issue by the Reform *American Israelite* to its traditional Jewish protagonists. "Will the Shulhan Aruck fundamentalists learn anything from the Scopes trial?" the editors questioned in a brief blurb on the editorial page, immediately going on to another brief synopsis of the death of fundamentalism: "If ridicule can kill a cause then fundamentalism as championed by [William Jennings] Bryan, should have one foot in the grave and the other very close to it at this moment." For much of the Jewish community, the Scopes trial defined Protestant "fundamentalism" as much as the Shulhan Aruck defined Jewish "fundamentalism."

In the preceding issue, the *American Israelite* editors compared the outcome of the evolution trial in Dayton, Tennessee, with the anti-Semitic attacks in Henry Ford's *Dearborn Independent.* "It has been said that no matter of greater importance to American Jewry has developed since the brutal onslaughts of Henry Ford," the periodical proclaimed. "The Scopes matter is of even greater moment, because upon the final decision of the highest courts will rest the fate of the Jews. For if education by the State is to be on a religious basis, then all freedom of thought and speech will vanish and we shall go back to the Dark Ages when Church was all powerful and was, in fact, The State." The deep fear of the respected Jewish editors clearly surfaced as they stated:

> If Mr. Bryan, as the accepted leader of this reactionary and fanatical Fundamentalist element has his way, we shall have an amendment to the Constitution which will disqualify the Jews under a religious test. They have taken great pains to avoid in any way giving the Roman Catholic Church directly any cause for complaint, but they are not afraid of the Jews, and they feel that if the public schools and other State supported institutions of learning and intellectual training can be Protestantized, it will be a very long step toward the goal they are seeking, to make this a Christian country—a Protestant Christian country, in the full sense of the word.[19]

"The trouble with those who are seeking to have religious exercises, or Bible reading, or both, in the public schools, or in connection with them, is that they promptly abuse every privilege granted," the editorial excerpts continued an oft-repeated axiom in *The American Israelite.* "This, unfortunately, has been the history of all the attempts thus far."

"There will be no real progress toward better religious education and training for the people-at-large so long as the churches of the dominant faiths refuse to recognize all other churches as their peers," a following editorial excerpt insisted. "Just so long as the present status continues, racial, religious and social prejudice and hatred will continue to set faction against faction." The Reform periodical also found the "arbitrary, domineering methods the Zionists have always employed toward those who do not share in their particular beliefs" particularly upsetting. After a lengthy discussion of the Scopes trial and an excerpt showing Europe's amusement concerning it, *The American Israelite* stated:

"Most of the Jews of this country who belong to the Reform wing are growing weary of being constantly called upon to furnish money for the glorious privilege of hearing themselves damned as traitors to 'Traditional Judaism.'"

It is interesting that Rabbi Jerome Mark of Knoxville, Tennessee, questioned William Jennings Bryan about Zionism while they waited for an afternoon session of the Scopes trial to begin. A Presbyterian, Bryan appeared to lack the prophetic bent of the premillennial fundamentalist-evangelical movement. As a politician, he was a conservative evangelical crusader of the nineteenth-century mold—the typical caricature of the "fundamentalist" many in the Jewish community pictured and *The American Israelite* portrayed. Bryan told the rabbi that he had "no interest" in the reestablishment of a Jewish homeland and no interest in the future development of Jewish history. This was in accordance with the standard Reformed (Calvinistic) theology. The rabbi ended his account, however, by questioning whether the "would-be statesman" should "not give a little trouble to the Jewish question." One wonders whether or not Rabbi Mark was aware of the prevalent prophetic movement among Protestants and was provoked by it to ask Bryan such a question.[20]

In this last issue of July, the editorial "William Jennings Bryan" appeared in *The American Israelite*—for the national figure had died unexpectedly. Noting that "Mr. Bryan was a striking example of misdirected energy," the editors decided that they could "speak kindly and gently of him." "Especially will we of the Jewish faith honor his memory, for at all times and under all the trying conditions of the World War he showed himself the unfailing defender and friend of the oppressed and persecuted Jews in the war-ravaged countries as well as at home." And yet, derogatory comments about "Shulhan Aruck" Jewish fundamentalists as well as "Bryan fundamentalists" followed on the heels of the tribute. Perhaps the statement that followed in the sixth paragraph below the Bryan "tribute" underscored the key problem between fundamentalist-evangelical biblicism and the liberal biblical views that were to dominate the Jewish milieu:

If there is anything purely, entirely, completely and absolutely Jewish, it is the Pentateuch, the Homesch, the five books of Moses, the Torah, The Law. To note the frenzy with which the Fundamentalist (i.e. Reactionary) fanatical Protestant Christians rush to the defense of that scripture, which was compiled by Jews, for Jews in the Holy Land of Jews, is to wonder if the literal acceptance of the story of The Creation occupies the mind to such an extent that neither logic nor reason can find lodgment therein.

While both traditional and liberal Jewish groups would deplore Christian evangelism and would fight against any appearance of the formation of a Christian state, the fundamentalist often would be viewed as fanatical, reactionary, bigoted, ignorant, anti-intellectual, antisocial, a redneck country bumpkin in the eyes of a liberally oriented Jew. Evangelicals and fundamentalists; pre-millennialists, postmillennialists, and amillennialists—all were often lumped in the same category of caricature and aspersion.

## FUNDAMENTALIST-EVANGELICAL ATTITUDES

At the World's Conference on Christian Fundamentals held in Philadelphia in 1919, the pastor of First Baptist Church in New York City, I. M. Haldeman, delivered the address "Why I Preach the Second Coming." Later that year, an expanded book of the same title appeared under his authorship—a book that is indicative of how most fundamentalist-evangelicals viewed Jews and their future between the world wars. Haldeman emphasized in the first four chapters that Jesus' second coming was the event most often recorded in the Bible, that every fundamental doctrine and promise was linked to it, that the redemption of humankind would be complete only when Jesus came back, and that the church would be exalted to "her true function of rulership over the world" only when Jesus Christ returned. In chapter 5, "Only at the Second Coming Will the Solemn and Covenant Promises of God to Israel Be Fulfilled," the New York minister conveyed what he believed the Bible taught about the Jewish people.[21]

"God sware to Abraham that he and his posterity should have the land of Palestine for an everlasting possession," Dr. Haldeman began. "Abraham never got a foot of the land under covenant promise. The only bit of ground he was able to call his was the burial plot he purchased with his own money. The children of Israel never entered the promised land under the Abrahamic covenant." Using a dispensational scheme, Haldeman explained how the Lord had delivered the ancient Hebrews from Egypt and dealt with them "in pure, unconditional grace till they came to Sinai." "There in all the pride and self-sufficiency of the flesh," the preacher declared, "they [the Jews] took themselves off the ground of grace and unconditional covenant and put themselves under the covenant of the law. . . a covenant of good behaviour."

Not able to keep the covenant of good behavior, the Jewish people for two thousand years lapsed periodically into idolatry and were led away into captivity. Rev. Haldeman asserted that "because as a nation guilty of manslaughter in slaying the Lord their covenant king, the Jews have been the wanderers of the earth, the people of restless foot, finding a home in every land but their own." While Haldeman believed that all men and women (including he himself) were responsible for Jesus' death, as so many Christians over the centuries he believed that the Jewish people were held accountable collectively for the death of Jesus. And God's chosen people, the Jews, were warned by the prophets of the woe and terror that awaited them. God used the nations of the world as "the rods of His anger, as the instruments of discipline" to "correct" his chosen people, but he also punished those nations who hurt the Jewish people. According to Haldeman, "he would not make a full end of his own people."[22]

The Baptist minister explained in a later chapter:

It was the original purpose of God to make the people of Israel the head of nations, place them in Palestine as the geographical center of the earth, make them its political center, send His own Son to be their incarnate king, use them as a channel of earthly and spiritual blessing and make this world the most perfect and happiest spot in all the wide universe. They failed to meet their opportunity. Then the Lord transferred the possibility of world rulership from the Jews to the Gentiles.

Rev. Haldeman took a dim view of such gentile rulership. "In all the twenty-five hundred years of this Gentile rule there have not been one hundred consecutive years of universal peace," he wrote. "It has been twenty-five hundred years of war, of rapine, murder and measureless lust." In the midst of modern preachers saying that the twentieth century would be a time of peace, the ravages of the Great War convinced Haldeman that his Bible remained the true measure of the heart and motive of human-kind.[23]

Dr. Haldeman seemed to be truly touched by the suffering of the Jewish people. "They have not only been wanderers in every land," he taught, "but they have suffered an agony no tongue can fittingly tell." He elaborated:

The men have been robbed. They have been broken on the wheel. They have been stretched on the rack. They have been flayed alive. They have been burned alive. They have been sent to sea by thousands as herded cattle; and they have been sent thither in rotting and sinking ships. Their wives and daughters have suffered worse than torture or death. Their children have been mutilated; and when they failed to bring a full and satisfactory price in the public market, men, women and children have been given away as worthless slaves, not worth even the price of a kennel dog. They have been hunted like wild beasts of the mountain. Like frightened beasts they have trembled at the sound of approaching footsteps and the sound of a shaken leaf has caused them to flee. If their Lord was a man of sorrows and acquainted with grief [an allusion to Jesus and Isaiah 53], truly may it be said of them that they have been through the centuries a nation of sorrows and acquainted with grief; but the sorrows were unlike those of their Lord. He carried the sorrows, the griefs and woes of others that He might relieve them; they carried their own sorrows put upon them by the wickedness and cruelty of others until tears were their meat and drink night and day.[24]

But I. M. Haldeman believed that God was faithful to God's Jewish people. "They should be the first to be restored to the land," he declared. "They would go back in unbelief [not accepting Jesus as their savior at that time]." "The stone cities are waiting and every stone in door and window seems to be crying out: 'We are waiting till they return whose right alone it is to live and dwell here,'" Rev. Haldeman exclaimed.[25]

As so many fundamentalist-evangelicals before and after the First World War, I. M. Haldeman underscored the point that the nations and the peoples who had hurt God's chosen people had suffered immensely and lost their ancient glory for touching the apple of God's eye, the Jews. Rev. Haldeman proclaimed in joy about the Jewish people's prophetic glory and future victory:

> There are fifteen millions of Jews to-day. They are the most vital and vigorous race on the earth. They are five times the number of all Israel who left Egypt; and they are but a sixth part of them—two tribes, Judah and Benjamin. They are the money makers and money loaners of the world. They are the merchants, the bankers, the musicians, the professors in school, in college and university. They are the philosophers, the scientists, the electricians and chemists. They have furnished prime ministers, statesmen, judges and generals. Such a statesman as Disraeli who glorified England, such a general as Massena whom Napoleon characterized as "the child of victory." If to-day you should seek a representative in every department of human genius and endeavour you would find that representative to be either a Jew or a Jewess. Fifteen millions of Jews! What are these fifteen millions of Jews but fifteen millions of proofs that the book we call the Bible is true, is inerrant, infallible? Fifteen millions of demonstrations and fifteen millions of indubitable proofs.[26]

"By so much as they prove that God keeps faith with His warnings of woe and judgment," Haldeman explained, "by so much will He keep faith with the promise of good He has made; by so much is it sure He will yet plant them as He said in their own land and will do so with His whole heart and His whole soul."

To Dr. Haldeman, Zionism was another proof of the inerrant Word of God. "Already the sound of their footsteps may be heard on the homeward march," the New York fundamentalist preacher wrote. "Zionism is now an immense fact." The pastor of First Baptist Church explained:

> The spirit of nationalism has come back to Judah. The blue and white flag of David has been unfurled. Diplomats in the nations' counsels agree there can be no settled peace between Europe and

the East till the Jew is back in his own land and Judah once more a recognized political state; that the Jews are the only people all the nations will agree should have Palestine, and the words, "Jewish State" are words repeated in common speech round the globe.

England has driven the Turk out of Jerusalem. The corner-stone of a five million dollar university has been laid upon that Mount of Olives where once the Son of God amid its lonely shades prayed and agonized, a begun fulfillment of the prophecy of Zephaniah that in the latter days the Lord would execute judgment on the Gentile nations that should be gathered there and to His restored and delivered people turn again a pure speech, no longer the stuttering and smattering phrase of Yiddish, but the old Hebraic tongue of their fathers. Already there are papers in Jerusalem published in Hebrew, schools are taught and many speak in ancient language.

"Many Jews are going back to Palestine," Rev. I. M. Haldeman insisted. "Many more are there now than returned from Babylon."

## "The Day of Jacob's Trouble"

As we have seen in the previous chapter, the premillennial prophetic interpretation of the fundamentalist-evangelical movement posited a period of tribulation and an Antichrist that would wreak havoc on the Jewish community and the world. Rev. I. M. Haldeman's *Why I Preach the Second Coming* was quite typical of fundamentalist-evangelical attitudes during the twentieth century. Although Zionism and the return of the Jewish people to the Holy Land were viewed as the fulfillment of prophecy, there was no implication that the Jewish people were drawing closer to a belief in Jesus as their Savior. The apostle Paul had written in Romans 11:7-10 that the Jewish people who did not accept Jesus had been "blinded" (the translation in the King James Version that Haldeman was using, but "hardened" in more accurate translations), and Paul had quoted from Isaiah 29:10 and Psalm 69:22-23 about the "spirit of slumber" that engulfed the Jewish community, that is, eyes that were darkened and could not see, ears that could not hear.

The Hebrew prophets had been quite stark in their pronouncements against the Jewish people, and Christians for centuries had repeated their statements. In fact, in the 1980s an American

Jewish woman who had just read for the first time the English
translation of the Hebrew Bible commented to a leader of the
American Jewish Committee that it was the "most anti-Semitic
book" she had ever read. In Romans 11, however, Paul continued
in the English version Dr. Haldeman was using: "I say then,
Have they [the Jews] stumbled that they should fall? God forbid:
but rather through their fall salvation is come unto the Gentiles,
for to provoke them [the Jews] to jealousy." He also reminds the
gentile Christians to "boast not against the [natural] branches" of
God's tree, the Jewish people (11:18). Fundamentalist-evangelicals were ever reminded that "if God spared not the natural
branches, take heed lest he also spare not thee" (11:21) and that
"blindness in part is happened to Israel, until the fulness of the
Gentiles be come in" (11:25).

It is in light of this chapter in the Christian Testament book of
Romans and other passages that Rev. I. M. Haldeman and other
fundamentalist-evangelicals constructed their view of the future,
formulating their attitudes about Jewish people and the Jewish
future. For example, after discussing Zionism and the return
of the Jewish people to the Holy Land, Haldeman wrote (and
preached):

> They [the Jews] are going back [to the Holy Land] as the Word of
> God foretold, in utter and absolute unbelief and bitter repudiation
> of the idea that Jesus of Nazareth was their foretold and foreor-
> dained Messiah.
>
> They are going back with the veil upon their eyes and as blind as in
> the day when their fathers caused Him to be crucified by Roman
> hands.
>
> They are going back to a time of anguish of which Jeremiah
> solemnly warns as "the day of Jacob's trouble," and our Lord
> describes as the tribulation, "the great one," the like of which the
> world has never seen and will never see again.
>
> They are going back to be set up by a league of ten nations and to
> enter into an alliance and covenant with its godless head as their
> political and false Messiah.
>
> They will suffer until there shall come upon that generation all the
> righteous blood shed upon the earth from the blood of the righteous

Abel to the blood of Zacharias, the son of Barachias who was slain between the temple and the altar, and the blood of the Son of God [Jesus] which they invoked in judgment on themselves and their children in that fatal hour when Pilate convinced of the innocence of Jesus and wishing to let Him go had washed his hands in water, putting the responsibility of the crucifixion upon them as a people. Then it was they cried that terrible cry: "His blood be on us and on our children."[27]

"But then as now, and always since the days of Elijah, there was and is an elect remnant in Israel," Haldeman explained. "For their sakes the Lord will come."

The pastor of the First Baptist Church of New York City held to the most popular fundamentalist-evangelical belief, that the Rapture would occur during which born-again Christians would meet Jesus in the air; the Holy Spirit would be taken out of the world with them, allowing the forces of evil in the Antichrist and his minions to flourish in a seven-year period of tribulation; and Jesus would return in his second coming to defeat the Antichrist and rule the earth from Jerusalem. Then the elect remnant of the Jewish people "will look upon Him whom their fathers pierced . . . will fall down in anguish before Him [Jesus] . . . will mourn for Him as one mourneth for his only son." According to Haldeman, the Jewish people on earth "will take up the fifty-third chapter of Isaiah and make it their confession of faith and bitter, self-accusing lamentation."

With a personal testimony that underscored why he preached the Second Coming, Rev. I. M. Haldeman concluded his fifth point:

And because there can be no permanent peace in the world till Israel has been restored; and because I wish to see, not only peace among the nations and Israel reaping the blessings of the unconditional covenant of God's grace and unchanged faithfulness, but because I yearn to see the hour when the Lord shall enter upon His own inheritance and justify Himself before heaven and earth as Judah's Lord, as Israel's God and turn the accusation of His cross: 'This is Jesus of Nazareth, the king of the Jews' into the paean of His coronation as such, I preach the Second Coming.[28]

Between the world wars, fundamentalist-evangelical teaching
that the Antichrist and a Great Tribulation were on the horizon
sensitized the members of the movement to the dangers that
both fascism and communism posed for the Jewish people (and,
indeed, for the world). "Lawlessness will not down," Arno C.
Gaebelein emphasized in *Our Hope*; "it will increase. The Bible
says so. . . . The world will find out yet the full power of the god
of this age—Satan—the murderer and liar from the beginning."[29]
In "Jews Facing New Massacres in Russia," Gaebelein asserted:

> Reports have reached England that almost every day mobs in some
> of the larger Russian cities march through the streets shouting
> "Down with the Jews." An eye witness declares that this cry "Kill
> the Jews" will most likely lead to the bloodiest pogrom that the
> world has ever seen. They are blamed for the outrages of Bolshe-
> vism. The ordinary Russian and the ignorant Moujiks (peasants)
> look upon the government as ruled and controlled by the Jews, and
> they blame the race for everything that has gone wrong. Trotzky, as
> it is well known, is a Jew and so is another leading Bolshevik, Zin-
> orieff. More and more the ignorant population blame the entire Jew-
> ish race for all the terror, mistakes and failure of the revolution. The
> passions of these Moujiks once aroused will know no bounds and
> if this cry of "Kill the Jews" does come, the present government will
> fall into a terrible slaughter of Jews and the innocent masses will
> suffer.[30]

"Believers should pray that God's mercy may be displayed in
behalf of those who are wrongly accused," Rev. Gaebelein concluded, "and that they may be delivered from these threatening
massacres."

Gaebelein continued to be dismayed that the Jewish people
were persecuted by both communist and anticommunist forces.
He wrote:

> One of saddest chapters of the world war and the aftermath is the
> suffering of the Jews. The full extent of their experience will perhaps
> never be known. Hundreds of thousands of families [who] have
> been driven from their homes are now homeless wanderers in East-
> ern Europe. Over 50,000 Galician Jews found a refuge in Vienna but
> now they are forced to leave that city as they are considered aliens
> and the food scarcity has made it necessary to evict all non-citizens.

Where they can go in this new exodus is a problem. The pogroms in Russia continue. It seems they suffer from the hands of different factions. The Reds accuse them of having supported the Anti-Red forces and when the Anti-Reds get control they persecute the Jews for having sided with the Bolshevik movement.[31]

And yet, Rev. Gaebelein felt that "too often the Jews have brought disaster upon themselves by meddling with the politics of the countries into which the Lord has scattered them." Because of this, "the innocent will then suffer with the guilty." To Gaebelein and many fundamentalist-evangelicals, this was a forewarning of coming events. "When finally they [the Jews] make a covenant political with that coming leader [the Antichrist] and when they turn away completely from the Law and the Word of God, the greatest sufferings will come. For this they are getting ready." Gaebelein had as little regard for "apostate" liberal and rationalistic Judaism as did the Orthodox rebbe. He believed many Jews would suffer for the compromise of irreligious Jews.

Nevertheless, during the 1920s and 1930s, anti-Semitic comments still riled Arno C. Gaebelein as they had in the 1890s. An editorial in *Our Hope* in 1926 is indicative of the many times he wrote and spoke on this subject between the world wars. He related:

> In speaking with a certain nominal Christian about a stranger who had passed, he said, "Oh! He is only a Jew." It was spoken in contempt. In spite of the good feeling which exists in our country toward the Jewish people there is still the same age-long antagonism to the Jew, and contempt for the members of this race. This prejudice is far greater in Europe; Antisemitism there is not on the decrease. Certain persons and societies try to foster it in this land also. No true Christian believer will ever say, "Oh! He is only a Jew" with a sneer on his lips. We owe the greatest debt to the race.[32]

The great fundamentalist-evangelical Bible teacher went on to declare in his editorial that the prophets, the apostles, the early church, and Jesus himself were all Jews. "Therefore, the contempt expressed by certain 'Christians' to the Jews, arises from ignorance, and is most ungrateful and ungenerous," Dr. Gaebelein added.

Arno C. Gaebelein was highly regarded in fundamentalist-evangelical circles, and his innermost feelings on the Jewish people are expressed in an article in the June 1928 issue of *Our Hope* entitled "The Middle Wall of Partition." In it Dr. Gaebelein responded to the question, "Who are these people [the Jews] who are set apart by themselves, who are viewed with suspicion as strangers and treated with discrimination as aliens?" His answer: "In spite of peculiarities of race, custom and tradition, just folks like ourselves, resentful of injustice, responsive to kindness, sensitive to disdain. . . . Nor should we forget that to this race—the race of Jesus—we owe our spiritual privileges."[33]

Little wonder that many fundamentalist-evangelicals (including Gaebelein) believed that a "true Christian" could not be an anti-Semite! And the movement as a whole not only spotted the anti-Semitism of Adolf Hitler, but also believed that the Holocaust was indeed occurring at a time when more liberal religious movements were labeling such reports "atrocity propaganda" (see next chapter). During the 1920s, for example, Gaebelein and other fundamentalist-evangelical preachers and theologians pointed to the rise of dictators in Europe, emphasizing Mussolini's growing power. At the end of 1930, Arno Gaebelein wrote in his "Current Events in the Light of the Bible" section of *Our Hope*:

> Adolf Hitler—Will He Be Germany's Dictator? . . . He seems to have a wild program of leadership. He is adored by thousands of women whom he seems to captivate. He is an outspoken enemy of the Jews . . . one of the most fanatical anti-semites of Europe. The near future will show if he will succeed.[34]

As Hitler's political party continued to garner votes, Gaebelein explained the danger the Jewish people faced. In "The Shadows of Jacob's Trouble" (August 1932), he related to the readers of *Our Hope*:

> Especially threatening is it in Germany. Adolf Hitler, the clever Fascist leader who is winning out in Germany and holds the power in his hands, is a rabid Antisemite. His leading Organ "Der Voelkischer Beobachter" (the people's observer) gives the advice to the

German Jews to leave Germany "while they have an opportunity to do so." The paper tells Jews to follow the example of Emil Ludwig (the biographer) to emigrate and seek citizenship elsewhere.[35]

To Arno C. Gaebelein, this was such an ominous threat that he felt the Great Tribulation for the Jewish people and for the world could well occur at any time. "Hitler declares and vows, when he has full power, to rid Germany of the Jewish plague," Rev. Gaebelein noted. "Similar dark clouds arise everywhere on the European horizon."

Throughout the 1930s and during the Second World War, books by fundamentalist-evangelicals appeared which detailed the persecution of the Jewish people and also fought against anti-Semitic stereotypes. Arthur I. Brown, a revered scientist, surgeon, and Bible teacher, wrote *Into the Clouds* (1938) for a fundamentalist-evangelical readership (Fundamental Truth Publishers published the book). While noting the "splendid qualities" that exist in the Jewish people, he related that Jews were "dominant" in the clothing business, secondhand autos, scrap iron and steel, tobacco buying, liquor, department stores, jewelry, pawnshops, radio, theater, and movies. "It may surprise some to learn that they do not control banking and finance in this country, nor the New York Stock Exchange," he added. "Those who see a Communist in every Jew are poorly informed in regard to Stalin's attitude toward them. If the Jews are his allies, he is certainly treating them as if they were bitter enemies. . . . These facts ought to give pause to those frantic exponents of anti-Semitism, who see Red every time they see a Jew."[36]

Dr. Brown continued by noting, "Christians especially ought to view these persecuted and much-criticized Jews, with fairness at least, remembering that our Lord was one of them. From Haman to Hitler there have been those actuated by the Devil who are seized with hatred and a determination to annihilate the Hebrews as a blot on civilization." Arthur Brown warned:

In no uncertain terms, God speaks in Isaiah 60:12: "That nation and kingdom that will not serve thee shall perish; yes, those nations shall be utterly wasted." These words sound the death-

knell of Jew-baiting nations and individuals, and this writer is glad
to speak a brief word of defense on behalf of this noble – often mis-
guided and sinning – race, who have placed us Gentiles under such
a debt of gratitude, when "by their fall, salvation came" to us. We
rejoice in the glorious days which are ahead for them, and sorrow
with them because, first, they must endure greater privations than
they have ever known.[37]

The first printing in December of 1938 of five thousand copies of
Dr. Brown's book was sold out in two months, requiring a second
printing of five thousand copies in February 1939.

In *The Lamp of Prophecy or Signs of the Times* (1940), Dr. H. A.
Ironside, pastor of the Moody Memorial Church in Chicago, entitled chapter 9, "Are the Jews as a People Responsible for the So-
called 'Protocols of the Elders of Zion'?" After relating the innocent Jews who had suffered from propaganda concerning these
documents, this respected fundamentalist-evangelical theologian insisted:

> It is, therefore, it seems to me, not only most unfortunate but really
> wicked to attempt to foist responsibility for the Protocols upon the
> people of the Jews. Whoever may have written these documents,
> certainly they were not penned by Jews entitled to speak for the
> race. In my judgment, Christian teachers would do well to stress
> this fact in order that they may not participate in putting upon
> Christ's brethren after the flesh a responsibility that does not
> belong to them and thus expose them to a persecution they do not
> deserve.[38]

"It is true that blindness in part has happened to Israel
because of their rejection of their Messiah when He came to
them in lowly grace," Rev. Ironside added. "It is true that they
joined with the Gentiles in crucifying the Lord of glory. It is true
that many of them hate Christianity and Christians as much as
some professed Christians hate them." But, quoting the solemn
words in the book of Obadiah, verses 12, 13, and 14, against
those who hurt or mock God's chosen Jewish people, Harry A.
Ironside remarked: "These are solemn words and may well be
taken to heart by the Gentile nations at the present time. Surely
no real Christian wants to be found in such company but rather

would seek to manifest the grace of Christ to those through whose fall salvation has come to us."

Dr. Ironside also condemned prejudiced statements about Jews that were "unfair and false." He declared:

I have noticed of late that certain teachers are constantly drawing special attention to anyone opposed to orderly government who happens to have a Jewish name. But in all fairness such should surely point out that there are far more men of Hebrew parentage who are in the forefront of civilization and progress than are to be found among those who are seeking to destroy the present order. The idea seems to be prevalent in many quarters that practically all the great financiers of France, Britain, and America are Jews. Look over the roster for yourself. Take the great banking houses of America and England with which I am personally more familiar than with those of France. How many Jewish names do you find among them? How large a proportion of the money barons of Wall Street are Jews? How many of the millionaires still left in America are Jews? By far the great majority are Gentiles, and it is absurd to think that the small majority of Jews could even if they would overthrow this or any other Gentile government.[39]

"It should be the business of Christians not to sow seeds of distrust and dissension among men," the fundamentalist-evangelical pastor and Bible teacher stressed, "but to exemplify so far as they possibly can, the grace that is in Christ Jesus, Who gave Himself a ransom for all, Whose Gospel is to be proclaimed to Jew and Gentile alike and in Whose mystical body, the church, there is neither Jew nor Gentile, but all are one in Christ Jesus." "We cannot afford to waste our time stirring up racial hatreds instead of seeking by all means to save some," H. A. Ironside concluded, quoting 1 Corinthians 10:32, "[giving] none offense, neither to the Jews, nor to the Gentiles, nor to the church of God."

Dr. Ironside was one of the many speakers at a national Congress on Prophecy, November 1–8, 1942, which met in the Calvary Baptist Church in New York City. A four-part "Manifesto" signed by leading fundamentalist-evangelical theologians was read to those assembled on the fifth evening and was unanimously approved. The fourth section, on anti-Semitism, read:

4. As to anti-Semitism. We believe that anti-Semitism in its present vicious world-wide manifestation, is incompatible with both the letter and the spirit of the gospel, and is to be shunned and guarded against by all who sincerely love our Lord Jesus Christ; that to do kindness and to show mercy to the seed of Abraham is a direct Christian obligation.[40]

# 4

## CONSPIRACY THEORIES, ANTI-SEMITISM, AND THE HOLOCAUST YEARS

The national Congress on Prophecy held in New York City in November of 1942 underscored the fundamentalist-evangelical's firm and historic opposition to anti-Semitism—hatred for Jews was antithetical to all that these prophetically minded conservative Christians believed. And yet, there were elements of the fundamentalist-evangelical belief system and popular attitudes that were extremely distasteful to members of the Jewish community. Between the world wars and during the Holocaust, evangelism was a primary concern of fundamentalist-evangelical preachers and teachers. In addition, as communism and fascism spread and as the world prepared for a second world war, the fundamentalist-evangelical prophetic interpretation of the Bible succumbed to conspiracy theories and rhetoric that was at times construed as anti-Semitic. Sometimes, anti-Semites tried to use prophetic rhetoric and fear of a Communist takeover to recruit conservative Christians. This chapter will analyze these elements as well as as certain fundamentalist-evangelical attitudes toward the Nazi debacle and the Holocaust.

## EVANGELISM

During the 1942 Congress on Prophecy, Dr. Charles Lee Feinberg, a professor at Dallas Theological Seminary, ended his sermon "What Israel Means to God" by detailing God's love for God's chosen Jewish people. Feinberg inventoried the points he made in his conference message and related:

> To summarize, then, it has been shown that Israel means much to God, for He has purposed to use them to witness to the unity of His Person; to show the blessedness of serving Him; to receive, preserve, and transmit the Scriptures; to show the sustaining power of the Scriptures throughout the centuries; to be the channel of the Messiah's incarnation; to show His long suffering in dealing with sinful man; to reveal to the world the futility of seeking to gain acceptance with Him by works of the flesh; to manifest His faithfulness to His promises; to use them as world-wide missionaries; and to spread abroad the glory and knowledge of Himself in the millennium.[1]

"If God can so use them [the Jewish people], do you not think they ought to mean a great deal to Him?" Charles Feinberg rhetorically questioned, answering for himself and those assembled, "The word to you and to me is clear: 'Ye that are Jehovah's remembrances, take ye no rest, and give him no rest, till he establish, and till he make Jerusalem a praise in the earth' (Isaiah 62:6,7)."

A Jewish convert to Christianity, Dr. Feinberg remembered fondly how his father, "after he had completed reading a portion of the Scripture for his own comfort and joy, would not close the sacred page before kissing it tenderly." To Feinberg, the Jew's reverence for and devotion to the Bible "has kept Israel buoyed up through the centuries when persecutions, that would have broken the morale of the mightiest of nations, came upon them like an overwhelming flood." "It is as though God had said: 'I desire to show to the world how powerful my Word is to sustain even though not always followed, and I choose Israel to convey this message to the world," Charles Feinberg noted. "Does not Israel mean much to God in this way?"[2]

Certainly, the Jewish community had been as appalled by the "Hebrew Christian" movement during the twentieth century as it had been horrified by missionary movements aimed at Jews. Ironically, the American Board of Missions to the Jews had been asked by fundamentalist-evangelical pastors and teachers to sponsor the 1942 New York Congress on Prophecy because of "its wide capacity organizationally, its peculiar fitness to promote such a conference, and its ability to distribute benefits derived therein.[3] In fact, Jewish converts to Christianity and missionary enterprises aimed at Jews were a constant means of information on Jews and Judaism for modern evangelicals, especially the fundamentalist-evangelical movement. And, while the Congress on Prophecy declared in its manifesto its horror at the "age-old hatred against the Jews" that had "shocked civilization with its revolting manifestations overseas," the prophetic conference members affirmed that "the Church has a supreme obligation to press upon the hearts of individual Jews the message of the gospel." In other words, the movement refused to give up evangelism among any racial or religious group in the world—including Jews.

### Moody Monthly

This is amply seen in the pages of the popular fundamentalist-evangelical magazine published by the Moody Bible Institute in Chicago. Beginning as a small biweekly paper in 1891 that acquainted former students with the news at the Institute, it was discontinued in 1893 because of the poor economic conditions in the United States that year. In September 1900 it began a new series as a copyrighted magazine printed monthly. Dr. James Gray edited it from 1907 to 1917 and enlarged its scope to be more of a Bible study magazine for fundamentalist-evangelicals, with practical helps for Christian service. In 1910 the name of the periodical was changed to *The Christian Workers' Magazine,* and in 1920 it was again changed to *The Moody Bible Institute Monthly.* In 1938, the name was abbreviated to *Moody Monthly,* the name it carries to this day.

In the early issues of this periodical, Christian evangelization techniques for use among Jews were highlighted side by side with "exciting" reports from Palestine. In the May 10, 1892, issue, Reuben A. Torrey's "Passages of Scripture to Use in Dealing with Various Classes of Men" not only dealt with Roman Catholics and Spiritualists, but also mentioned Jews. "The best way to deal with a Jew is to show him that his own Bible points to Christ," Torrey wrote. "The most helpful passages to use are Isaiah 53; Daniel 9:26; Zechariah 12:10." While Jewish evangelism received one paragraph, the Roman Catholics received six![4]

Students of Moody Bible Institute had the opportunity in 1904 to hear a series of lectures by Rev. Samuel H. Wilkinson of the Mildmay Mission to the Jews in London, England, when he toured the United States for two months. Rev. Wilkinson believed that the restoration of the Jewish people to Palestine would be in two stages. During the first stage, Jews would be partially restored and would incur the "ill will of the Gentile people." They would return to Palestine "in unbelief," rebuild the Temple, and "reestablish Mosaic ritual." The Antichrist would persecute them at this time, and then the second stage would occur, when Jesus Christ reappeared to deliver them and to set up his millennial kingdom. Wilkinson had visited Russia ten times and brought twelve hundred feet of motion picture film, which included scenes of military processions, prisoners, police, and the Kishinev massacre, as well as his mission work. His lectures were published in a two-article series in *The Institute Tie*, and thus students and readers alike benefited from his exposé of the horrible atrocities perpetrated against the Jewish people.[5]

In 1909, Rev. Louis Meyer, a Jewish convert to Christianity and the first Hebrew Christian minister of the Reformed Presbyterian Church, spoke to students at Moody Bible Institute on "The Jewish Problem and Its Solution." While he believed that the only correct manner of solving the problem was through evangelization, he also recounted the "guilt" of the Christian church. According to Louis Meyer, the greatest cause of guilt was the Christian church's persecution of the Jewish people, while prejudice against the Jew ran a close second.

While he believed it was true that Jewish "unbelief," belief in their own righteousness and tradition and unwillingness to listen to the message of salvation through Jesus Christ, was a stumbling block that Jewish people placed in their own path, Meyer insisted that Christians were guilty of placing obstacles in the path of the Jewish people as well. He emphasized that Christians were also inconsistent at living Christlike lives for their Jewish neighbors to see and were indifferent about the spiritual needs of the Jewish people. They lacked information about the Jewish people and lacked sincerity of purpose with regard to the Jewish community. The Hebrew Christian minister asserted that more prayer instead of pressure would let God work in the lives of Jewish people. Rev. Louis Meyer became the field secretary for the Chicago Hebrew Mission (the mission William E. Blackstone founded) and was the second editor of *The Fundamentals.*[6]

By the latter part of 1917, the fundamentalist-evangelical periodical rejoiced at the movement of Zionism and that the British forces had taken Gaza, Hebron, and Beersheba. No capture sent the fundamentalist-evangelical camp into an uproar of rejoicing more than the capture of Jerusalem. "Every Christian heart thrills at the tidings that Jerusalem after twelve centuries of almost unbroken Moslem rule, has surrendered to the British forces," Moody Bible Institute's *The Christian Workers' Magazine* reported.

In stating "every Christian heart," the editor left out a great number of more liberal Christians or conservative amillennial Christians who had little regard for Jewish restoration to Palestine or the premillennial prophetic interpretation of the fundamentalist-evangelical. Liberalism's *The Christian Century,* for example, had misgivings about the British policy of encouraging "aggressive Jews to claim the country as a 'homeland' for their people." In stark contrast to this liberal Christian opposition, fundamentalist-evangelical periodicals reprinted the letter of Arthur J. Balfour, the foreign minister of Great Britain, to Lord Rothschild (later referred to as the Balfour Declaration). "By Mr. Balfour's letter, the Allies become the champions of Zionism," *The Christian Workers' Magazine* exulted.[7]

As has been shown in these excerpts from thousands of pages of early editions of Moody Bible Institute's popular Christian magazine, the philosophical and theological elements found in the issues of *Moody Monthly* between the world wars were evident and grounded long before. Fundamentalist-evangelical attitudes toward the Jewish people and anti-Semitism were formed in the latter decades of the nineteenth century and the early decades of the twentieth.

For instance, in the October 1938 issue of *Moody Monthly* Wilbur M. Smith continued the series "With My Bible Around the Mediterranean." As he considered Palestine, he lamented the effects of anti-Semitism throughout history. "For centuries Israel has been a persecuted, hated, hounded people," Dr. Smith told fundamentalist-evangelical readers. "She has always known what insult means, what hatred can do, the tragedy of being driven into ghettos like cattle, and denounced as the leprous nation of the earth. But since the fall of Jerusalem over eighteen hundred years ago, Israel has not known such suffering and persecution as she has experienced since the World War." The fundamentalist-evangelical professor and pastor informed the readers of *Moody Monthly* that anti-Semitism "is the only compound word in our language to express hatred of and opposition to a nation, and that only one nation."[8]

He found anti-Semitism to be "one of the strangest sociological phenomenon in the world today." "After all the reasons why the nations of the earth have a perpetual hatred for the Jews, it still remains a mystery," Rev. Wilbur Smith wrote, "and the Word of God again reveals its supernatural origin in its clear predictions of exactly this condition to obtain in Israel's history at the close of this age."[9] Dr. Smith related anti-Semitism to the current conditions of 1938:

The hatred of the Jews in Palestine today differs from the hatred poured upon them in other countries. In Germany and Austria the persecution is by the German government, not by the people. It is a part of national policy. In Palestine the government is pro-Jewish, supporting and attempting to carry out the Balfour declaration; but the people of the land, the Arabs, hate the Jews, and are continually warring against them. It is something worse than war. Wars are fought, and lost, and won, and conquered peoples adjust themselves to the new situation. But there is no war officially declared in Palestine. There is hatred, and this is almost daily resulting in bloodshed, in bombings of busses, and cold-blooded murders, often of most innocent and helpless persons.[10]

"The hatred of the Arab for the Jew is deep," Wilbur Smith related. "If it were not for the presence of British soldiers in Palestine, the Arabs would slaughter thousands of Jews and attempt to rid the land of them."

With prophetic premonition and additional insight from his extensive travels to Europe and the Middle East, Dr. Smith felt that there was little prospect for peace outside of the return of the Messiah. "It will grow worse instead of better," he asserted. "All Europe will yet be fevered with this poison of anti-Semitism, and the Jews will crowd into their land more rapidly than ever, hoping there to find rest for their souls." Alas, biblical prophetic passages told Smith that "the king of the North," whom many fundamentalist-evangelicals believed to be Russia, would "swoop down upon the land of Israel with a great army," and the "king of the South" would come up against them from Egypt. Tribulation would occur, and the Jewish people in the land would "turn to Jehovah for deliverance." There was no doubt in Wilbur Smith's mind that Jesus Christ would return to save the Jewish people, and he was thrilled that out of 360,000 volumes in Hebrew University in Jerusalem, more than two hundred were labeled under the subject "New Testament."[11]

Evangelism was, therefore, ever on the mind of Rev. Smith and *Moody Monthly*. They hoped to spare a "remnant" of the Jewish people from the Great Tribulation to come. Calling Dr. Judah Magnes, president of the Hebrew University, "one of the most remarkable Jews in the world today," and quoting from him about the "great testament of literature" in the Hebrew University on Mount Scopus, Wilbur M. Smith dreamed in the conclusion of the first part of his article:

> Some day it may be, in the Providence of God, that a student mining in the riches of this library, will come upon a volume that will bring him to accept and adore the Saviour, and so inspire him to witness to David's greater Son [Jesus Christ], that all that land may

hear the gospel of the one who came of Judah, to deliver Israel from
her enemies, and all men from their sins!

In the second part of his article (which appeared in the November 1938 issue), Dr. Smith related that the Arabs would be certainly punished by God for all their vicious cruelties toward the Jewish people.[12] Numerous articles in *Moody Monthly* referred to the evils of Nazism and communism. Gleaning information from Jewish periodicals and Christian missionary enterprises concerned with the welfare of European Jews, fundamentalist-evangelical readers not only kept up with the horrible persecution facing the Jewish community, but in prophetic indignation believed each report. The May 1940 excerpt, "Jewish Notes," is indicative of such portrayal:

> More than 250,000 Jews have been wiped out in Poland by military operations, disease, and starvation since September first, according to an estimate released by the Joint Distribution Committee. It added that 80 per cent of the remaining 1,250,000 Jews in the German occupied area have been reduced to beggary. Typhus epidemics are raging in Warsaw, Lodz, and many other towns, and their virulence is augmented by widespread starvation and exhaustion. Economic life has been completely strangled. Hundreds of thousands of families, uprooted from their homes, wander along open roads, seeking a shelter. Women, aged men, and children are subjected to countless indignities.
>
> In Nazi Poland 2,500 Jews are reported to have committed suicide, and the number is being increased daily, according to the committee's report, while many hundreds have been summarily executed.
>
> Not the least of the hardships confronting the Jews of Poland are their fears for the future. The institution of a ghetto in Warsaw was officially ordered. This would crowd 250,000 people into a few square blocks, half of whose buildings were destroyed by bombardment or fire. The execution of the order has been delayed because of fear that epidemics might spread to the rest of Warsaw's population.[13]

This excerpt was taken direct from *Jewish Missionary Magazine*, and one finds fundamentalist-evangelicals looking for any piece of information on anti-Semitism and the plight of the Jewish people. Nevertheless, in the same issue, a page-long advertisement in the form of an article was sponsored by the Million Testaments Campaign. A picture of Orthodox Jews, with a few more modernly dressed individuals, was centered on the page with the two-line caption: "A STREET FILLED WITH JEWS IN A CITY IN EUROPE. They sorely need the healing balm of the Word of God!" The title read: "'It's Suicide or Christ': Giving God's Word to Jews throughout the world to win them to Christ." The quotation came from "one who has labored for years on the Continent," and followed an introductory quotation from the chairman of the World Jewish Congress on the plight of the Jews in Europe. The article continued:

> We are in the midst of a campaign to place the life-giving Word of God, in the form of attractive Testaments, in the hands of the sorrowing and suffering Jews of Europe; and among the refugees and other Jews in Palestine, America, and other lands. Israel's extremity is our opportunity. Giving God's Word to Jews is the best way to lead them to a saving knowledge of Christ! It is surely God's appointed hour to place New Testaments in the hands of the Jews throughout the world!
>
> In spite of the war, the work of distributing New Testaments among Jewish people in Europe is still going forward. Many workers are cooperating in giving New Testaments, in Hebrew and other languages to Jewish people who agree to read them. How sorely they need the healing balm of God's Word in this hour of terrible affliction![14]

"Jews in Palestine are now eagerly receiving New Testaments in Hebrew and English," the following section on "Open Doors in Palestine" went on to say. "Missionaries and workers are cooperating heartily in the distribution. Two missionaries visited 160 of the 300 colonies in Palestine." Testaments distributed to Jewish refugees and a campaign to reach the United States and Canada from coast to coast were detailed as well.

To the fundamentalist-evangelical, those who did not accept Jesus Christ as their "saviour and Lord" were destined to a worse fate than Nazi extermination, that is, they would spend an eternity in hell. And while these prophetically minded Christians believed that the Nazis would receive the vengeance of God for their deeds toward the chosen people, evangelism was seen as a means to at least acquaint the Jewish people with the gospel of Jesus Christ and "their Messiah," so that sorrowing Jews would recognize the events surrounding his return (and, perhaps, "believe in Jesus"). Such evangelism was at best viewed by Jews as deceptive preying on a persecuted people—at worst, the attempt to turn Jews into Christian believers was viewed by Jews as another form of extermination of the Jewish community.

Some readers, however, questioned whether or not Jews should be evangelized. In the "Practical and Perplexing Questions" section of the August 1940 issue, a reader from Rochester, Michigan, asked: (1) Should missions to the Jews be supported? (2) How about Romans 11:25 (". . . that blindness in part is happened to Israel, until the fulness of the Gentiles be come in")? (3) Will the time come when those who love Jewish work will be obliged to withdraw from our churches? *Moody Monthly* columnist Grant Stroh replied:

> (1) By all means. At first the Jews predominated in the Church. "The Jew first" is still in good order. At the present time, God is greatly blessing missions to the Jews. (2) As a nation Israel has been rejected and the Gentiles favored. Yet even among the Gentiles, only a few are being saved at the present time. When Christ returns "all Israel shall be saved" (vs. 26). (3) In view of the treatment of the Jews, especially in certain European countries nominally Christian, we are unable to predict what will happen to those who are interested in their evangelization. Yet we are under obligation to give them the gospel.[15]

The magazine announced that the November 1940 issue would venture "on something entirely new—a Jewish number." Explaining why the "Jewish issue" of *Moody Monthly* was necessary, the editorial notes stated: "In these tragic days for Israel there is an opportunity, strategic and demanding, for bringing the gospel to your Jewish friends and neighbors."

The November 1940 "Jewish Number" gave little doubt as to what was happening to the Jews of Europe. On the inside cover, Joseph Taylor Britan detailed the tribulations of the Jews (whom Britan calls "the people of God"). Using information from *Opinion:*

*A Journal of Jewish Life and Letters,* the fundamentalist-evangelical told of severe repressive legislation enacted once Romania was partitioned—legislation that aimed at the elimination of Jews from the economic, industrial, and cultural life of the country. Britan also told of the "anti-Jewish and other fascist-nazi statutes" that the Pétain government had instituted after the Nazis captured France. Quoting the Jewish journal, the article stated: "Synagogues were burned, Hebrew Schools demolished and Jewish owned buildings dynamited. The internment of Jewish refugees, seizure of Jewish property, the publication of violently anti-Jewish diatribes and charges of rebellion, looting, assault and illegal executions marked the outbreaks."

The Jewish refugee problem and the accompanying starvation are detailed in the article, and Joseph Britan specifically asks that fundamentalist-evangelicals (including pastors, Sunday school superintendents, and leaders of missionary societies) send money to the Friends of Israel Refugee Relief Committee in Philadelphia to feed the Jewish refugees in Europe. He noted that no salaries or office space were paid to this committee, so that the large majority of funds could feed the Jewish people who were in distress. Unlike the Evian Conference, which refused to specify that the large majority of refugees were "Jewish," the fundamentalist-evangelical had no difficulty in pointing this fact out. "When the Son of Man [Jesus Christ] shall come in His glory and in the glory of the Father with His Holy angels and shall sit on the throne of His glory judging the nations of the earth," Joseph Taylor Britan warned, "it is distinctly written that the principle of judgment shall be their treatment of the Jew." All anti-Semites in the church, Nazis, communist persecutors, and even those indifferent to Jews, would receive the wrath of God.[16]

Other articles in the issue noted the appalling conditions that engulfed Jews and Hebrew Christians, human beings who faced the living terror of the Gestapo. Rev. Jacob Peltz, general secretary of the International Hebrew Christian Alliance, had just returned from travels to Germany, Austria, Czechoslovakia, Hungary, Romania, and Poland, as well as meeting refugees in the major cities of Europe. "I have listened to the harrowing tales of Jewish mothers whose husbands have been murdered and whose sons have suffered indescribable tortures in Nazi concentration camps," Rev. Peltz related. He was beginning a nationwide speaking tour in churches on "What I Saw in Nazi Germany," "The International Situation in the Light of Prophecy," and "The Triumphs of the Gospel Amongst the Jews of Europe."[17] Like Peltz's messages, the *Moody Monthly* "Jewish Number" contained much more material on how to evangelize the Jewish people than on the conditions in Europe. In fact, the conditions seemed to dictate to these fundamentalist-evangelicals the imperative to escalate conversion efforts; and Hebrew Christian missionary enterprises dominated the November 1940 issue.

Again, other Christians (many whom fundamentalist-evangelicals only considered "professed Christians") resisted evangelizing Jewish people. Some just did not care enough about what happened to Jews, and preferred that Jews would go to hell (a new twist on prejudice). Others, however, felt that Christians had no right to go to the Jewish people with the Christian gospel. "The Jew has his religion, let him alone" was their cry. *Moody Monthly* editors had just heard Rev. Jacob Gartenhaus, the head of Jewish missionary enterprises for the Southern Baptist Convention, declare: "We have had more Jewish conversions to Christ during the past year than in the preceding ten years." Now, in the "Jewish Number," they excerpted an article Gartenhaus had written for the September issue of *Southern Baptist Home Missions.* Gartenhaus, a former Moody Bible Institute student, answered Christian critics of Jewish evangelism by writing:

> It is amazing that in our consideration of the ever-present problem of the Jew, we of the Christian faith are so remiss in pressing the one obvious solution – which is the conversion of the Jew to Christianity; not by persecution, but by treating him exactly as we would treat any other non-Christian.

In answer to Jewish critics of Christian evangelism, Rev. Gartenhaus quoted an "unnamed American rabbi":

> The intelligent Jew knows that the entire missionary idea is borrowed from Judaism and the motive behind it is admirable. The

sincere Christian who feels that by virtue of the admonition of Jesus it is his duty to share Christianity with his fellow man, is only displaying genuine loyalty to his faith.

Relating the above, the editors of *Moody Monthly* concluded: "Not in condescension or in any mere spirit of tolerance should we go to the Jew with our gospel, but with a heart of love. He has experienced enough of the world's hatred. Let us now show him the love of Christ released through us."[18]

## CONSPIRACY THEORIES

Fundamentalist-evangelical theology not only necessitated a belief in evangelism, but also encouraged Christians to watch "the signs of the times." Jesus had told his followers, "Watch therefore, for ye know neither the day nor the hour wherein the Son of man cometh [Jesus' second coming]" (Matt. 25:13). He related, however, that there would be "wars and rumors of wars," famines, pestilences, earthquakes, and false prophets that would precede the "abomination of desolation" of which the prophet Daniel spoke—when the Antichrist would attempt to set himself up in the Holy of Holies of the rebuilt Temple in Jerusalem (see Matt. 24, especially v. 15; compare Dan. 8:11–13; 9:27; 11:31; 12:11).

In like manner, the apostle Paul spoke of a "lawless one," the Antichrist, wickedly deceiving with signs and false wonders (note 2 Thess. 2). It is this individual along with the enemies of the Jewish people that fundamentalist-evangelicals believed Jesus would return to defeat. Most prophetic Bible teachers in the movement taught that Christian believers would be "raptured" before the Great Tribulation took place, meeting Jesus in the air seven years before his second coming. They used the apostle Paul's words in 1 Thessalonians 4:13–18 (KJV):

> But we do not want you to be uninformed, brethren, about those who are asleep [dead], that you may not grieve, as do the rest who have no hope. For if we believe that Jesus died and rose again, even so God will bring with Him those who have fallen asleep in Jesus. For this we say to you by the word of the Lord, that we who are

alive, and remain until the coming of the Lord, shall not precede those who have fallen asleep. For the Lord Himself will descend from heaven with a shout, with the voice of the archangel, and with the trumpet of God; and the dead in Christ shall rise first. Then we who are alive and remain shall be caught up together with them in the clouds to meet the Lord in the air, and thus we shall always be with the Lord. Therefore comfort one another with these words.

Since the forces of lawlessness and the birth of the Antichrist preceded this "rapture," Bible teachers sometimes were caught up in trying to ascertain who the Antichrist would be. Famines, earthquake, and war only served to further fuel the speculation.

Many respected fundamentalist-evangelical Bible teachers disdained such activity. Arno C. Gaebelein, for example, wrote in *Our Hope* in September 1933 that "a normal, scripturally well balanced believer looks for the Lord Jesus Christ and not for the Antichrist—Stop the wild guesses!" Dr. Gaebelein determined never to preach on world conditions (such as communism's spread) or on prophecy in a Sunday morning sermon, nor to begin an issue of *Our Hope* with such material. Such times, Gaebelein felt, were reserved to preach or write something that would "glorify the Lord."[19]

Nevertheless, Arno Gaebelein and some other fundamentalist-evangelical Bible teachers believed that the Antichrist would be an apostate Jew. Since Jesus was Jewish, they believed the apostate Antichrist controlled by Satan would try to counterfeit Jesus in origin, and would present himself as a "messiah" and "king." As in the days of the ancient Hebrews, many Jews would be led away into apostasy by this deceiver. Thus, some fundamentalist-evangelicals watched for Jewish apostasy as much as they railed against modernistic Christian apostasy. "Here we must call attention to the fact that while there is an on-sweeping apostasy in Christendom, there is also a corresponding Jewish apostasy, or rather infidelity," Arno C. Gaebelein wrote in his most controversial book, *The Conflict of the Ages* (1933). He noted:

Any Christian will honor the orthodox Old Testament believing Jews, who still cling to the hope of a coming Messiah, and who pray for His coming and expect him. They know the promises of the kingdom and the promises of a glorious future, yet there is upon them a judicial blindness. They keep their feasts year in and year out, generation after generation, hoping for the promised day when their wanderings among the nations of the world are ended and they can get back to the promised land.[20]

"But they are becoming less," the seventy-two-year-old Gaebelein explained. "The greater part of Jewry has become reformed, or as we call it 'deformed.' They no longer believe in the law and in the prophets."

Gaebelein's early mission work in the Lower East Side of New York City had given him a deep respect and love for religious Jews, although he felt they were given to law and works—blinded to their "messiah, Jesus Christ." His fight against rationalistic Christianity matched the traditional Jew's fight against rationalistic Judaism. Now, in the light of the horrors of Stalin and the spread of communism; now, in the midst of the Great Depression and the talk of socialism; now in the valley of fascism and despotism that signaled the end of times, Gaebelein was upset over apostate Judaism's combining with apostate Christendom to bring the world under the control of the Antichrist and Satan. He wrote:

The Messiah and the glorious future is looked upon as a delusion. One of them [a Jew] said years ago—the Messiah we love is the dollar—Jerusalem we do not want, Washington is our Jerusalem. Turning away from the hope of their fathers and their own Scriptures, they become infidels and finally through their reaching out after material things and power they become a menace. The lower elements become lawless. As we have shown, these infidel Jews were prominent in the revolutionary propaganda during the nineteenth century. Karl Marx, the author of the "Communist Bible" was an infidel Jew; so was Lasalle and hundreds of others active in the socialistic and communistic activities. Trotzsky and at least two score other leaders of the Russian revolution were apostate Jews. They make themselves felt in our country and in other civilized countries. Watching the names of those who were arrested in anti-government demonstrations we find that a large percentage are Jews.

We must mention another fact. Apostate Christians, by which we mean professing Christians, who have turned against supernatural Christianity, like Drs. Sherwood Eddy, Harry Emerson Fosdick and hundreds of others, fraternize with the rationalistic Jewish elements. They are bedfellows in socialistic organizations. There is a strange coming together; infidel preachers invite infidel Jews to their "pulpits" and reformed Jewish rabbis welcome modernistic preachers to their synagogues. The Religious "Book-Club" of New York, under the leadership of several outstanding modernists has recommended books, written by rationalistic Jews, to their "Christian" club members. It is an indication that as this age ends the infidel Gentile and Jewish forces will unite to make opposition to God and to His Christ, and when that man of sin appears, the antichrist, he will be accepted by the apostate Gentile-Christian, for he denies the Father and the Son, just what the apostate denies . . . and that same man of sin will be acceptable to the Jew for he will deny "that Jesus is the Christ," the Messiah (1 John 2:18–23). He will be accepted by the infidel Jews as their Messiah.[21]

"Jew and Gentile will then fulfill, through Satanic delusion and power, what is written in the second psalm," Gaebelein continued. "Gentiles rage, people imagine vain things and finally there is a confederacy 'against the Lord and against His anointed (the Christ).'"

Some Hebrew Christian missionary organizations viewed Gaebelein's book as anti-Jewish in tone and, certainly, it appears to be his only venture into conspiracy theory in his fifty books. The Jewish studies program at the Moody Bible Institute would view it with suspicion as well. Although he believed in 1933 that authorship of the Protocols of the Elders of Zion would "never be ascertained," and later signed a statement against the Protocols in 1939, Gaebelein insisted in *The Conflict of the Ages* that "throughout the twenty-four Protocols we have a very pronounced restatement of the principal theories of Illuminism and Marxism." He then quoted a section of the Protocols to prove his point. Gaebelein quoted many other sources, including statements of his friend, Rev. Dr. George A. Simons, former superintendent of the Methodist Missions in Russia. Dr. Simons had testified before the Overman Committee during the "Red scare" in 1919. Simons told the committee concerning Bolshevik agitation in New York City that "more than half of the agitators in the so-called Bolshevik movement were Jews." Dr. Simons added:

> I do not want to say anything against the Jews as such. I am not in sympathy with the anti-Semitic movement, never have been, and do not ever expect to be. I am against it. But I have a firm conviction that this thing is Yiddish, and that one of its bases is found in the east side of New York.

The *London Times* (March 29, 1919) is also quoted by Gaebelein in his *The Conflict of the Ages* as stating that of the twenty or thirty commissaries or leaders who provided the central machinery of the Bolshevik movement, "not less than 75% are Jews." Other respected newspapers and journals are quoted in *The Conflict of the Ages* to show apostate Jewish involvement in bolshevism. Even the *Jewish Chronicles* (April 4, 1919) was quoted as stating: "There is much in the fact of Bolshevism itself that so many Jews are Bolshevists, in the fact that the ideals of Bolshevism at many points are consonant with the finest ideals of Judaism."[22]

Because of such statements, Arno C. Gaebelein at times would be accused of anti-Semitism in his latter years. And yet such accusations would appall him, and he would never desist from his statements of love toward the Jewish people. When the League of American Writers (which included the head of the Communist Party in America) in 1939 listed Our Hope Publishers and Gaebelein among "anti-Semitic publishers," claiming that the periodical's "main purpose is to promulgate Aryan, Gentile and White supremacy" and that it "attacks Jews as 'Red Anti-Christs,'" Gaebelein fought back in print. He pointed out *Our Hope*'s forty-five-year history of Bible study and instruction, and its consistent opposition to Aryanism and racism. To the charge of anti-Semitism, Rev. Gaebelein responded:

> This is slander number three. There is not a drop of anti-Semitic blood in our veins. Nine of the best years of our life were devoted to the welfare of the Jewish people. From 1890 to 1896 thousands of Jews, driven out of Eastern Europe, arrived in New York. The Editor had a church and a mission in downtown New York. At that time we helped hundreds of families with food and clothing. The Editor's love for Israel has never undergone a change. One of

America's leading Rabbis said a few years ago, "The Jews in America have no better friend than Dr. A. C. Gaebelein." The late Governor of Idaho, the Hon. Moses Alexander, a fine Jewish gentleman, while in office became our friend. He invited us to his home to dine with his family. In listening to a sermon we preached on the national future of the Jews he offered to write to every mayor of the larger towns of his state to urge the people to invite the writer just to give this lecture. He thought so highly of the Editor of "Our Hope" that he appointed him a commissioner to a certain National Convention to represent him and his state. The commission with his signature and the state seal is in our possession.[23]

When Ralph Lord Roy repeated the anti-Semitic charge in 1953, linking Arno C. Gaebelein with Gerald Winrod in his book *Apostles of Discord,* Roy had to retract "his error" when he reviewed the written evidence. Gaebelein's son, respected Christian educator Dr. Frank E. Gaebelein, was able to state categorically that he had never heard an anti-Semitic statement in his home as a youth or from his father (with whom he worked closely) in later years. Furthermore, a half century of pages from *Our Hope* exhibited only a deep respect and love for the chosen people, the Jews. Arno C. Gaebelein despised anti-Semitism as being a deceptive tool of Satan. Nevertheless, Dr. Frank E. Gaebelein, who was headmaster of the private Stony Brook School (a Christian school which throughout its history welcomed Jewish students), had to refuse far-right groups permission to reprint *The Conflict of the Ages* after his father's death.

As for the reception that *The Conflict of the Ages* received in 1933, glowing reviews are found in *Moody Monthly, Christianity Today* (not the current evangelical periodical founded in 1957, but one published by Westminster Seminary), *Southern Churchman, Bibliotheca Sacra, Revelation, American Lutheran, The Sunday School Times,* and numerous periodicals that transcend denominational lines. Many newspapers, such as the *Minneapolis Journal* and the *Toronto Globe,* gave it high praise. And individuals as diverse as Rev. Kenneth McKenzie, well-known Episcopal rector in Connecticut, a number of physicians, evangelist Billy Sunday, Professor Leander S. Keyser of Hamma (Lutheran) Divinity School in Ohio, J. Hampton Baumgartner, special representative of the

Delaware, Lackawanna, and Western Railroad Company, and Sir John Sandeman Allen of the British House of Commons gave it favorable reviews and comments. To this broad spectrum, Dr. Arno C. Gaebelein had keen insight into history as well as into the modern world and into the forces that attempted to control it. Nevertheless, Gaebelein never attempted a work such as *The Conflict of the Ages* again, and in 1939 he signed a petition by Keith Brooks and other fundamentalist-evangelicals repudiating the Protocols of the Elders of Zion.

## Oswald J. Smith

Rev. Oswald J. Smith (1889–1986) was pastor of the Toronto Gospel Tabernacle in Canada when he wrote books such as *Antichrist and the Future*, *Prophecies of the End-Time*, *Is the Antichrist at Hand?* and *When Antichrist Reigns*. His congregation would become the missionary-minded Peoples Church in Toronto, and Oswald J. Smith would be noted in evangelical circles as an evangelist, preacher, missionary statesman, author of nearly thirty books published in thirty-five languages, poet, hymn writer, radio preacher, editor, and avid traveler. His life spanned nearly a century, and he was one of the few early fundamentalist-evangelicals who would view both world wars, the formation of the State of Israel, the Vietnam conflict, and the 1967 and 1973 Arab-Israeli wars. Billy Graham, recounting how Smith's books had touched his own life, once stated: "The name, Oswald J. Smith, symbolizes worldwide evangelization."[24]

In 1932, *Antichrist and the Future* appeared, and the book is indicative not only of Oswald J. Smith's biblical literalism and premillennial eschatology, but also of his worldview and political analysis. In the midst of the Great Depression, Rev. Smith prefaced his text with the questions: "Whither are we bound? Where are we headed? What next? These are the questions that men are asking today. Is there an answer? There certainly is." He answered:

> If we are living, as many believe, in the End-Time Days, then we may rest assured that conditions are not going to improve, not just

yet. The financial situation will grow worse and worse. Industrial and economic problems will increase. Governments will rise and fall, war clouds gather, and the general depression become more serious than ever.

No statesman can solve the financial problems of the world today. No government can deal successfully with the unemployment situation. Men's hearts are already failing them for fear, and everywhere there is perplexity among the nations. Thus will it continue until—Until, in due time, after all others have failed, a man will arise who will settle every problem that confronts the world today. He will solve the financial problem. He will deal with unemployment and every man will be given a job. There will be plenty of money and an abundance of work. None will be idle. He will be heralded far and wide as the saviour of the world, the deliverer of humanity. Statesmen will gladly put everything in his hands. Governments will appoint him to supreme positions of authority and power. He will be big enough for the job.[25]

"Thus, prosperity will return," Rev. Oswald J. Smith insisted, noting that the depression would end, problems of finance would be solved and a seeming golden age ushered in. As all nations and peoples "idolize and worship" the great man who accomplished this, they would discover that "he is none other than the Antichrist himself." The world would have a costly salvation, "saved by the devil's Christ." According to Smith, the Great Tribulation would then occur.

In the book, Smith chided those who felt that they were going to "christianize" the world. Although he and his church were supporters of missionary movements around the world, they did not believe that the world would become Christian or the governments of the world could become Christian. Rev. Oswald J. Smith declared: "There is not a nation on the face of the earth that is going to be christianized in this age. There is not a government that will accept the teachings of God's Word."[26] Smith explained:

God's ideal government is not a democracy but an absolute monarchy, an absolute monarchy however, with Jesus Christ as the Monarch. And when Jesus Christ is on the throne as the absolute Monarch, you can trust that kind of a government. My friends, that is what we are heading toward. And when the millennium is set up, the Golden Age ushered in, and God's kingdom established over all the earth, with Jesus Christ reigning on the throne of David, let me tell you, it is going to be an absolute Monarchy in the final sense of the word, for His commands will be obeyed. He shall rule them, the Bible says, speaking of the nations, with a rod of iron.[27]

"And as I think of it—and I think of it and dream of it and visualize it again and again—I grow weary and tired of the governments of man," Rev. Oswald J. Smith confided. "You can show me the best government on the face of the earth . . . but I want to tell you that there is not a government on the face of this earth today that satisfies me for a single moment, not one."

Smith explained to his readers that "when the Jews expected Jesus Christ to establish a literal kingdom upon this earth [in the first century] with themselves in power, and the Gentile forces subdued, they were not missing the mark." "Jesus did not rebuke them," Rev. Smith related. "He simply told them that the time had not yet come; that was all." According to Oswald J. Smith, the Jews of Jesus' day were correct in looking for a messiah and a literal kingdom—"their aspirations were all right."[28]

The Jewish book of Daniel, however, related how the modern Antichrist would deceive the Jewish people into a false sense of peace and security, making a covenant with them and pretending to be their protector. Then the Antichrist would break the covenant and initiate the anti-Semitic Great Tribulation. Smith concluded:

Then will commence to burn the terrible fires of the Great Tribulation which will break in all its fury upon the Jewish people. Neither man nor woman will be spared, neither boy nor girl saved. On every side they will be slain, slain like so many sheep, with the exception of those who will be fortunate enough to escape to the mountains and to hide in the dens and caves of the earth. It is thus that the antichrist commences his diabolical work. The covenant made three and a half years before will be broken. And only after another three and a half years have passed will our Lord return to destroy his armies and bring to an end the terrible career of the antichrist himself. Desolation, indeed, will be the order of the day when the wrath of the antichrist is poured upon the Jewish nation.[29]

"My friends, I cannot but believe that the hour of the fulfilment is at hand," Rev. Oswald J. Smith concluded. "I believe that the last seven years of this age are soon to commence, that we are close to the seventieth week of Daniel's prophecy. I would not be surprised to hear that the antichrist is now living, and if so, he will soon be revealed."

As most fundamentalist-evangelicals, Oswald J. Smith believed that the Antichrist would arise in Europe, in a ten-nation confederation of a type of revived Roman Empire. He used the book of Daniel as his guideline in this interpretation, incorporating passages from the Christian Testament's book of Revelation. "The governments of the world are going to become bitter and strong in their opposition against the Lord and His Anointed," Smith explained at the outset of his book. "More and more they are going to throw off the yoke and turn away from the principles and the teachings of the Bible. And at last they are going to arise in one great, final government, the revived Roman Empire, made up of ten great nations, with a ruler over all, an Emperor sitting in his Seat at Rome, the antichrist of Scripture, and that government is going to be the last great government of Gentile world dominion."[30] Little wonder that some prophecy teachers had great interest in Mussolini in the latter 1920s and early 1930s. Adolf Hitler would also rise in the prophetic consciousness of some fundamentalist-evangelicals as he increasingly gained power.

Nevertheless, like many Americans, fundamentalist-evangelicals were concerned with Stalin and the growing strength of communism. In fact, some Jews in Germany had been fearful of movements to the left. When James G. McDonald, League of Nations high commissioner for German Refugees, 1933-1935, addressed the Cincinnati Jewish Welfare Fund's campaign on November 28, 1937, he explained that "some of Germany's best-informed Jews thought—in Adolf Hitler's early days—that it was better to support Hitler than to support leftist movements. They thought they saw a greater peril in communism than in Hitler." McDonald chided that "Jewish communities of the entire world have been slow to appreciate the magnitude of that which has been happening in Germany under Hitler. They have been slow to respond." In 1937 on the editorial staff of *The New York Times*, McDonald recalled:

> I talked with Hitler in the spring of 1933; he was quite clear in his attitude as to what he meant to do to the Jews. When I told Hitler that anti-Semitism would hurt Germany, he replied: "Even if we have to draw the belt tighter, because of hunger, for an entire generation in Germany, that would be a small price to pay for ridding Germany of the Jews." The Nazis have eliminated the Jews from cultural, juridical and similar fields. They will eliminate the Jews from economics and finance.[31]

"The Jewish community in Germany is doomed," the eminent Christian statesman continued, later adding, "The tragedy of the Polish Jews cannot be exaggerated."

Rev. Oswald J. Smith was fearful as well—terrified of communism. A prophetically minded fundamentalist-evangelical, he believed that Russia as the power "of the North" mentioned in the Bible would someday attack the Jewish people in the Holy Land and would be involved in Armageddon. Bible teachers had consistently pointed out that the Bible predicted the rise of Russia, "the king of the North." The premillennial eschatology of fundamentalist-evangelicalism held to this view when Russia appeared to be weak and of little significance on the world scene. Now, as Bolshevist Russia was becoming a world power under Stalin, these biblical prophecies seemed to be uncannily accurate. And Communist Russia insisted that it was atheistic and bent on world conquest. Such were the ingredients for the rise of conspiracy theories—theories that could promote the vicious anti-Semitism that the large majority of fundamentalist-evangelicals abhorred; theories that could affect such a well-known evangelical as Oswald J. Smith and cloud his judgment concerning Adolf Hitler and the rise of Nazism in Germany.

In 1936, the forty-six-year-old Smith traveled to eighteen countries, including Germany. It would be one of fifteen world tours made in his lifetime.[32] Adolf Hitler was in the midst of his "Clean Up Germany" campaign before the 1936 Olympic Games to be held in Berlin, and on July 8 Smith traveled from Paris to Berlin.

Smith's article, "My Visit to Germany" appeared in Gerald Winrod's *The Defender Magazine* in September 1936. As will be shown below, Rev. Winrod would become a classic example of prophetic conspiracy theory gone awry, but in the 1920s and 1930s he would be noted in evangelical circles for his effective anticommunist stance. In the latter 1930s, Arno C. Gaebelein would label Winrod a "secret follower of Hitler," and his esteem dropped quickly in prophetic circles.

"And now it falls to my lot to write about the New Germany," Oswald J. Smith began, "not the Germany I had seen in 1924 and 1929, but the Germany of Adolph Hitler." Admitting that what he had to say would be favorably received by some and rejected by others, the evangelical statesman wanted to "be fair" and "impartial" in judgment—writing only of what he knew. Rev. Smith explained:

> During my stay in Berlin I preached twice. I conferred with Christian leaders. Germans who had lived in Germany from the days of the Kaiser to the present, freely talked to me of the New Germany. Gladly and without hesitation they answered all my questions. I was able to get inside information. They were not afraid to talk for they knew me personally. In fact, some of them had known me for twelve years, and they knew they could trust me. For hours we conferred together.

> No where in Europe did I feel as safe as in Germany. No one at any time sought to molest me. In Spain I trembled. In France the air was full of uncertainty. But in Germany there was no alarm. I felt secure. Fear is a thing of the past. Confidence has been restored.[33]

"Everywhere I found an awakened people, a people full of optimism and hope," Oswald J. Smith insisted to the ninety-four thousand readers of *The Defender*. "Their faces fairly shone. They greet you with a smile. There are no signs of discouragement. It is the difference between slavery and freedom. They are most polite. . . .

"Talk about optimism—I thought I knew the meaning of the word," Dr. Smith continued. "But here in Germany I have witnessed a practical manifestation of optimism the like of which I have never seen before. Germany has awakened." He exuberantly reported about Adolf Hitler and the German people:

> What, you ask, is the real attitude of the German people toward Hitler? There is but one answer. They love him. Yes, from the highest to the lowest, children and parents, old and young alike—they love their new leader. Their confidence in him cannot be shaken. They trust him to a man.
>
> "What about your elections?" I asked. "You have no choice. It is Hitler or no one. There is no opponent." "We don't want another party," they replied, with indignation. "We have had enough of parties. We want a true leader, a man who loves us, and works for our good. We are satisfied with Hitler." And that feeling exists everywhere. Every true Christian is for Hitler. I know, for it was from the Christians I got most of my information, and right or wrong, they endorse Adolph Hitler.[34]

Smith added that German Christians did not like all the "Little Hitler's" serving under Hitler. These men did not have their Leader's spirit. But the people rationalized, saying that Hitler could not "personally attend to everything" and "must of necessity leave much to those under him."

The Christians in Germany had impressed on Rev. Smith the desperate situation of Germany in 1932. In his words, one sees how conspiracy theory and deception could work together to undermine the sensitivity and common sense of a fundamentalist-evangelical. Smith related:

> To understand the present situation, as my German friends pointed out to me, one must needs know something of the past. The outside world does not realize the depths to which Germany had sunk in 1932, the year before Hitler came on the scene.
>
> It was bad enough when I was last in Germany. That was in 1929. But by 1932 the situation had become desperate. Immorality had gripped the entire nation. More than seven millions, one tenth of the entire population, were out of work. It was not safe to be on the streets after dark. People, famished by hunger, became a menace to everyone. Male prostitutes openly solicited in the cafes and dance halls. Women, nude and unashamed entertained their melancholy audiences.

The Bolshevicks were preparing to take over the country. When
their offices were raided, lists of the pastors of Berlin were found,
marked for death. There was no hope, no future. Germany was
doomed. Then came Hitler, and just in time. Two days later, and Communism would have been in complete control. Now all is changed. All
is different. It is German freedom instead of Soviet slavery. Hitler
has saved Germany. He has put new hope into the hearts of seventy million people.[35]

Smith listened "spellbound" to the contented, happy people.
"All must work. There is no time for dissipation," he wrote.
"They have a saying in Germany now—'Strength through Joy'
. . . Hitler knows well the value of holidays, and he has made
abundant provision. For again it is 'Strength through Joy.'"[36]

Rev. Smith was impressed that the "ideal family consists of
four children" and "all girls are trained to be mothers." Furthermore, the fundamentalist-evangelical was excited that mass
immorality was being corrected. He explained:

Before the days of Hitler, women, like the women of the United
States, used paint and lip-stick. "We don't need these things,"
declared their new leaders, and cosmetic firms had to close for lack
of trade. In all my travels through Germany I never saw a German
girl with artificial color on her face or lips. And oh, how fresh and
natural they looked! How much more attractive!

Before Hitler's days, Spiritism flourished. Almost every corner had
its medium. Now occultism of every description is banned. Hitler
has enforced the laws of Saul. Spiritism was sending the people to
the asylums. Today it is no more.

To Oswald J. Smith, the Nazi banning of birth-control "preven-
tives" and punishment of those advocating abortions had further advanced the morality of the nation. His "German friends"
even convinced him that sterilization had an important purpose,
and that the Nazi purges were a corrective to homosexuality.[37]

Smith was more than thrilled that Russellism (Jehovah's Witnesses) was banned as "dangerous to the nation." "And anyone who knows Russellism, knows that it is a pernicious her-
esy," Rev. Smith asserted, adding that "Judge Rutherford cannot

propagate his pernicious doctrines in Germany." The fundamentalist-evangelical suggested that the "United States and Canada could learn a valuable lesson in this regard." In actuality, both Oswald J. Smith and the German church were to learn that when one person's religious freedom is violated, all religious freedom is on the chopping block as well.

German Protestant Christians explained to Rev. Smith that Roman Catholics were being prosecuted because they were smuggling church monies across the border and because priests and nuns were guilty of having sexual intercourse with those children in their asylums and institutions. "Can we blame the Government for its attitude?" Smith questioned. "Germany needs her money and needs it badly." He declared that Hitler had nothing against Roman Catholicism as a religion, but that "he is against the political influence of the priests and the vile practices that have been proven against them."[38]

It should come as no surprise that a Christian minister who could be so duped by such arguments in defense of the policies of Adolf Hitler would also fall for Nazi propaganda about Jews. Nevertheless, Rev. Oswald J. Smith's prophetic bias toward "God's chosen Jewish people" and in defense of their right to settle in the Holy Land could only succumb to a Communist conspiracy story with immoral overtones. "And now about the Jews," Dr. Smith related under Winrod's caption "Jews and Bolshevism." "A single incident will clarify the situation." Smith wrote what was told to him by German Christians:

> Last September the director of a Business College for girls was hailed into court. He was a Jew. Evidence was given by more than four hundred parents. They claimed that he had violated the chastity of their four hundred daughters during the preceding ten years.

> The charges were carefully investigated one by one and proven to be true. The man was sentenced to ten years imprisonment. The case created such hatred in the hearts of the German people of the community, against the Jews, that with one accord they raided their places of business, and many innocent had to suffer with the guilty.

That, in part at least, illustrates the present attitude. Every time such a case was proved, sentiment broke loose against the unfortunate unfortunate Jews. It is charged that most of the places of commercialized vice were run by Jews prior to the rise of Hitler, as is the case in America.[39]

"I am sorry that the good Jews have had to suffer with the bad," Smith rationalized. "But who can differentiate in an hour of mob rule and violence? Even Hitler could not restrain his followers." "Today there can be no mixed marriages," he added. "The government has enacted laws that make it difficult for the Jews." And yet, Smith seemed to find solace in the fact that some Jews continued in business. "Yet there are still Jewish establishments all over Germany that carry on unmolested," he noted.

Rev. Smith also succumbed to the arguments about "Jewish Bolshevism." He continued:

It was conclusively proven that the Bolshevicks who organized and planned the overthrow of the German Government were nearly all Jews. But they were not all German Jews. Many were from the south of Europe who had crossed the border and entered Germany with the set determination of stirring up strife, murdering the clergy, and handing the country over to Moscow.[40]

"Not for a moment would I say anything against the orthodox, God-fearing Jews," Smith insisted. "I would be the last to make their lot harder than it is, for I love them. But they have been betrayed by their renegade brethren who have become their worst enemies, and they know it not."

Ironically, it was Rev. Oswald J. Smith, a minister and missionary statesman who would never have considered being "anti-Semitic," who had been betrayed by his "renegade brethren." He was convinced that the German people were on the threshold of a spiritual revival. "France, I do not trust," he declared at the end of his article. "France is Red, immoral and godless. Germany is Protestant. It was from Germany that Luther came."[41]

## The Defenders

A number of fundamentalist-evangelicals such as Smith were duped by Gerald Winrod as he progressively leaned toward

Adolf Hitler and Jewish conspiracy theory. One of the best examples of prophetic interpretation and fear of communism being used to promote anti-Jewish thought and rhetoric is found in the life and ministry of Rev. Gerald B. Winrod, the editor of *The Defender Magazine*. Winrod published the articles of many fine Christians in his magazine, as well as advertising some respectable Christian literature and Christian colleges. At the same time, his articles in *The Defender* (like his books and tracts) talked incessantly about "Jewish communism," the "Jewish government of France" and other countries, "international Jewry," "Jewish bankers," and Mussolini as the possible fulfillment of Revelation 13:1 ("And I stood upon the sand of the sea, and saw a beast rise up out of the sea"). Winrod was convinced that Mussolini in connection with the Roman Catholic Church could very well turn out to be the Antichrist.[42]

Christian followers of Winrod called themselves "Defenders." Their theme song was "Faith of Our Fathers"; their motto was "Back to the Bible." These Defenders experienced an agonizing period when they finally discovered that their leader had become an anti-Semite and a secret follower of Adolf Hitler. Like Stalin and the Communists that they despised, their leader Rev. Gerald Winrod did not come out directly and declare himself as such, but he steadily injected his anti-Semitic poison into the periodical and organization. Even the February 1937 issue, on the importance of the home and the family, carried an appeal by Winrod to defeat an impending measure to close the postal service to Christian periodicals and to make it a felony to send the New Testament through the mails. Winrod insisted "the Jews" were responsible. He wrote:

The outstanding Communist leader of the United States is a Russian-born Jew by the name of M. J. Olgin. He is editor of America's largest red publication, the New York Morning Freiheit—a Yiddish newspaper. Olgin openly advocates the overthrow of our government by force. . . . He devoted a full column to an explanation of how Jews should proceed in silencing certain publications which are exposing the true Jewish facts behind Communism and the present program of world revolution.[43]

"When religious Jews align themselves with the apostate, Communist conspirators of their race," Rev. Winrod warned, "it makes the efforts of Christian leaders exceedingly difficult who are trying to discriminate between 'good' Jews and 'bad' Jews." "Communism," Winrod summarized, "can no more be separated from apostate Jewry than a sunbeam can be separated from the Sun."[44]

After 1934 Gerald B. Winrod accepted Nazi justifications for their anti-Semitic policies, even praising Germany as a nation brave enough to defy Jewish communism, Jewish radicalism, Jewish occultism, and Jewish finance. When Jews were persecuted (as in the Crystal Night pogrom in 1938), Winrod countered by asking why no one showed remorse for the millions of Christians persecuted by the Communists. And, yet, Winrod too proclaimed an "utmost respect" for devout Jews. When he entered the Republican primary for United States Senator from Kansas in 1938, he curbed his anti-Catholic and anti-Jewish rhetoric until he began to be opposed as a closet Nazi. Then he claimed "Jewish financial interests" defamed him and engineered his defeat. In 1942 the name of this dispensationalist fundamentalist headed a list of twenty-eight men and women indicted for conspiracy, and his war years would be consumed with defending himself while trying to decipher his present troubles in the light of prophetic events.[45]

By 1938, many fundamentalist-evangelicals were onto Winrod, and word passed swiftly in the following year that he was anti-Semitic and pro-Hitler. Today, the parent organization of the Defenders has dissociated itself from any form of anti-Semitism and is a friend and supporter of Israel. Nevertheless, *The Defender Magazine*'s circulation reached a high of 110,000 by 1938—a potential vote base and petition base for Rev. Winrod that could not be ignored. Some Defenders soon recognized not only the peril of Winrod's rhetoric, but also the danger that anticommunism and conspiracy theory could become full-fledged anti-Semitism. One such individual was Rev. Elmer A. Josephson.

A graduate of Bethel Institute (the Bible school of the Baptist

General Conference), with additional courses at the Moody Bible Institute of Chicago, Elmer Josephson had been called to be the young minister of the Calvary Baptist Church at Leavenworth, Kansas. Interested in world affairs and imbued with an interest in Bible prophecy from his schooling, he subscribed to a number of publications that dealt with these subjects. It was in one of these publications that he learned of Dr. Gerald B. Winrod and the work of the Defenders. Rev. Josephson would later write:

> In 1937 the fear of Russian communism was sweeping America. Alarmists were "finding communists" under every bed and in every basement. It seemed rather exciting. Dr. Winrod was one of America's top communist-fighters in those days, and since my sympathies lay that way I wrote inquiring further how I might help. (The rumor was circulated later that he [Gerald Winrod] had made several trips to Germany to see Hitler.) I considered becoming Gerald B. Winrod's "lieutenant" so I drove to Wichita to see him, to become better orientated and to make future plans.
>
> Before this I had been given a copy of The Protocols of the Elders of Zion. It looked very official and I reasoned, "If Henry Ford, Sr. endorses this document it must be the truth." It told of a purported international communistic plot by world Jewry to take over the governments of the nations and related the terrible ensuing things Jews would perpetrate on Gentile society. Believing this propaganda, I became a staunch anti-Semitic communist-fighter.[46]

"I wanted to do something on as large a scale as possible and so began to plan for a city-wide rally at Leavenworth," Rev. Josephson recalled. "Since our new church sanctuary was not completed, I tried to secure the city auditorium for the meeting. However, the Jewish business men, through the city fathers, blocked this attempt. This, I felt, confirmed what I was being taught; that communism was an international Jewish plot."[47]

When his new church sanctuary was finally completed, Rev. Elmer A. Josephson invited another "communist fighter" from Michigan to speak and show films of the Detroit Ford Plant riots. He noted of this eminent Communist fighter:

> This man showed me his 38 caliber revolver which he always carried "to protect himself from the communists." However, shortly

afterward, it was evident through experience and observation, that this man carried a gun, not to protect himself from communists, but rather from revenge-seeking, irate husbands!

"I began to take a second look at my anti-Semitic leanings through careful study of the Scriptures and found that I was traveling a very perilous path," Rev. Josephson confided. He never toyed with anti-Semitism or conspiracy theory again. Continuing his prophetic studies, he founded Bible Light, Inc., in 1956, a nondenominational organization to foster better understanding between Christians and Jews. Taking his first trip to the Middle East in 1960, he and his wife finally moved to Israel, living there from 1969 to 1974.

## Opposition to the Protocols

Although a few fundamentalist-evangelicals would continue to insist that the Protocols were genuine, the leaders of the movement brought great pressure to bear on those who used the documents. For example, William Bell Riley continued to believe that the Protocols were a legitimate Marxist program for world conquest, but his book *Protocols and Communism* created such a stir in fundamentalist-evangelical circles that he felt forced to take it off the market. In October 1939, Rev. Keith L. Brooks, president of the American Prophetic League, Inc., published a fundamentalist manifesto in his *Prophecy* magazine. The heading proclaimed: "America's Most Honored Fundamentalists Hereby REGISTER THEIR PROTEST Against Anti-Semitic Propaganda in a Guise of Fundamentalism. BEWARE of any who use the Scriptures as an excuse for such an attitude while they preach the protocols and associate with known Nazis. Note carefully the names of these Gentile Christian leaders. Extra copies of this MANIFESTO free." It is profitable to quote the entire Manifesto, because it incorporates the basic fundamentalist-evangelical theology opposing anti-Semitism, the penchant for prophetic interpretation, an awareness of the dangers of conspiracy theory, and the inability of the movement to exclude evangelism. The Manifesto declared:

BEARING FALSE WITNESS is a sin. Maligning Jews is also a sin. Both are solemnly condemned in the Scriptures of Truth, that Word which shall judge us in the last day.

Inasmuch as for some two or three years there has been carried on in our free country a persistent propaganda of Jew-hatred,

Therefore we who have subscribed our names hereto declare that we are opposed to anti-Semitism in whatever form it may take, as inconsistent with our heritage of liberty and fair play as citizens of America, and as unworthy of those who bear the name of Christian. And we further declare that any attempt to use the Scriptures as an excuse for an anti-Semitic attitude is a perversion of God's Word and irreconcilable with the spirit and teaching of the Lord Jesus Christ.

We beseech every Christ-honoring child of God to show kindness to the Jew. Pray much for his salvation. How much he needs your prayers in these tragic days!

We wish our lives to be worthy of the Gospel of Christ so that the Jew may differentiate between the Gentile who is a Christian and the one who is not. And wherever there are those seeking to make the Jewish people acquainted with the contents of the Christian message, we wish to uphold their hands in prayer and sympathy, knowing that the Gospel of Christ is "the power of God unto salvation to everyone that believeth; to the Jew first, and also to the Greek." Romans 1:16.

To the Jewish people we declare: —We have for you a heart full of sympathy. The One we love most, and the One who has done most for us, was Himself a Jew in the flesh. To Him we owe all that we are and ever will be, and our hearts yearn that everyone of you might share with us the blessing of eternal life through Jesus Christ our Lord. We have no part in the stirring up of base passions against you. And we want you to know that those who are thus guilty do not express the love which the Lord Jesus Christ has commanded us to show you. We rejoiced to learn that on May 14, 1935, the Cantonal Court of Berne, Switzerland, openly denounced the so-called "Protocols of the Elders of Zion" as "forgeries, obvious plagiarism, immoral, and manifestly prepared for the purpose of inciting popular passion against the Jews." N.Y. Evening Post, May 14, 1935.

We look forward to that blessed day foretold by the Prophets, when through a converted Israel the whole world will learn of salvation through the Lord Jesus Christ. Then, it will be that "ten men . . .

shall take hold of . . . him that is a Jew, saying, We will go with
you: for we have heard that God is with you!" Zech. 8:23.

To that end may the God of Abraham and Isaac and Jacob, give His
approval and multiplied blessing, to this our united testimony.[48]

Included among the sixty-seven prominent fundamentalist-
evangelical leaders who signed Keith Brooks's petition when con-
tacted were President J. Oliver Buswell of Wheaton College; President Lewis Sperry Chafer of Evangelical Theological College
(later named Dallas Theological Seminary); David L. Cooper of
the Biblical Research Society; Arno C. Gaebelein, editor of *Our
Hope*; Dan Gilbert, General Secretary of the World's Christian
Fundamentals Association; President Will H. Houghton of Moody
Bible Institute; Harry A. Ironside of Moody Memorial Church;
Roy L. Laurin, editor of *King's Business*, Bible Institute of Los
Angeles; President Alva J. McClain of Grace Theological Semi-
nary; President Robert S. McQuilkin of Columbia Bible College;
Dean Kenneth M. Monroe of the Bible Institute of Los Angeles;
William L. Pettingill, former dean of Philadelphia School of the
Bible; William E. Pietsch, secretary of the Fundamental Churches
of America; Charles G. Trumbull, editor of the *Sunday School
Times*; and H. O. Van Gilder, editor of the *Independent Baptist*. Pastors with large fundamentalist-evangelical churches among the
Presbyterians, Methodists, and Baptists also signed the Manifesto, as well as some early fundamentalist-evangelical prophetic
teachers from the post–World War I era. Over fifteen thousand
copies of the Manifesto were distributed to fundamentalist-evangelical churches and organizations for posting, requiring an additional fifteen thousand copies to be published in a larger, more
attractive format by May of 1940.[49]

## *OUR HOPE* AND THE HOLOCAUST YEARS

To their credit, almost all fundamentalist-evangelicals believed
that the Holocaust occurred and that six million Jews were exter-
minated. In addition, as the persecution unfolded, the large
majority of fundamentalist-evangelical periodicals believed the

reports of atrocities, refusing to question them as "atrocity propaganda" (as some more liberal Protestant periodicals were prone to do). The fundamentalist journal *Our Hope*, is indicative of this trend. Because it incorporated Bible study and current world news in a volume without advertisement, *Our Hope* provided some of the most extensive news coverage among fundamentalist-evangelical periodicals. Its readers came from a large spectrum of denominational affiliations and vocational backgrounds. Dr. Arno C. Gaebelein had cultivated friendships throughout the world, was a voracious reader, and, by 1934, had edited *Our Hope* for forty years.

In February 1933, Gaebelein briefly analyzed the plight of the Jews in the excerpt "European Jewish Conditions." He explained that riots against Jews had occurred in many of the prestigious European universities, among them the University of Berlin and the University of Vienna. "A good part of Germany is seething with anti-semitism," the seventy-two-year-old Gaebelein wrote. "Hitler and the Nazi movement are outspokenly against the Jews." Polish and other Eastern European Jews also had dire circumstances. He emphasized:

> The plight of Polish Jewry is appalling. Over 100,000 have registered in Warsaw alone as being helplessly impoverished. Thousands have been driven back to the soil, and some sixteen new, exclusively Jewish villages have sprung up. The distress in the Ukraine, in Latvia, in Roumania and elsewhere in eastern Europe is equally great, if not greater than in Poland.[50]

"This Jewish distress," Gaebelein summarized, "is another harbinger of the nearing tribulation." He noted, however, that "conditions in Palestine were never as bright as they are now," with a Jewish population of nearly two hundred thousand.

When Adolf Hitler became chancellor in 1933, Gaebelein gave his impression of the Nazi leader in "Hitler Successful in Germany." He wrote:

> After years of perseverance Adolf Hitler has become the Chancellor of the German Republic. Hitler is a Roman Catholic, but what we have seen coming from his lips and pen proves that he is an

unbeliever. He has a tremendous following in Germany, and seems to lean toward the Monarchists. The only good side is that he is a sworn enemy of the Reds. On the other hand, he is a regular Haman, a Jew hater. More than once he has promised that if he gets power and leadership he will purge Germany of the Jews, whom he charges with being responsible with all the ills of Germany and Europe.[51]

Gaebelein detailed Nazi disruptions in and boycotts of Jewish department stores. Tear-gas canisters were thrown into crowded stores. In Vienna and Bucharest similar anti-Semitic incidents were noted, including the painting of swastikas on tramcars. The swastikas were "the anti-Semitic device" and the leaflets declared, "Don't buy anything for Christmas from those who crucified Christ." "The Editor believes the next six months will bring serious disturbances in Germany," Arno Gaebelein surmised. "The hopes of recovery in Germany were bright, but now the election and victory of Hitler brings a setback."

Although Gaebelein had been a Bible and prophecy teacher for forty years, recording events in *Our Hope* and diligently watching the "signs of the times," he had no patience with those who tried to pinpoint or date prophetic events or those who would try to guess who the Antichrist might be. His philosophy is well illustrated in his statement in the November 1933 issue:

> The Editor has no use for day-and-year-setters, nor has he any use for figuring out the duration of the times of the Gentiles, nor has he any sympathy with men who prophesy that Mussolini, Hitler, Feisal or any other person is the Antichrist. It is a morbid condition which seems to suit certain minds. We wonder whom they will name next. At any rate why should a Christian have any interest at all in that coming man of sin? We have nothing to do with that lawless one. Our interest must be in Christ and not in Antichrist.[52]

In this same issue, Gaebelein explained the various fascist groups to his readers, from the Nazi "brown shirts" of Germany to Mussolini's "black shirts" in Italy, as well as the origin of the term "fascism." To Arno C. Gaebelein, fascism meant that "the political conditions of the entire world are breaking up."[53] He would provide his readers with the latest update, but refused to be a modern prophet on the dates.

In subsequent months, *Our Hope* detailed such events as the alliance between Germany and Japan, Hitler's attack on Hebrew Christians, the Hitler Youth Movement, the Confessing Church in Germany (including Martin Niemöller), German revival of Teutonic paganism, and the rise of anti-Semitic acts throughout Germany.[54] In "The Devil Marches On in Germany" in the February 1936 issue, Dr. Gaebelein was horrified at Hitler's attack on Christianity's Jewish root. He found the Nazi outlawing of German hymns in which Hebrew names appeared (such as "To Thee, Jehovah, I Will Sing" and "Rejoice, Daughter of Zion") ludicrous. "If Hitler and his unbalanced minions had any sense whatever," he told the readers of *Our Hope*, "if they read the page of history, they would know that their task is one which will not only ignominiously miscarry, but that they will go down ere long in everlasting shame and ruin."[55]

Even in 1936, the Nazi's repressive measures against the Jewish people were appalling to Gaebelein. "The conditions in Germany among the remaining Jews are outrageously inhuman," he protested and then explained:

> The city of Leipzig, not far from where the Editor spent his boyhood days in his Thuringian home, is a city of culture and art. Yet from that city comes an urgent S.O.S. call from Jewish institutions, citing facts of the actual starvation of Jews there. It is impossible for Jews to earn anything, they are even not permitted to be peddlers. Large numbers of them even have not the means to buy bread.[56]

To add to the Jewish grief, Gaebelein found "an alarming increase of anti-Jewish propaganda" in Transylvania, Romania, and Greece. Even in Syria, "five Jews were attacked recently by Arabs carrying daggers in the streets of ancient Damascus." The medieval accusation that Jews needed the blood of Christian children to perform rituals was being circulated again in various countries. Gaebelein cited Lithuania as an example in 1936, where Jews were beaten by a Gentile mob when a Christian girl disappeared.[57]

In 1936 the Olympic Games were held in Germany. Adolf
Hitler used them as a great propaganda ploy. Overt persecution
of the Jewish people was hidden as much as possible from jour-
nalists, tourists, and statesmen in the latter half of this year and,
as we have seen above, even Oswald J. Smith was duped by the
vibrant pro-Nazi testimonials of his Christian friends. Arno C.
Gaebelein was not deceived, and he reported with disdain how
David Lloyd George (1863–1945), the British statesman, was
fooled by the Nazi propaganda. After visiting Germany and
spending time with Hitler, Lloyd George "brought back a glowing report of the bettered conditions in Germany and that the
people are happy." Gaebelein was appalled at such naïveté.[58]

As 1937 approached, Dr. Arno C. Gaebelein at seventy-six
years of age instinctively felt the turmoil of nations rearming
themselves in an unprecedented manner. He published a chart
of standing armies, reserves, and airplanes for various nations,
mocking "certain postmillennial preachers and teachers" who
speak of Europe "as being composed of 'Christian nations'" and
who declare that the world is "surely becoming Christian." Gaebelein instead affirmed: "Europe is a vast armed camp and, as far
as we can see, unless God intervenes soon in a supernatural way,
a frightful world-war must come." In his first issue of 1937 he
insisted: "The whole world is a smouldering volcano."[59]

Throughout the early 1930s, Arno Gaebelein had mentioned
to the readers of Our Hope that he wanted to take a trip to Germany to visit relatives (he had immigrated to the United States in
1879). It was not until August 16, 1937, however, that he and his
wife, Emma, sailed for Central Europe. Here he gained a firsthand view of the Nazi regime. He sent home reports for seven
issues, giving his observations of Hitler, Goebbels, Streicher,
Rosenberg, Hitler Youth, and others in the Nazi regime. Unlike
Rev. Gerald Winrod, Gaebelein came back unimpressed with
Hitler's philosophy and held the firm conviction that the Jewish
people in Europe were in deep trouble. Gaebelein noted the trouble Nazis had caused a Jewish woman on their train and the Nazi
confiscation of foreign newspapers. "This is done to keep unde-
sirable information from the German citizens," Dr. Gaebelein

explained and then continued, "Well, we appreciated our American liberties, that no policeman goes around to confiscate newspapers. Evidently the entire German Press is under the supervision of the government."[60]

The fundamentalist-evangelical editor was not pacified by Adolf Hitler's declaration that national socialism stood "on the Foundation of real Christianity" and that it held religious confessions to be "valuable helps to uphold our people." Rather, Arno C. Gaebelein questioned in 1938 that if Chancellor Hitler was sincere, why had he appointed Alfred Rosenberg, a known anti-Semite and anti-Christian, to receive the first national prize of one hundred thousand marks. Gaebelein believed that Hitler was actually proposing a new religion in his "New World View." He stated to readers of *Our Hope:*

> But what is this German brand of New World View? It might be expressed by two sentences, "We are the people. We are superior to other races." The hatred of the Jew is its backbone. . . . Out of this anti-Semitic agitation has sprung the New World View. Its prominent leader, as stated before, is Alfred Rosenberg. Others are Willhelm Hauer, Ernst Bergmann, von Reventlow, and several more.[61]

Rev. Gaebelein was appalled that the German's "New World View" accused the Jews of defiling and ruining the Nordic race. He documented the fact that it was a crime for an "Aryan" to marry a "Jewess," and the fear that Christians had of finding a Jew in their family tree. He pointed out to Christian readers that the denial of Jewish chosenness was logically extended beyond anti-Semitism to a denial of the authority of the Bible, objections to Paul (because Paul was a Pharisee), and the necessary Aryanization of Jesus. That Jesus was characterized as an anti-Semite by this "arrogant" Germanic religion was particularly shocking to the fundamentalist-evangelical editor.[62]

Alas, 1938 proved to be discouraging to Gaebelein as the persecution of the Jewish people increased and spread. *Our Hope* documented the incidents, listing the anti-Jewish measures instituted in Romania, Poland, and Germany, while noting that Austria, Latvia, and Lithuania "also have anti-Semitic tendencies."

Of Poland, the fundamentalist statesman commented that "there has been more Jewish blood spilled there than possibly anywhere else, except in Russia and in Palestine." He sadly related that "after Hitler and his minions took over Austria," even converted Jews were not safe from Nazi wrath. The case of a dispossessed physician and his wife was related, and Arno Gaebelein exclaimed: "This is worse than inhuman, it is a diabolic cruelty. But there is a day of reckoning coming. God will deal with the enemies of His people and when judgment comes, as it surely will, this modern anti-Semitism will find its ignominious end."[63] Unfortunately, it was not yet the end.

When Benito Mussolini made his anti-Semitic statements in Triest, Gaebelein labeled him "another modern Haman." He expressed compassion for the "homeless millions" of Jews and reminded Christian readers of Jesus' compassion for the Jewish multitudes. The editor of *Our Hope* stated: "As Christians we are moved with the same compassion; we pray for them [the Jewish people] and know the day will come when the Lord will deal with the nations for their cruel treatment of the Jews."[64] In a following excerpt, the fundamentalist-evangelical leader mentioned that refugees from Germany and Austria were arriving in the United States at a rate of one hundred a day, but the U.S. Embassy in Berlin was not accepting any more applications from German and Austrian Jews because the quota was filled for the next two years.

The acts of the German government in 1938 increasingly appalled Gaebelein. "What is being done to Jewry in Germany is satanically cruel," he wrote, relating that the latest laws were against Jewish professionals. Jewish doctors' permits were canceled; one thousand Jewish dentists were purged on October 5 when the conference of the Dental Association convened. By January 1, 1939, Jews were required to have a name that showed their Jewish origins or they must add "Israel" or "Sarah" to the name they possessed. As *Our Hope* went to press on November 14, news of *Kristallnacht* infuriated Gaebelein, who passionately reported "the outrageous happenings in Germany" during Crystal Night. "The three leaders, Hitler, Goering and Goebbels, permitted and encouraged the vicious and murderous outbreaks against the Jews, destroying millions of dollars worth of property," Arno Gaebelein asserted. "How many were killed we do not know. It is devilish from start to finish."[65] His feelings, like those of the vast majority of fundamentalist-evangelicals, were quite a contrast to Gerald Winrod and his analysis in *The Defender Magazine.*

One gains some indication of the interest of the readers of *Our Hope* in world events from the fact that some readers requested more information on the fate of Czechoslovakia, and Gaebelein responded by publishing the ten-point compromise plan "hatched out in Munich." Anti-Semitic legislation in Czechoslovakia, Hungary, and Romania was detailed in the early months of 1939. Gaebelein commented: "As the march continues toward the East, Hitler's great ambitious anti-semitism develops right along the line." In response to an "official" report on the increase in church membership in Germany from 1934 to 1936, he predicted that the report for the years 1937 and 1938 would show "an astonishing decline." Rev. Gaebelein lamented: "The deplorable thing is that the German youth are turning their backs on the churches; they have become 'Hitlerized.'"[66]

Arno C. Gaebelein continually asserted that those who persecuted God's "Chosen People," the Jews, would come to a disastrous end. This is fervently proclaimed, for example, when Alfred Rosenberg suggested that all the Jews be settled on "reservations" in British Guiana or in Madagascar. *Our Hope* quoted him as saying, "I stress the word reservation for there can be no talk either at present or in the future about a Jewish state." Gaebelein responded to Rosenberg's comments:

> Poor mumbling, blind Rosenberg! He hates God's Word. He despises the Old Testament! He wants to have it thrown out! German youth is warned against reading it. Soon the day will come when not a Jewish state, a Jewish reservation or anything like it, will be established, but when the kingdom will be restored to Israel, when God's covenant promises to His earthly people will all be fulfilled, when his glory will dwell in "Immanuel's Land."[67]

"Poor Rosenberg, Streicher, Hitler and others," Gaebelein chastened, "you are not fighting the Jews, you are fighting God, God's Son, our Lord, God's purposes and God's Word. What a terrible defeat and fate is awaiting you!"

Dr. Arno C. Gaebelein's premillennial bias toward the Jewish cause in Palestine during the Arab violence is clearly seen in his evaluation of Jewish funds and migration to Palestine in the 1930s. He had no illusions about the struggle in Palestine and reported vicious attacks on Jewish settlements in Samaria. "They burned down houses and shot at people, while others broke into the stores to steal," he wrote of Arab atrocities, "uprooted newly planted trees in the widely known Balfour Forest." But he observed that "in spite of the Arab opposition, Ishmael's sons rising against Isaac's earthly offspring, Zionism continues to flourish." Of Great Britain's new recommendation in 1936 to create independent sovereign Arab and Jewish states, Gaebelein declared: "The suggested division of Palestine among Jews and Arabs has been a great shock to Zionism. It is too early to say much about it. It seems to us it is altogether against the program of prophecy." To the fundamentalist-evangelical leader, the separation of Jerusalem from "Israel's" rule, the lack of Jewish control of the lighting and irrigation networks they had built, and the lack of a sound biblical basis made the plan appear to be absurd.[68]

In June 1939, E. Schuyler English became associate editor of Our Hope, relieving the seventy-eight-year-old Gaebelein of writing the "Current Events" section. A president of Philadelphia School of the Bible and a staunch fundamentalist-evangelical, Dr. English and Arno Gaebelein agreed on prophecy and on the Jewish people. During the crucial days of the Holocaust, Schuyler English would write in Our Hope that "the best friend that the Jew has is the Christian, who knows God's Word, His love for His Chosen People, and their place in the prophetic plan." He castigated those theologians who told the fundamentalist-evangelicals that "God is through with the Jews" and was particularly upset with the theologian who asserted that "the Jews have no more place in God's plan for the world than have the Japanese."[69]

While Dr. Gaebelein continued to receive each excerpt written by Dr. English ahead of time and authorized it for publication, these men were so enmeshed in the fundamentalist-evangelical milieu that no check was necessary. This agreement extended to the support of Zionism as well as of the Jewish people. For example, *Our Hope* noted soon after English joined the staff that the Jewish people would return to Palestine, "their own land," in spite of the British White Paper of 1939. "How and when the White Paper will be repudiated we do not know," *Our Hope* maintained, "but that in the end it shall be non-effective is a certainty." The fundamentalist journal concluded: "[Political] Zionism, though it is not influenced one whit by God's Word, may be His chosen instrument to effect their return to Palestine."[70]

Perhaps nothing disturbed the editors of *Our Hope* more in 1940 than anti-Semitism within the United States. It reported the "rumor" that leaders of American anti-Semitic organizations were combining forces, and warned its readers to "be careful" of what they read. So beguiling was the anti-Semitic literature that *Our Hope* feared Christian acceptance of it. One of the anti-Semitic propaganda leaflets being circulated in the United States was *Why Are the Jews Persecuted for Their Religion?* The fundamentalist-evangelical editors explained that the pamphlet purported to quote from the Talmud, but the fact of the matter was that "the 'quotation' is a misquotation." The editors explained to their Christian readers that the Talmud does not state that a gentile girl can be violated by a Jew after three years of age; nor does it conclude that all property of other nations belongs to the Jewish nation. *Our Hope* sadly concluded: "The enemies of Israel will stop at no end to accomplish their purposes to persecute them, and to drive them out. When will anti-Semitism take hold in this land? Perhaps it may be sooner than we think."[71]

Most Jews would not be happy to learn that *Our Hope* regarded this anticipated American persecution as a reason for the fundamentalist-evangelical to "be instant in season and out of season, to preach the Word to Israel [Jewish people], before this persecution sets in!" Nor would Jews be overjoyed with the fundamentalist emphasis that this persecution would eventually "be a blessing to the Jews'' and would cause some to ''go back to their own land [Palestine]'' as the editors of *Our Hope* clearly stated. Our study of the evangelistic thrust of the fundamentalist-evangelical movement should prepare us for this emphasis. Nevertheless, it must be stated that the fundamentalist-evangelical editors of *Our Hope*, young and old, recognized the potential for anti-Semitism in the United States in 1940, dreaded it, and warned fundamentalist readers not to become a part of it. In addition, the fundamentalist-evangelical movement had believed that the Nazi atrocities were occurring as soon as they came to light. *Our Hope* was no exception.

As the Nazis formed ghettos to starve out the Jewish people, *Our Hope* reported the particulars it had at hand. The starvation conditions in Lublin, Poland; armbands in Antwerp; and the spread of anti-Semitism in Spain and France are a few of the topics discussed in 1940–1941. One of the early reports about the Warsaw Ghetto read:

> All the Jews in Warsaw, about one half a million of them, are now required to live within a concrete wall constructed by German decree. The wall is eight feet high and surrounds more than one hundred city blocks. This is not, say the Nazis, an anti-Semitic edict but a health measure, to protect the Poles as well as the Jews from pestilences![72]

*Our Hope* could not accept the ''official'' Nazi version. It did, however, believe that as the anti-Semitic tentacles spread, a glorious future awaited the Jewish people. It declared in an earlier account about anti-Semitism: ''The barbed fist of persecution is crushing the Jews, or trying to do so. Where will Israel go? To THE LAND— PALESTINE.''

During 1942, *Our Hope* documented ''the ugly shadow of Anti-Semitism'' arising in the British Isles. The British were discussing Jewish domination of the black market. *Our Hope* complained that the news coverage always headlined the few ''Cohens'' while saying little about the large number of ''Smiths'' (*Our Hope* added that these names were fictitious, to illustrate the point). At the same time the editors of *Our Hope* pointed out the consternation that Zionist leaders, such as Chaim Weizmann, experienced from the British over a "tragedy" such as the *Struma*, or British intransigence toward allowing Jews in Palestine to defend themselves. The fundamentalist-evangelical periodical stressed the *Struma* incident:

> Dr. Weizmann's associates pleaded with authorities to allow the transfer of 760 certificates of entry into Palestine to be assigned by and from the Jewish Agency in Britain to these unfortunates living like rats in their 200 ton ship at Istanbul. Consent was delayed, but at length permits were written, for sixty children – but too late! The Turkish Government by that time had ordered the Struma to leave port, and she went down in heavy seas.[73]

Dr. Weizmann's declaration served as the critical comment on British actions: "One is horrified to think what sort of people are those who rule the destinies of Palestine – people without understanding, without compassion and without pity."

In October of 1942 Arno C. Gaebelein, the editor-in-chief of *Our Hope*, summarized the exploits of "Monster Hitler." Rev. Gaebelein declared: "Not gradually, but suddenly Monster Hitler developed a devilish mania to persecute and exterminate the entire Jewish race, an ambition which he has pushed more and more to the front and in which he persists today as never before in his bloody and despicable career." Gaebelein insisted that Hitler had instituted "the worst program of Anti-Semitism known in history" and reminded his readers that Hitler also persecuted Christian believers and that Hitler hated the Jewish book, the Bible. He informed his readers of Nazi executions of Jewish people. Of the executions in Wilno in May 1942, he exclaimed:

> Men, women and children were taken in trucks to a suburban village where they were stripped of their clothing and then machine-gunned. Similar reports come from Latvia, the terrorism of hell continues in Czechoslovakia, Bulgaria and elsewhere.[74]

Gaebelein quoted a long excerpt from *The Contemporary Jewish Record*, a publication of the American Jewish Committee (*Commentary* would succeed it in 1945), on the Nazis' methodical starvation and execution of Jewish people. He suggested that his fundamentalist-evangelical readers subscribe to the Jewish periodical as well, noting that it was "trustworthy."

Gaebelein ended this article by assuring his readers that "Hitler's master, Satan, is after all a stupid fellow" and that the Nazis would make blunders that would lead to their downfall. In a later article in the series (June 1943), Rev. Gaebelein refused to underestimate the Nazi atrocities. He asserted:

> The horrors of Anti-semitism continue. During the first World War many atrocious deeds were reported only to be found later untrue. But this is far from being true in this war of barbarism. If anything the number of Jews killed is underestimated. Reliable sources mention not less than two million Jews murdered since Hitler went on his devil-controlled mission.

Arno Gaebelein then probably shocked his conservative readers by relating a typical incident by Hitler's "beasts of lust." He wrote:

> Crimes against women go unabated. A pathetic incident became known through a letter successfully smuggled out of Poland. It reports the suicide of 93 young Jewish girls. They were between the ages of 14 and 22, students in a religious school. Some of Herr Hitler's beasts of lust had herded them together for transportation to houses of prostitution in Germany. These 93 young Jewish heroic girls preferred mass suicide to degradation.[75]

These accounts overwhelmed the eighty-two-year-old fundamentalist editor to such an extent that he burst forth: "But we cannot continue with such rehearsals and pass by other reports of a similar nature. How long! How long! Oh Lord!"

In stark contrast, liberal Protestantism's respected journal *The Christian Century*, in September of 1944 continued to label such accounts "atrocity stories." Of a *New York Times* account by W. H. Lawrence of the extermination of "persons" [CC did not use the word "Jews"] at a German concentration camp near Lublin, the liberal Protestant editors of *The Christian Century* smugly stated: "Many newspapers gave the Lublin charges the big headline of the day, but the parallel between this story and the 'corpse factory' atrocity tale of the First World War is too striking to be overlooked. That story started in 1917 and was not finally discredited until 1925."[76]

In July of 1943, *Our Hope* used the Warsaw ghetto as an example that there was absolutely no improvement in the treatment of European Jews. Gaebelein reminisced in "The New Great World Crisis: XXIV":

> When about 50 years ago the Editor took walks through that noble city (Warsaw) he admired its stately buildings, synagogues, churches, schools, libraries, public parks, etc. The greater part of it is now a thing of the past. In 1934 the Jewish population was 336,600. When the Nazis came 5 years later they herded all Jews into a miserable Ghetto. Then came regular reports of their increasing reduction by cold-blooded massacres and by cruel removal. Rabbi Irving Miller of New York City, the Secretary General of the World's Jewish Congress, has given horrible information. It is most shocking. The 40,000 Jews remaining in the Warsaw Ghetto had revolted against the inhuman treatment of the Nazis and killed sixty German officers and men. As a result these Jews have been murdered and forcibly removed. Nazis rolled through streets in giant tanks, leveling stores and houses and silencing the feeble guns of the defenders, in the final stage of extermination. "Every living soul was either butchered or uprooted and moved to some other part of the country," the rabbi added.[77]

Dr. Gaebelein emotionally responded about the Nazis: "What judgment storm is brewing and gathering against these incarnate demons!"

A few issues later, *Our Hope* published a chart entitled "Extermination of the Jews," which related to its readers that at least two million Jews were known to be dead and five million were in danger of "extermination." "That this people Israel has been the great prey of the Axis powers, Hitler in particular, and the great sufferer of World War II, is too well known to argue," *Our Hope* maintained. "Surely American Jews and Gentiles, for humanity's sake, will want to succor them. When victory is won they will be repatriated [to Palestine], without a doubt."[78] In stark contrast, the liberal Protestant editors of *The Christian Century* (November 8, 1944) published an appeal from the anti-Zionist American Council for Judaism in the first pages of their issue which declared in part:

"We oppose the establishment of Palestine or any locality as a Jewish State or Commonwealth."

With the July 1943 issue, *Our Hope* had embarked on its Jubilee year as a fundamentalist-evangelical periodical. The associate editors, Dr. E. Schuyler English and Dr. Frank E. Gaebelein (the youngest son of Arno), used the November 1943 issue as a "Jubilee Issue" to honor Arno C. Gaebelein. An assortment of articles that the editor had written for *Our Hope* over the years were reprinted and dated. Included was an early excerpt from 1898 that stated that there was "no doubt" that the process of "Israel's restoration" to Palestine was beginning; and an excerpt from the July 1932 issue entitled "Trembling Judaism." This latter excerpt mentioned the rise of Adolf Hitler and the increase of anti-Semitism in universities and other institutions. It stated:

> Dark clouds are gathering over Judaism in many lands. Anti-Semitism is rising. Adolf Hitler, with his rising and powerful influence, is a rabid, fanatical Jew Hater. He evidently is heading for the same end and the same fate as Haman in the book of Esther.

Also published were thirty-nine "testimonials" to the importance of Dr. Arno C. Gaebelein and *Our Hope.* Many of the leading evangelicals gave high praise in this section, underscoring *Our Hope*'s widespread influence on the fundamentalist-evangelical movement. And yet, signatories encompassed a broad spectrum of Protestant denominational affiliations.[79]

Throughout 1944 and into 1945, *Our Hope* detailed the setting of "Herr Hitler's star." Blunders made by Hitler and his generals were given significant coverage. This proved to the editors of the fundamentalist-evangelical journal that those who persecute the Jewish people would be cursed by God. E. Schuyler English proclaimed: "There is no place for anti-Semitism in any land which calls itself Christian, and we who are the Lord's will feel for the Jews and do all in our power to succor them in their present distress in lands across the seas." The "Editorial Notes" of this issue ran the caption "Never before!" and related the shocking details of the methodical extermination of the Jewish people.[80] Later in 1945, Dr. English lamented: "The poor Jews! 6,000,000 of them died under Nazi persecution. Had Palestine been opened many of them might have escaped."

As news of the fate of the Nazi leaders reached *Our Hope*, the horrid details of the concentration camps overwhelmed the editorial staff of the fundamentalist-evangelical publication. Under the caption "Better and Better?" was printed:

> We wonder what the evolutionists and others think who have seen the world getting better and better all the time! And what of the theologians who maintain that man will work himself into a millennium of peace and righteousness? They must have a hard time convincing themselves, after reading about and seeing the pictures of the wholesale atrocities perpetrated in German prison camps. If nothing else could persuade them, we should think that the horror scenes and graphic accounts that have come out of Buchenwald, Dachau, Belchen, Berga, Ziegenham, Orbke, Belsen, et al. . . . These organized murders and sadistic maltreatments were not the work of one man, or one small group of men. They were devised and carried out by thousands of Nazi beasts, the product of modern Germany.[81]

*Our Hope* reminded its readers that these atrocities did not occur "in the jungles of Africa" or "the uncivilized islands of the sea," but rather in what some considered the epitome of world civilization. Then the fundamentalist-evangelical journal questioned: "Is this what civilization does to man? If man evolved from some protoplasm, and then developed through the ages to his present state, what happened to Germany between 1939 and 1945?" To the fundamentalist-evangelical, the answer to this rhetorical question was quite evident.

Dr. Arno C. Gaebelein died at the age of eighty-five on Christmas Day in 1945. He lived long enough to see the fall of Adolf Hitler, the "modern Haman" whom he predicted God would punish. He did not live long enough to see the reestablishment of the State of Israel, a Jewish state that he had declared for nearly sixty years would one day be restored according to "God's Word, the Bible." Toward the end of his life his youngest son, Dr. Frank E. Gaebelein, a graduate of Harvard, traveled sixty miles from his position as headmaster of the Stony Brook School to visit Arno on his sickbed. "Papa, would you like me to read something from the Bible?" Frank would instinctively ask him. "I'd like that," Arno would answer. "What would you like me to read?" Frank asked one day. "Anything!" Arno C. Gaebelein replied. "Anything in the Word of God is good!"

Frank Gaebelein never forgot those words of his father. He and Schuyler English were characteristic of the next generation of fundamentalist-evangelicals, a generation that today has nearly slipped away. This is the generation that would enter into the period of the Cold War with communism, struggle with the plight of the fledgling State of Israel, encounter the age of the atomic bomb, deal with the rock-and-roll generation, and nurture a young evangelist named Billy Graham. This is the generation that would simply call themselves "evangelicals," becoming part of a broad religious sea that spanned centuries and nearly defied definition.

# 5

## THE COLD WAR

With the defeat of Germany and Japan at the end of the Second
World War, a power vacuum was left in Europe and in Asia. The
two great world powers that remained were the Soviet Union
and the United States. To the chagrin of the Truman government
in the United States, Russian communism began to spread into
the vacuum, later joined by the Chinese Communists. The United
States began to oppose its recent Communist allies in an effort to
stem the flow of Communist power and influence. With a monop-
oly on atomic weapons, the United States appeared to hold the
upper hand, but by 1949 the Russians had exploded their own A-
bomb. A "cold war" developed quickly as the United States
sought to build allies among its former enemies (Germany and
Japan) and sought through NATO to solidify an alliance with
Great Britain, France, and other nations against the Communist
menace.

Hearing the news that the expansionary Soviet Union had har-
nessed the dreadful power of atomic weapons, the American
public became increasingly fearful that traitors within its own
government were delivering the world to the Communists. Loyalty boards were instituted in March of 1947 to investigate the allegiance of federal employees, and Communist sympathizers were
ferreted out. Representative Richard M. Nixon of California
declared in 1950 that "traitors in the high councils of our own
government have made sure that the deck is stacked on the

Soviet side of the diplomatic tables," and the accusations of Senator Joseph R. McCarthy of Wisconsin culminated in televised congressional hearings in 1954. Although Joseph McCarthy turned from public hero to villainous buffoon before the television audience as he attacked the beloved President Dwight D. Eisenhower, the Cold War continued to escalate. The Russian Communists had turned their drive toward the Middle East.

In religious circles, conservativism began to spread and grow with evangelistic fervor during the Cold War years. Rev. Billy Graham rose as the prominent revivalist of the period. A fundamentalist-evangelical, Graham was a friend of President Eisenhower and Vice-president Richard Nixon. Most of the Jewish community, along with their more liberal Christian colleagues, were not amused. A "cold war" escalated between liberal religion and conservative religion during these years—a cold war that drew Jews and fundamentalist-evangelicals into its sphere.

## THE JEWISH STATE

Near the end of World War II and after the war, the fundamentalist-evangelical movement continued its fervent support for a Jewish state in Palestine. Their Bible and prophecy teachers told them that God had assured the Jewish people that Palestine belonged to them. This is clearly evident in the messages delivered at the Colonial Hills Prophetic Conference held in the Colonial Hills Baptist Church in Atlanta, Georgia, March 19–26, 1944. One of the major Southern prophetic conferences during that year, it included prominent fundamentalist-evangelicals such as Louis S. Bauman, Charles L. Feinberg, Howard W. Ferrin, Dan Gilbert, Vance Havner, J. Palmer Muntz, W. H. Rogers, and Robert J. Wells. The lectures presented at this conference were published in the volume, *Prophetic Messages for Modern Times*, and had wide exposure during the end of World War II.[1]

One of the messages of Charles L. Feinberg, "The Right of the Jews to Palestine," clearly indicated that the Christian Zionism of these fundamentalist-evangelicals had not waned during the Second World War. Dr. Feinberg told the large audience:

You may be aware that the year, 1944 happens to be the year in which falls the consideration of the White Paper which England issued with reference to their policies with regard to Palestine. They issued a certain manifesto in the year 1939 which comes up for reconsideration in 1944.

The subject is vital. It is a burning question. The question is this: Does the land of Palestine belong to the Arabs, or does it belong to the Jew? Who has the right to Palestine? Who has the right to the land—the Canaanites, the Philistines, the Turks, the Arabs, the English, or the Jews.[2]

Wasting no time mincing his words, the Dallas Theological Seminary professor proclaimed: "The Jews, Israel and Israel alone, have the right to Palestine." He then proceeded with a battery of "Scriptural evidence" to prove his point.

Dr. Feinberg emphasized to the large crowd of fundamentalist-evangelicals that although the Promised Land bore the name of a foreigner ("the natural will always try to usurp the heritage of the spiritual," he asserted), there was "a three-fold, indestructible chain that gives Israel, the Jew, the right to Palestine." First of all were God's promises found in Genesis 12:1–3, 7; 13:14–15; 15:18; and God's unconditional covenant stressed in Deuteronomy 28–30. Secondly, Feinberg noted that the Jews had occupied the land "for more than a millennium," and thus "the land is Israel's because of their possession of it." Thirdly, the Christian theologian declared, "The land is theirs because of the prophecies of resettlement." He read large sections from Isaiah 49:14–23 and ch. 60, and then added Amos 9:14–15: "And I will bring back again the captivity of my people of Israel, and they shall build the waste cities, and inhabit them; and they shall plant vineyards, and drink the wine thereof; they shall also make gardens, and eat the fruit of them. And I will plant them upon their land, and they shall no more be pulled up out of their land which I have given them, saith Jehovah thy God."

Dr. Feinberg concluded with a story about two Jewish rabbis:

Is the land Israel's? It is theirs of a surety, because God has given it to them by His promise, and by their actual possession of it, and by the predictions and prophecies of resettlement. They tell us that a little while after the destruction of Jerusalem, two Jewish rabbis, walked over the ruins and were greatly affected by the mournful sight. But while they were emotionally stirred, one of them wept profusely and the other one laughed. The one who wept was naturally surprised that his companion laughed and said: "How can you smile when you see our holy city laid low in ruins? How can you smile?" The other one said: "Nay, rather, let me ask you a question. Why do you weep?" "Why do I weep?" he asked. "I weep because I behold around me the fearful judgments of the Almighty God. Our beautiful city is no more. Our holy temple is laid waste, and our brethren—where are they now? Scattered to the ends of the earth." The other one said: "Oh, that is the reason! The reason I laugh is because I see how sure God's judgments are. But, I also know God has said, 'I will destroy Jerusalem,' so He has. But, I also know God has said, 'I will rebuild Jerusalem.' Shall I not believe His Word when He is ever more ready to show mercies than judgments?"[3]

Using this story, Dr. Feinberg maintained that "the very fact that the Jew is scattered over the earth is a surety, is a substantiation of all the predictions of punishment and warning; and now, they are by their literal fulfilment the very pledge that God will literally fulfill all of the promises of blessing and of prosperity and of fruitage, of awakening, and of glory for his people, Israel. God's promises are yea and amen altogether. He has given Israel the land of Palestine and it shall be theirs forever."

Relating the horrors the Romans perpetrated on the Jewish people, Dr. J. Palmer Muntz in his lecture, "The Jew in History and Destiny," insisted that the "dispersion of Israel is one of the greatest tragedies of history." He added:

How bitterly and relentlessly have the Jews been persecuted! They have been shamefully treated and downtrodden, ruthlessly plundered, abominably abused, diabolically tortured and barbarously martyred. But Israel, dispersed and persecuted, is also the miracle of history in her preservation. No other people could have survived such treatment without extermination or utter degradation. . . . And in spite of the damnable devices of a Hitler, God has by His providence kept them and always have they been strangely distinct from all other peoples, always separate, never effaced. Why has not persecution destroyed them? Simply because God is not yet through with the Jews. God has used mighty nations as His rod to chastise His chosen people, and then has thrown the rod away. But He has promised to keep His own and He is going to fulfill His promise.[4]

"It is true," Dr. Muntz admitted, "that Israel has not deserved to be kept nor have they been faithful to their God. But unfaithfulness on the part of Israel would not justify unfaithfulness on the part of God. . . . Their calling was for world blessing and there is no divine blessing of nations apart from them. The end of Israel's history is not in dispersion and persecution, but in restoration and conversion. In accordance with the word of prophecy, Israel is going back to Palestine.

"There is no understanding of the Scriptures unless the literal restoration of Israel is clearly seen," J. Palmer Muntz asserted. Alluding to the Zionist gains and Arab perfidy in the past few decades, the premillennialist fundamentalist-evangelical minister related:

The number of Jews in Palestine has increased from 55,000 to 500,000 since the [First] World War, and the present struggle [World War II] has caused but a temporary hiatus in that emigration to the land. Of course, the Jew has gone back in unbelief, but he has gone back with money in his pockets. In recent years, hundreds of millions have been invested in Palestine and like amounts are awaiting expenditure, for the Jew has unquestionably been successful in his foster lands. That some of Israel's wealth was used to buy the land back from the Arabs was the cause of much trouble in more recent years. When the Zionists invaded Palestine with money in their hands instead of a sword and offered it for farm lands, the Arab owners welcomed them. Thousands of them sold out, laughing in their sleeves at such easy victims, and for a little while felt rich. But soon the money was gone and the Zionists had the farms, and there was such a protest as had never before been heard. "These aliens," the Arabs wailed, "have taken our farms from us. They are stealing our land."[5]

To Dr. Muntz, the "Rapture of the Church" could occur at any moment—the "next thing in the order of events" in his estimation. Then would the old Roman Empire be reestablished, the Antichrist revealed, a treaty with the Jews made, temple worship restored, the treaty nullified, and "Palestine will again become a battleground of the world and every foot of it drenched in blood." Muntz insisted that when things looked the worst for the Jewish people and as "Israel calls upon Jehovah," Jesus Christ would be revealed as their Messiah and would deliver them in power and glory. Fresh from the vision of their Messiah, the Jewish people would then "become a missionary people so that through them all the ends of the earth may hear the glorious gospel preached and see the salvation of God. Then shall the earth's golden age be ushered in. (Psalm 67:7; Zechariah 8:22, 23)."[6]

As a fundamentalist-evangelical, J. Palmer Muntz was direct about his biblical interpretation and his prophetic analysis. It certainly was not a welcome theological interpretation in Jewish circles and actually was condemned in many other Christian circles. And yet, as so often was stressed by these fundamentalist-evangelical Bible and prophetic teachers, God's attitude toward anti-Semitism was firm and direct as well. Dr. Muntz and other premillennial interpreters taught their audiences that God's attitude toward God's chosen people should be the Christian's attitude. Muntz asked those assembled in the Colonial Hills Baptist Church auditorium: "In the meantime, what is to be the attitude of the Christian in these days of Israel's trials?" He responded: "Certainly it should not be one of hate and persecution. It should not be forgotten that God is surely going to judge the enemies of the Jews, whether they be nations or individuals." Anti-Semitism would be judged swiftly by God, and any Christian who succumbed to it would pay dearly. To the fundamentalist-evangelical, the Bible was clear about this.

Nevertheless, to these fundamentalist-evangelicals, the church's antipathy toward the Jew was evident not only in overt anti-Semitic acts, but also in the church's neglecting to acknowledge its heritage from the Jewish people and neglecting to present the gospel to those it considered wretched outcasts – the Jews. Muntz believed this was anti-Semitism as well. He preached:

> Do we criticize the Jew because he has failed to learn the purpose of his being scattered today? Possibly the Gentile has failed to learn why God has put the Jew in his midst. The Church, rather than the Jew, has become the custodian of Gospel truth. We can read large

the record of unwillingness of the Jew to bow under the rod of divine punishment, but we must also recognize the failure of the Gentile in the Church to mediate the grace of God that has come to him. Notwithstanding the fact that there is a veil over the eyes of Jews today, their rejection of Christ at Calvary is one thing and their continual rejection of Him today is another. Are we not, in the measure that we have not presented the Gospel to him, to blame for his present rejection?[7]

"Christ has been ignored by Israel; Israel has been ignored by the Church; and both have suffered loss in consequence," Dr. Muntz concluded. "Remember what a great heritage is yours—from the Jew! He has the greatest possible claims on you. He preserved the sacred Scriptures for you. He prepared the world for your Saviour. Can it be that sometimes you forget that Christ was a Jew?"

"It behooves us as Christians to give the Jew the message of Him Whom they know not, and apart from whom the Jews of this present generation will be eternally lost," J. Palmer Muntz asserted, ending his presentation by stating: "There is no other way of salvation. 'There is none other name under heaven given among men, whereby we must be saved' (Acts 4:12). The terms are the same for the Jew as well as the Gentile."[8] As we shall see in the following pages, fundamentalist-evangelical response toward the right of the Jews to be restored to the Promised Land was firm throughout the era of the Cold War—grounded in their biblical interpretation. Just as firmly grounded, however, was their belief that there was salvation only through Jesus Christ, and love for the Jewish people mandated that "true Christians" must share the gospel with God's chosen people, the Jews.

Their premillennial prophetic interpretation of the Bible also led them to watch carefully the development of Russia and the Communist movement. Even during this conference in March of 1944, Louis S. Bauman predicted the escalating conflict between Russia and the Western world, a conflict he believed might well lead to World War III! Dr. Bauman emphasized: "It is my sincere conviction that this present war [World War II] is setting the stage perfectly for World War No. III, and, that that war will be

the war described so vividly by Ezekiel in chapters 38 and 39. 'And
the word of Jehovah came unto me, saying, Son of Man, set thy
face toward Gog, of the land of Magog, the prince of Rosh, Meshech, and Tubal, and prophesy against him.''' Bauman quoted
from a notation in the *Scofield Reference Bible* on this passage to
prove that the primary reference in this passage was to Russia
(Meshech and Tubal as Moscow and Tobolsk). "Never before in
human history has any great government officially ordered God
to pack His trunks and to clear out of her dominion," Bauman
declared of the Communist regime in Russia. "Thus, as we 'peep'
into 'the closet' of prophecy, we behold Russia even as she is
today—a brazen, defiant hater of all that is called God—Russia
with her mighty fists raised against the heavens."[9] Amazingly,
the fundamentalist-evangelical's eschatology was in vogue for
the Cold War even before the end of the Second World War.

Fundamentalist-evangelical periodicals, such as *Moody Monthly,*
also drew the connection between the "spirit of Hitler" and communism. In an excerpt entitled "The Spirit of Hitler," an editor of
*Moody Monthly* stated in January of 1944: "It will be a glorious day
when the war comes to an end, but the cessation of hostilities will
not be the end of our problems. One wonders what the fate of
Hitler will be. He merits whatever of punishment can be meted
out." The writer pointed out, however, that "the end of Hitler
doesn't mean the end of the spirit of Hitler." He explained:

Hitler is the symbol of an age. In the last analysis the difference
between the various forms of totalitarianism is only a difference of
degree. In essence, Communism and Nazism are the same. And
the modified State Socialism, now evident in the United States and
Great Britain, is rooted in the same soil.

You must remember there is a great difference between the positions of Mussolini and Hitler. Mussolini seized power. Hitler
reached his dictatorship by constitutional means. It is plain silly to
place all the blame for Hitler upon Hitler. The German people voted
him into being. He is the expression, visible and vocal, of the Germany of our day.

It has been said before, that every nation gets the kind of government to which it is entitled. Rulers are but the embodiment of the

ideals of the ruled. The ideals of the day around the world are all in the direction of the deification of the state. It's a repetition of the tower of Babel, only this time the tower is a political philosophy.

Students of prophecy will be interested because they see in all of this the possibility of a world state and the preparation for a world dictator. And it all presents fine evidence of how self-deceived humanity is, that with all of its discussion of freedom it is desperately hunting for someone to whom it might surrender control.[10]

A later editorial bluntly stated: "Because we are Christians, we are forever opposed to Communism."[11]

The fundamentalist-evangelicals' support of the Jewish state was as fervent as their belief in the necessity of evangelism or their dislike of communism. Upon the establishment of the State of Israel, *Our Hope* welcomed the new nation with the ten-paragraph commentary, "Israel Becomes a Nation Again." It declared: "The State of Israel, one of the world's oldest sovereignties, became the world's newest sovereignty at midnight on May 15 [the correct date was 14], 1948." Alerting its readers to the retreat of High Commissioner Sir Alan Gordon Cunningham, the selection of the new premier David Ben-Gurion, the "recognition" by President Harry S. Truman, and the impending attack by five Arab nations, *Our Hope* exclaimed that "Britain has mystified the world by having disarmed the Jews and armed the Trans-Jordan Arabs."

Recounting the message that had been delivered in hundreds of thousands of fundamentalist-evangelical sermons and lectures in pulpits and at conferences, *Our Hope* explained that the Bible had given the land to the Jewish people. "There are many Bible references to this restoration," *Our Hope* asserted, quoting one passage in full:

Behold, the days come, saith the Lord, that I will raise unto David a righteous Branch, and a King shall reign and prosper, and shall execute judgment and justice in the earth. In His days Judah shall be saved, and Israel shall dwell safely: and this is His Name whereby he shall be called THE LORD OUR RIGHTEOUSNESS. Therefore, behold, the days come, saith the Lord, that they shall no more say, The Lord liveth, which brought up the children of Israel out of the

land of Egypt; but, The Lord liveth, which brought up and which
led the seed of the house of Israel out of the north country, and from
all countries whither I had driven them; and they shall dwell in
their own land. (Jeremiah 23:5–8; cf. Matthew 24:30, 31.)

"Observe," E. Schuyler English concluded in this "Current
Events in the Light of the Bible" section of *Our Hope*, "that in
God's sight it is their own land."[12]

## Liberal Responses

Mainstream liberal Protestant responses were quite a contrast.
Although some liberal theologians, such as Reinhold Niebuhr
and Paul Tillich, continued in their support for a Jewish state in
Palestine, they were a distinct minority. *The Christian Century*, a
liberal Protestant magazine that would in the 1980s support PLO
representatives to the United Nations, in January 1945 opposed
the attempt to seat Jewish representatives on the board of
UNRRA (United Nations Relief and Rehabilitation Administration) and all other organizations of the United Nations. While
European Jews still suffered in extermination camps, the editors
of *The Christian Century* patronizingly stated:

We are all aware of the anxiety which gave birth to these resolutions.
The Jews have been so victimized, persecuted, knocked about that
it is to be expected they would wish in every possible way to protect
their position in the postwar world. Nevertheless, we believe that
the adoption of the resolutions [of the second session of the American Jewish Conference in Pittsburgh concerning Jewish representatives to the United Nations] was a blunder. Instead of accomplishing
what their authors wanted—that is, protecting the future of the
world's Jews—they will simply raise again old questions that have
done much to expose the Jews to suspicion and discrimination in
the past. No single factor has done more to render insecure the position of the modern Jew than the charge that he is not completely,
wholeheartedly, first, last and all the time a citizen of the country in
which he resides, but that he attempts to hold a dual citizenship
which in actuality works out in a divided loyalty, with his primary
loyalty given to an allegiance other than the land in which he lives.[13]

"We do not believe that this is true for the overwhelming majority
of Jews in this and other countries," the editorial stated. "But the
resolutions adopted by the Pittsburgh convention are well calcu-
lated to revive this ancient charge." The liberal Protestant periodical's use of the words "overwhelming majority" ironically cast
doubt about the implied Jewish minority that in the editor's view
had a divided loyalty.[14]

Abram Hirschberg, rabbi emeritus of Chicago's Temple Sho-
lom, agreed that the resolution "rendered a great disservice to
the cause of the Jew," but he wrote to the editor of *The Christian
Century* to remind him that "dual citizenship" was not the issue
when it came to anti-Semitism. Rabbi Hirschberg expounded:

> Anti-Semitism sinks its roots far deeper in an unreasoning, illogical,
> inherited and centuries-old prejudice that has been fostered by such
> oft-repeated and unjustified charges as the Jewish blood-guilt for the
> crucifixion of Jesus as well as by the Shylock myth of William Shake-
> speare. The minds of the masses have been poisoned for centuries
> by these false accusations. And lately the rising tide of anti-Semitism
> has been given fresh impetus by the brutal mouthings of a fanatical
> Hitler and by the clamor of a lunatic fringe here in America.[15]

Reminding the liberal Protestant editor that Jews across the board
were good American citizens, Rabbi Hirschberg explained: "I
know, too, that there are many of my own people who feel that
we are a homeless people, who believe that we are in exile and
that the fulfillment of the destiny of the Jew demands the creation of a Jewish state. Most of these, however, are unwavering in
their devotion to America and the American dream of a truly
democratic and civilized world."

In spite of such friendly reminders, *The Christian Century* continued to portray insensitively any spark of Jewish nationalism
and Jewish peoplehood. In a long editorial (June 13, 1945) which
listed the possibilities of the German people's true attitude
toward Nazi ideology, the liberal Protestant periodical stated:
"We do not believe the German people want to become another
Jewry. They have not lived long enough with their ideology of a
unique and privileged race." In the face of the horrors of the
Holocaust, the *Christian Century* editorial continued that such

"ideology" required centuries to generate "long enduring patience under self-inflicted ostracism which the martyr spirit
demands." As it had done so often, the prestigious liberal journal omitted any mention of the extermination of six million Jews
(although "martyr spirit" was callously applied to Jewish chosenness by implication).[16]
    James M. Yard, director of the National Conference of Chris-
tians and Jews in Chicago, was astounded at such crassness from
liberal Protestantism's celebrated journal. He wrote to the editor:
"I read your editorial on 'Germany's Regeneration' in *The Christian Century* of June 13. I was shocked beyond words and could
hardly believe my eyes when I came across the sentence that dealt
with the Jews." Yard explained:

> First of all, it was dragged in by the ears without rhyme or reason.
> Second, by implication it made it appear as if the Jewish doctrine
> of a chosen people as found in the Bible was on a par with the nazi
> ideology of a master race. Had an avowed anti-Semite written that
> article, or an ignoramus on matters biblical, I could have under-
> stood it. You do not qualify as either. You know that the idea of a
> chosen people in the Bible bears no similarity to Hitler's master
> race idea.[17]

"Haven't the Jews, after suffering from the starvation, asphyxia-
tion and assassination of Hitlerism," James Yard pleaded, "suffered enough without being pilloried by one of the most influential Christian journals?" The editors of *The Christian Century*
made no apology to the readers, to Yard, or to the Jewish people,
but merely mentioned the context of the editorial and restated
the offensive sentences once again! This time the sentences were
followed by " —The Editors" so that there could be no doubt that
they not only stood by their statements, but also agreed as an editorial staff to their content.
    Certainly the *Christian Century* editors and other liberal Protes-
tants were victims of their own personal theological biases, and
yet certain segments of the Jewish community had reinforced
such views. President Lessing J. Rosenwald of the anti-Zionist
American Council for Judaism had been given the first two full
pages of the November 8, 1944, issue of *The Christian Century* to

publicize his open letter to Secretary of State Cordell Hull (October 19, 1944). Asking only "equality of rights and obligations" of Jews with their "fellow-nationals," Rosenwald insisted that any policy that would "continue to segregate" the Jewish people would depart from the principle of full equality. The support of the United States government for a separate Jewish state in Palestine was viewed by the American Council for Judaism as one such "segregation." On behalf of his fellow Jews in the ACJ, President Rosenwald declared:

> We oppose the establishment of Palestine or any locality as a Jewish State or Commonwealth. We regard as fundamentally undemocratic the procedures involved in such an establishment, such as a preferred status in immigration to those of one religious faith and an arbitrary and indefinite postponement of self-government.
>
> Such proposals will, we believe, embroil Jews now in Palestine in continuing civil strife and place in jeopardy the equality of status of Jews everywhere who are integrated in their respective homelands and do not wish to be party to a Jewish State or Commonwealth. Our emphasis therefore, is on attainment of the status for Jews of full equality for citizenship—its rights and its responsibilities.[18]

A tear-off slip that allowed *Christian Century* readers to either join the American Council for Judaism or receive the anti-Zionist literature followed the long letter. The influence of the American Council for Judaism on liberal Protestant ministers and their organizations should not be underestimated.

Within Reform Judaism, the debate over the establishment of a Jewish state in Palestine was heated and divisive, even after the details of the Holocaust atrocities had been proved. The delegates to the thirty-ninth biennial Union of American Hebrew Congregations (March 3-6, 1946) in Cincinnati, Ohio, went on record "officially and unanimously" to pledge official neutrality on the question of political Zionism and to uphold the right of individual choice on the same question. "The UAHC delegates gathered for the first peacetime convention (its first convention since 1943), in an atmosphere of tension regarding the controversial issue of Zionism," *The American Israelite* reported, "reports of pre-convention caucuses in both camps, and official efforts to avoid commitments that might threaten existence of the Union itself."[19] In an editorial the following week, Henry C. Segal, the editor of America's oldest English-Jewish weekly, approvingly wrote: "In a day when Jews are all too willing to enter the lists in ideological combat with one another, it is indeed refreshing to find one organization with the intelligence and courage to decide: 'There are plenty of organizations in which the question of Zionism can be debated. Let us make our group religious in fact as well as in name.'"[20]

In its November 19, 1947, issue, *The Christian Century* furthered the influence of the American Council for Judaism on the eve of the United Nations partition debate by publishing a special twenty-two-page section, "Palestine and the Jew: A Study of the Future of the Holy Land and of Judaism," by anti-Zionist ACJ stalwart Morris S. Lazaron. "Jewish nationalism has corrupted American Jewish community life!" Rabbi Lazaron proclaimed. "It has created discord and ill-feeling inside the Jewish community and anti-Semitism outside it. . . . The immeasurable misery of the Jews of Europe evoked deepest sympathy among Jews and Christians, and these instinctive humanitarian impulses were exploited to promote the political aims of Zionism."[21] "Present-day Jewish nationalism is an infection caught from the Streptococcus viridans nationalism which plagues our world," he raged. "Jewish nationalism is a new manifestation in recent history, especially since the First World War." "*Erect a Jewish state and Judaism loses whatever moral authority it has in the world*," he continued in italics on the next page, later explaining that with "a Jewish state in Palestine sustained and promoted by a nationalism embracing all the Jewish communities among the nations, we Jews would lose our very raison d'être."[22]

Rabbi Morris S. Lazaron sought to influence the readers of the Christian periodical by quoting a letter "from a Christian friend, a valiant supporter of the Stratton bill, a distinguished lawyer who as a Christian hates anti-Semitism and as an American fears it." Insisting that Zionism breeds anti-Semitism, Lazaron pointed out that the letter "represents the judgment of an increasing number of friendly non-Jews." The letter from the Christian lawyer began:

There is no doubt that the Zionists are doing everything they can to force our government to "take the lead" in urging the United Nations to support the majority recommendations of the Palestine Commission. I greatly regret that there are apparently many people who have been fundamentally opposed to Zionism but who are nevertheless prepared to support partition and a Jewish state. There is also no doubt that the Zionists, if they achieve partition and a Jewish state, will try for more and more with increasingly disturbing consequences to the international situation and, as I have long been convinced, with disastrous consequences to the millions of our fellow countrymen of Jewish faith, who have one wholesouled allegiance — allegiance to the United States of America. The Zionists seem to have achieved, at least temporarily, a Jewish bloc which, however effective for the moment, is contrary to all that is best in the American tradition, and, I am still convinced, does not truly represent the deepest convictions of the vast majority of Americans of Jewish faith. It is my feeling that most Americans of Jewish faith have been confused, as some Christians have been, by a clever and dishonest mixture of the humanitarian and the political aspects of the Palestine situation. As you well know, it is my sad conviction and prophecy that the Zionists will have done more, in the long run, to promote anti-Semitism than all the vilest forces of anti-Semitism.[23]

"The tactics of the Zionists, as you well know, are so disgracefully slanderous," the Christian lawyer continued, "that Christians of standing are simply unwilling to expose themselves to them."

Rabbi Lazaron, who since 1915 had been rabbi of the Baltimore Hebrew Congregation and who was a member of the Central Conference of American Rabbis, agreed with this assessment, ending his article in *The Christian Century* with the plea:

We Jews have a greater mission than upbuilding a single refuge or creating a Jewish state in Palestine. Profound sentiment and ancient memories attach to the Holy Land as the birthplace of Israel, but history has placed us in every advanced nation. Let us be worldwide carriers of the ideas of liberty and equality, evangelists for human rights for everybody everywhere. Then "homeland" for Jews as well as Christians will be universal, not parochial.[24]

Three weeks later in the first editorial of the December 10, 1947, issue, *The Christian Century* noted that it was "frankly dismayed at the moral and military responsibilities which the United States assumed in forcing this vote [the United Nations partition vote on Palestine, November 29] through an obviously reluctant Assembly."[25]

In the letters that followed Lazaron's "special section," there were some who disagreed with the rabbi's contentions. "The 'new' approach which you claim Morris S. Lazaron has brought to 'Palestine and the Jew' is the old, discredited and disreputable one of bigoted and irrational anti-Zionism," Theodore N. Lewis of the Progressive Synagogue of Brooklyn, New York, wrote. "It does not contain a single new idea, thought or challenge." Lewis told the editors:

> Not only does it repeat all the ancient and dishonest misrepresentations, but it also repeats the old slanders and accusations which have become the chief stock and trade of anti-Zionists, Jewish and Christian.
>
> It is a vulgar falsehood that "the creation of a Jewish state will affect the position of Jews in other lands." A Jewish state will no more affect my loyalties to America any more than the existence of Ireland affects the loyalties of Irish Americans in America. As an American Jew, I deeply resent this base charge, resent it not only for myself, but for the entire American Jewish community, which will continue to be as zealously patriotic after the establishment of a Jewish state as it was prior to that.[26]

Henry J. Berkowitz of Congregation Beth Israel in Portland, Oregon, concurred. "The article is such an eye-bulging hodgepodge of inaccuracies and contradictions, all in the name of clarification, that it can only arouse increased confusion, and some concern for a rabbi whose thinking is so utterly befuddled," he wrote. Bedros Baharian, executive secretary of the Council of Churches in Quincy, Massachusetts, pointed out to the editors that Lazaron's article "represents the point of view of the American Council for Judaism, which represents less than 10 per cent of Jewish thinking in the United States." Nevertheless, other letters found the article an indication of the journalistic quality of *The Christian Century*, and W. T. Couch, director of the University of Chicago Press, asked for "more public discussion of this problem at this high level" to greatly improve civilized solutions.

In contrast to the fundamentalist-evangelical euphoria upon the recognition of the new State of Israel on May 14, 1948, the liberal Protestant *Christian Century* labeled its excerpt on "the independent Zionist state of Israel" and the United States government's "instant recognition" of it "The Palestine Tragedy (Continued)."[27]

As Christians were swayed by the rhetoric of anti-Zionism, the American Council for Judaism found fewer Jewish adherents clinging to their cause. As early as the summer of 1945, Alfred Segal, a card carrying member of the ACJ and columnist for *The American Israelite*, complained that the American Council for Judaism's program lacked positive attributes. He questioned in print the wisdom of sending in his two-dollar dues to belong to an organization that devoted itself exclusively to the negative task of attacking Zionism. Immediately, the hierarchy of the ACJ attacked him, but was surprised that even a founding member of the Council came to Segal's defense. "I am thoroughly in accord with his point of view," wrote Rabbi Leonard J. Rothstein of York, Pennsylvania. "For some time I have felt that there has been something missing in the outgivings of the Council."[28]

The major Christian organization combating the ACJ was the American Christian Palestine Committee (ACPC), which had from 1946 carried on the work of the combined American Palestine Committee (founded in 1931) and the Christian Council on Palestine (founded in 1942). Under the energetic young executive secretary and liberal Protestant minister, Carl Hermann Voss, the ACPC was able to bring together a diverse theological spectrum of liberal and conservative Christian supporters of the Jewish state. The task was formidable, especially among the academics and Ivy-League establishment, because of the social, intellectual, and religious pressures that were brought to bear on anyone who appeared to be pro-Zionist. Reinhold Niebuhr and Paul Tillich looked to Voss when crises in the Middle East arose and when their colleagues brought immense pressures on them to renounce their Zionism. Very few liberal Protestants could stand the test in the face of the views propounded by *The Christian Century,* their seminaries, their denominational hierarchy, and, above all, their missionaries. Liberal Protestant missionary organizations lined up en masse against the Jewish state to protect their interests in Arab countries. Carl Hermann Voss was later to write:

> It was difficult to structure a definite, consistent program, except to stir public opinion and carry on as broad and specific an educational project as possible, especially through pamphlets and booklets, radio debates and public forums. We had to rely on letters to the editor and petitions to Congress, protests to the State Department and pressure on the American Delegation to the United Nations, especially in the final months from the August 1947 Report of the Special Committee on Palestine through the adoption of partition by the General Assembly in late November, 1947, on to the incredible reconstitution of the Third Jewish Commonwealth on May 14, 1948. Christians did play a part but not as significantly or as definitely as they should have. . . . Despite the uncertainty and timidity of many Christians, however, there was indeed a Christian voice; and it was expressed, though imperfectly and often ineffectually, by the American Christian Palestine Committee.[29]

Among the large percentage of Jews who supported the State of Israel and liberal causes, the minority of liberal Protestant ministers and academics, such as Dr. Carl Hermann Voss, who stood by the Jewish state throughout their lifetimes was appreciated and acknowledged. And it is these liberal Protestants who are the first to acknowledge that anti-Zionism has increasingly become anti-Semitism in the bastions of gentile liberalism.

## "I AM UNSAVED"

Nevertheless, Jews and most liberal Protestants were wary of the "easy solution" gospel of the postwar fundamentalist-evangelical. This liberal response to revivalism often provided a comaraderie that no amount of fundamentalist-evangelical Zionism could counteract. During the famed Billy Graham Los Angeles Crusade in 1949, for example, a deacon of a suburban church showed up at the door of Alfred Segal, the Cincinnati-based "Plain Talk" columnist for *The American Israelite*. Alfred Segal responded to the evangelistic witness of this Christian with the November 3 column, "I Am Unsaved."[30] It began:

The tall, thin man was a stranger who said that for years he had admired me from afar until this moment when he had come to call on me. He had been reading my column in the daily press 20 years and from that he had concluded I was worth his attention. His name was Atkinson.

"There's only one thing the matter with you," he said.

Oh, Mr. Atkinson, only one thing? Without preparation for giving such an accounting I can recite offhand many things that are the matter with me. My wife herself could tell you a number of things that are the matter with me. She's always reminding me of them.

Mr. Atkinson insisted that in his book there was only one thing wrong in me. He had called to tell me about it with the best of good will and to do something to improve me. . . "I might say I am your best friend, though we became acquainted only a few minutes ago" . . . He was worried about my soul.

[Speaking like a father to a son who was not going in the right way, the Christian deacon told Alfred Segal: "You are doomed if you continue in your present state." Heaven was an enjoyable place, "But I feel bound to tell you you are not going there." Segal responded that he had not thought much about going to heaven. His idea was that if he was a fairly decent citizen, he didn't need to worry about his future. Segal wrote about the deacon's feelings about this attitude:]

"But you are a Jew, Mr. Segal". . . Mr. Atkinson was saying in the friendliest way. . . "As a Jew you are an unbeliever and unredeemed. You can not share in salvation. There is no salvation except in being a Christian."

Mr. Atkinson was saying that not only he but other officers as well as ordinary members of his church had been worrying about me. . . "If you hadn't shown yourself to be a decent man in your column they wouldn't bother about you". . . They had decided to try to save me because they regarded themselves as friends of mine. They had sent Mr. Atkinson to make overtures toward a salvation that would make my future secure.

"To make it short," the deacon summarized, "We are inviting you to be a Christian."

"Mr. Atkinson, this is too sudden. After having been a Jew some 2000 years and more, a man can't make himself over in a moment." Mr. Atkinson said: "We'd be happy to take you into our church next Sunday though. That should be time enough. At your age you can't take too much time deciding whether or not you want to be saved."

Segal wrote:

> He reminded me how suddenly a lot of middle-aged men have been dying. . . "All unready to die, Mr. Segal". . . He thought I was at an age of life to be thinking of my future . . . "We'll give you a week."

He mentioned the fact that on the earth it wasn't too pleasant to be a Jew . . . "It's one thing and another for a Jew on this earth, Mr. Segal. If you accept my proposition you can make yourself secure now and in the eternity to come. We hope to have a big celebration on your account in our church next Sunday."

"Well, Mr. Atkinson, I must say your proposition is flattering. You say that no later than next Sunday I can escape all the disabilities of being a Jew on the earth and in heaven. It's something to think about."

Mr. Atkinson's eyes flashed brightly . . . "I knew you wouldn't turn me down. I can make a hopeful report on you to the congregation tomorrow. All our prayers will be for you at our Wednesday prayer meeting."

"But, Mr. Atkinson," Segal thoughtfully responded, "I'm thinking: Suppose I did become a Christian. Wouldn't I be an awfully lonely man? A solitary Christian in crowds of Gentiles!"

You see, if I became a Christian I would like to take it seriously. I might become a Christian who would make himself obnoxious.

You see, I might get up in the most unexpected places and start telling Gentiles it's about time they were Christians. Maybe I'd tell them about the unChristian way of treating Negroes and get them down on me by saying that the black boy is a brother, too, and is entitled to a fair break. I'd feel it was a Christian's duty to say these things.

Mr. Atkinson interrupted to say that if I got into that sort of thing I wouldn't be talking religion . . . "That would be politics. That would be mixing religion with politics. We don't stand for that in our church."

Then, Mr. Atkinson, I might talk about the slums in our town. They aren't Christian either. The way kids are being bitten by rats in our slums is more like a jungle than Christianity. I might tell them it's about time for Christianity to do something about slums. Maybe as a Christian I might lead some Gentiles toward the Christian conscience. Certainly the Christian conscience should care about slums.

Mr Atkinson asked: "But wouldn't that be getting into business matters, such as real estate?" His congregation wasn't interested in that sort of thing but only in me, to save and get me ready for salvation and my portion of the heavenly reward.

"We stick to salvation, Mr. Segal—the saving of souls," the deacon replied.

"And, in the end, Mr. Atkinson," Alfred Segal recounted his conversation, "I might be the loneliest of Christians, unpopular and despised as a subversive person." Segal said:

Finally I would be denounced as a damn Jew. (Please excuse the expression.) So, though I took the confessions of your church, I wouldn't be considered a Christian, after all, just an annoying Jew.

No, Mr. Atkinson, I don't like to be a lonely man. I want company, such as poker games, such as the convocations of Jewry in which we quarrel and have fun, such as those meetings of Jews in which we talk about being a Jew and what should be done to make ourselves deserving of the identity. In this way we reach for salvation in our own way. Sorry, Mr. Atkinson, don't think I can join your church next Sunday.

"I looked like a hopeless case to Mr. Atkinson," Segal concluded in the 'Plain Talk' column, "and much more in sorrow than anger he left me."

Alfred Segal's view of such evangelistic witness in the name of Jesus was certainly indicative of widespread Jewish attitudes. It also indicates that some Jews were quite familiar with the fundamentalist-evangelical's "gospel message" and abhorrence of a social gospel. And yet, Segal had shown over the years that as a liberal Jew he harbored no ill will toward Jesus. In fact, in a column entitled "Jesus and Jews" written three and one-half years earlier, Segal took to task a textbook used in Catholic parochial

schools that held the Jews responsible for Jesus' death, but he
firmly stressed his respect for the teaching of Jesus. Alfred Segal
wrote at that time:

> Enlightened Jews themselves hold no ill will against Jesus, despite
> all that Jews have been made to suffer in his name. They honor his
> teaching as a good way of life and hope for the time when all who
> call themselves Christians will go that way.
>
> The suffering of the Jews is only part of the suffering which the
> Christian world, as it is called, has inflicted upon itself by keeping
> Jesus nailed to the cross and refusing to let him come down to walk
> among men with light-giving.[31]

After the column "I Am Unsaved," Alfred Segal was asked by
Jewish mothers whether or not they should make an issue of
Christmas celebrations in public schools that were predomi-
nantly Jewish in population or had a considerable Jewish population. His response was surprising, for he believed that through
participating in such celebrations Jewish children could be led
from bigotry toward Christianity to better understanding their
Christian neighbors. He even related his own experience as a
child. "Besides, it is damaging arrogance for Jews to attempt to
deny Christmas to Christian children in schools in which Jewish
children predominate in numbers or in which Jewish children
are in large percentage," Alfred Segal maintained. "It is arrogance that undermines our own claims for tolerant treatment as
a religious minority. It is a denial of the ethical upbringing which
our prophets tried to give us."[32]

## "SOOTHING DISTORTION"

Most Liberal Protestant groups believed in evangelism by Christians nearly as much as did fundamentalist-evangelicals. They
proposed, however, that their evangelism and evangelistic
methods were quite different from those of their conservative
brothers and sisters in Christ. Reinhold Niebuhr had emphasized that Jews did not need to be "converted" by Christians
and that they should not be "evangelized." Nevertheless, his

bi-weekly journal, *Christianity and Crisis*, ran an editorial entitled "Evangelism" in the February 3, 1947, issue. It began:

> Evangelism is a word that has had connotations for most Americans. It suggests high pressure emotional appeals to suggestible crowds. It suggests narrowness and intolerance and spiritual imperialism. It suggests unfortunate encounters with professional evangelists, perhaps today more often met in novels than in real life. But evangelism is neither more nor less than the effort to confront people with the claims of the gospel, the witnessing to the truth of God's revelation in Christ. It is the effort to bring those who are now outside into the fellowship of the Church. No amount of general exhortations about the fallacies of secular philosophies, or about the actual or potential contribution of the Church to the life of the world can be of much use in the long run unless men and women come into the Church, not primarily because the Church is good for the world, but primarily because its faith is for them the deepest truth about life, about their own lives, because in its worship they find their God.[33]

"Undoubtedly the conventional methods of evangelism now prove inadequate in our situation," the liberal Protestant member of Niebuhr's editorial board, John C. Bennett, admitted in this editorial. "Where they do have the greatest apparent success, as in the 'Youth for Christ' movement, they are used to present a soothing distortion of the Gospel that offers a promise of salvation for the individual without, first of all, making him aware of the searching judgment of God upon him in every phase of his life." Bennett noted, however, that such fundamentalist-evangelical movements as Youth for Christ did "show up the failure of the Churches to find a way to bring to youth both Christian judgment and Christian promise."

Bennett found that the churches "are themselves so often obstacles to the persuasiveness of their message" and fail "to grasp the full depth and range of the Christian gospel. . . . " "The call to the Church to go out and seek the millions at its very door who have never acknowledged Christ," Bennett wrote, "is always at the same time a call to the Church to be changed in its own life." And yet, the very liberal John C. Bennett, like many postwar liberal Protestants trying to breathe life and social conscience into

Christendom, sounded like a fundamentalist-evangelical when he stressed the need for evangelism. He insisted:

There is another cause of the weakness of evangelistic efforts of the Church, a perennial factor and yet in our time more than usually pronounced. It is the distance between the Christian gospel and the natural assumptions and expectations and desires of men. In all ages the Cross has been a stumbling block to the Jews and foolishness to the Greeks and in all ages Christian faith and commitment have required a change of mind that is not easy.

But when all of these difficulties have been weighed there is one consideration that today seems more important than any of them. It is the fact that many millions of people, perhaps scores of millions, in our own nation, in all classes, have never in their lives heard a comprehensive and relevant presentation of the Christian gospel. Christianity for them has always meant some poor stereotype that any man with a feeling for reality would reject. When once such rejection has taken place, the inhibition against opening the mind and heart to Christian truth is very powerful.

Believing that "Christianity does not set a premium upon superstitious self-deception, that it is not narrowly legalistic, that it is not irrelevant idealism," Dr. Bennett called for a removing of these obstacles, concluding:

Now is the time to concentrate on the responsibility to give every one a chance to hear the Gospel, the full range and depth of it, for the alternative faiths that have most believers in America, especially the faith in man's control of his destiny through self-sufficient science, become daily more incredible. The urgency of this is to be measured not only by the threatening sickness of civilization but by the fact that in the case of every individual there is not much time to decide by what faith he is to live or die.[34]

*The Christian Century* concurred. In the editorial "America for Christ" (October 19, 1949), the liberal periodical supported the America for Christ campaign, an ecumenical effort to win people in the United States "to Christ." Still using the word "evangelical" to express the best in this type of liberal evangelism, the editors declared:

The die is cast. American Protestantism is committed. On October 3, thirty-eight denominations set out to win as many as possible of the 70 million unchurched people of this country to a living evangelical faith. Under the banner, "America for Christ," the largest cooperative endeavor of its kind started a 15-month march against the pagan secularism, spiritual illiteracy and open unbelief of the majority of our citizens. Using a variety of tested methods on a wide scale, the United Evangelistic Advance seeks to enlist the prayers and efforts of 35 million members of the cooperating churches.[35]

"It deserves to succeed," the liberal Protestant periodical proclaimed of the evangelistic thrust, "It must not fail."

The postwar editors of *The Christian Century* continued to believe that modernism as a theology was rooted in "evangelical faith" and evangelical ecumenism. America for Christ was the cooperative effort of all twenty-seven denominations of the Federal Council of Churches (the forerunner of the National Council of Churches), and its sixty-two-member national committee was headed by E. G. Homrighausen of Princeton Theological Seminary. The liberal Protestant participation was on a par with the Key '73 evangelistic thrust of the 1970s. The devotion of *The Christian Century* to the endeavor and the liberal Protestant commitment to this Christian missionary enterprise is evident in the wording of the editorial. It continued:

It will succeed if it manages to impress members of the churches with the fateful consequences with which this effort is inescapably invested. Achievement of its purpose will vitally affect for good the character and influence of the American people and all their institutions, including the church. It will trumpet the dawn of the new day toward which millions look with hope and longing. Failure to make recognizable and unchallengeable progress toward the objective of this movement will proclaim to the world that evangelical Christianity is spiritually bankrupt. It will reveal that Protestantism has wasted its magnificent American heritage and is no longer the major spiritual force in the mature life of the nation it brought to birth, cradled in infancy and guided in youth.

In either case, the outcome cannot be hidden. For better or for worse, this movement will bring America to an hour of decision concerning the free and evangelical faith which has found expression in the daily life and attitudes of its people as well as in its most fundamental institutions. . . . Spiritual power can be measured by the effectiveness of the church in maintaining and extending its life through its witness to the gospel of Jesus Christ. Such a test is now to be made on a nationwide scale in the United Evangelistic Advance.

"Of course America cannot be won for Christ by organization, however inclusive and extensive," *The Christian Century* admitted. "But such organization is an inevitable expression of Christian fellowship, especially when it is informed by a majestic and compelling purpose." The editors did find that a "major omission in the announced plans is a mission to labor." They noted that the "efforts should call forth the cooperation of literally millions of church people, and they must do so if 'America for Christ' is to become anything more than a slogan."

But, above all, the liberal Protestant periodical (and, it is assumed, the large majority of its Christian readers) was quite positive on this mainline, ecumenical, evangelistic thrust. "It is expected that voices will be raised declaring that the gates of heaven cannot be stormed by mass assault, and they are right," the editors emphasized. "But the point is irrelevant." *The Christian Century* editorial triumphalistically gloated:

> In this enterprise heaven's cooperation is assured, providing we make its cooperation possible. Christ wills the conversion of America. Of that we can be sure. But do we desire it above everything else? Are the churches prepared to risk it? When Christ wins America every local church will be transformed, every community changed, every denomination identified with the larger life of the ecumenical church. Did those who launched this movement realize that it might have such effects? Whether they did or not, there is no turning back now.[36]

To *The Christian Century*, the results of the "America for Christ" campaign depended on church members and ministers. "If they look upon this as another pious chore, another headquarters' brainstorm that has to be endured until it has blown over, then the second half of the 20th century will see the decline of Protestantism in America," the editorial decreed. "But if church men and women are sobered by the judgments that have fallen on our world and the worse catastrophes that threaten to descend, if they are moved by the promise of new light yet to break forth from God's word and by love which will not let us go, then 1950 will see a momentous turning point in Christian history."

How the Jewish community reacted to this endeavor, or if they understood that it was supported quite completely by liberal Protestants, is debatable. Perhaps they took comfort in their assumption that many liberal Protestants were Unitarians (an erroneous view that downplayed liberalism's commitment to Jesus Christ). Perhaps the Jewish community took comfort that the campaign was geared to reach "unchurched people," and liberal Protestants did not seem to desire to convert Jews. Perhaps they did not read the rhetoric of "conversion of America," "every community changed," commitment to "witness to the gospel of Jesus Christ," reference to "when Christ wins America," and reference to Protestantism as the "major spiritual force in the mature life of the nation" in this and other liberal Protestant editorials. From the rhetoric, perhaps most Jews felt that these Christians were actually fundamentalist-evangelicals. Fundamentalist-evangelicals, however, often believed that such movements were "of man" rather than "of God." Only the return of Jesus himself could convince a whole nation or a whole world. The Antichrist could very well work through a vast ecumenical church movement such as "America for Christ." Liberal Protestants often associated the word "fundamentalism" with "antiecumenical," as attested by the many editorials in *The Christian Century* using "fundamentalist" in connection with Carl McIntire's attacks on the Federal Council of Churches and other ecumenical enterprises.

Was liberal Protestantism anti-Semitic in supporting this evangelistic enterprise? Apparently not. Triumphalism is evident (couched in the language of Christian enlightenment), but not anti-Semitism. Assimilation seems to be implied, but not physical genocide. Both *The Christian Century* and *Christianity and Crisis* would be wary of fundamentalist-evangelical Billy Graham's evangelistic crusades and would oppose his "soothing distortion." Like Graham, liberal Protestant leaders would oppose communism and fear nuclear war, but in later years would mellow and question the Cold War between the United States and Russia. The vast majority of liberal Protestants could not accept Billy Graham's Christian Zionism or his "bias toward the Jewish people." Even in the same issue as the "America for Christ" editorial, *The Christian Century* featured an article by Francis J. Bloodgood, archaeologist and former chaplain to the Anglican Bishop of Jerusalem, criticizing the Zionists and calling for "an international government in the Jerusalem-Bethlehem area."[37] A cold war would continue to exist between fundamentalist-evangelicalism and liberal Protestantism. A cold war would also continue to fester between liberal Protestantism and the Jewish State of Israel.

## FUNDAMENTALIST ZIONIST ATTITUDES

The evangelical publication *Christian Herald*, with a circulation approaching 400,000 in 1948, claimed to be interdenominational and undenominational. Its editor was Dr. Daniel A. Poling, a member of the (Dutch) Reformed Church of America and honorary member of the Ohio Conference of the Evangelical United Brethren Church (his father's church, in which his own ministry had begun). A self-proclaimed "gentle Fundamentalist," Poling was a firm believer in premillennialism and was senior minister of the Baptist Temple in Philadelphia. A national cochairman of the American Christian Palestine Committee, Dr. Poling worked closely with Dr. Carl Hermann Voss and his executive committee on Israel's behalf. Answering unequivocably a reader's question in October 1947, Daniel Poling declared to the *Christian Herald* readership: "I am a Christian Zionist who believes that Palestine should become, as promised, the Jewish state." Welcoming the new State of Israel, he never wavered from that position.[38]

Although firmly committed to his fundamentalist-evangelical belief system, including the evangelization of the world, Poling clearly cared for Jewish people. Deeply touched by the horrors of the Holocaust and the extermination of a generation of Jewish children, Dr. Poling worked diligently as the treasurer for the Children's Memorial Forest in Palestine. In fact, the August 1947 issue of the *Christian Herald* carried an article on the Children's Forest and its importance.[39] Even though the periodical was supposed to represent the varied views of evangelicalism, the *Christian Herald* often reflected the fundamentalist-evangelical Zionism of its editor.

For example, in his "News Digest of the Month" (May 1944) in the *Christian Herald,* Christian news analyst Gabriel Courier reported about "the tinderbox of the Middle East," the Palestine situation:

> The pattern of World War I has been more or less repeated. There have been promises made to both Jews and Arabs; there has been doubledealing, and frustration of both Arab and Jewish hopes; there have been zealous pressure-groups at work all over the world, trying to get the Jew in or to keep the Jew out. We haven't made much progress since Lawrence rode in Arabia.
>
> The Arab in this situation has but one argument. He says this is his land, the land of his fathers. He objects to turning it over to "foreigners": i.e., the Jew. He pities the Jew, but he wants Palestine to remain an Arab state. The Jew counters with the argument that this is his land, and the land of his fathers. He points out that thousands of Arabs have sold their land—particularly their farms—to the Jews. He says there are also Arabs by the thousands who have learned new agricultural methods from the Zionists, and improved their lot. He insists that in many areas Jews and Arabs live in perfect peace together. He says there is room enough for both, in the Near East.[40]

"Both seem to us to be right," Gabriel Courier explained, "but frankly our sympathies (speaking personally now, and not for CHRISTIAN HERALD) lie with the Jew. He has turned a desert into a garden in Palestine; the Arab failed to do that, though he held the land for centuries." Indicating that the land could shelter millions of Jewish refugees "at least temporarily," Courier reminded his readers that "the Jew is pro-Ally, the Arab pro-German. That will mean something at the peace-table. . . . The Arab will fight the British—and the Jew."

By January 1946, Gabriel Courier was concerned about the Arab League and its actions. "The Arab League is not yet one year old," he wrote. "A mere baby. And an enfant terrible." Concerned about the deadly Arab riots against Jews in Cairo as the League met there, Courier related:

> They fight the Jew—specifically they fight further Jewish immigration into Palestine and the establishment of a Jewish state in Palestine. They fight a people who have come into that country to make the land blossom into an unexpected productivity—after the Arab, living there for centuries, had failed to make it produce. They fight a people with a claim as good as theirs to that land.[41]

"The Jews ask for a ridiculously small section of land on which to build their state; the Arab could grant it and never miss it," Courier concluded. "We wonder why he doesn't, and thus end the slaughter."

As the riots and bloodshed continued in Palestine, Courier noted that the British "have bound themselves fast to the Arab money-lords, and that they dare not cut loose now, in fear that they might lose that oil!" When Sir Edward Spears, former British minister to Syria and Lebanon, claimed that "Arab unity [is] essential to the progress and stability of this [Palestine] area," Gabriel Courier told his readers that "he tipped his British hand, badly." Courier retorted:

> The truth is that the Jew has brought more progress and stability to the land of Palestine than that land has known since King David. The Arab likes what the Jew has brought so much that he has come to consider Palestine not as a land to emigrate from, but a land to immigrate to. The Arab birth rate and life expectancy, thanks to Jewish hospitals, doctors and public health services, has shot up. Land that had gone fallow and laid useless for years has been reclaimed by Jewish irrigation and scientific farming; the Arab never made that land pay as it pays now. Industry has been brought to a higher level of productivity and efficiency under Jewish methods than it has ever known. If that isn't progress and stability, then we've lost the meaning of those words.[42]

What also irked the editor of the "News Digest of the Month," however, was that the Arab "money-lords" that the British were appeasing were "backward and oppressive," making themselves rich and powerful by grinding down the Arab commoner "by what amounts to slave labor—and he does not want to lose his grip." Gabriel Courier declared: "What the British must choose between is human rights and the continuation of that archaic system now in the hands of the rich and ruthless Arab princes. Some day, whether the British are there or not, the system will change. It must. And the quicker the better."

In August 1946, Courier ridiculed "Mr. Bevin, talking double" and deplored "the 'escape' of the traitorous, treacherous, Nazi-minded Grand Mufti of Jerusalem on the one hand, and the unfulfilled promises to the Jews on the other." He told the *Christian Herald* readers that this left "the British in a position that is anything but respectable." "It's time for a new deal in Palestine," Gabriel Courier exclaimed.[43]

By the end of 1946, the Palestine situation seemed like a play—a play without the key actors participating. In "Without Hamlet," Gabriel Courier began his news from abroad:

> The long awaited council of Jews, Britishers and Arabs has met—minus the Jews. Object: to find a solution to the Palestine problem. Accomplishments to date: exactly nothing.
>
> Nothing, we believe, was accomplished at this meeting. The Jews were not there. It was like trying to play Hamlet without Hamlet, without even the ghost. The British sought a solution while they completely ignored the most potent dynamite in the whole situation: they acted as though there were no such thing as Zionism.
>
> The Arabs will have none of it, either; they might as well have stayed home, too. They will not listen to talk of partition in Palestine; they say they will fight if the British try that. Who will supply them with arms? The Arabs have spoken before of seeking aid from—Russia. . . . The Arabs call for the UN to step in. If the UN did step in, would the Arabs abide by the UN decision? We think not.[44]

"Is there, then, any peaceful solution for the Palestine problem?" Gabriel Courier rhetorically asked. "As things stand now, we think not. It is time for the UN to take over, and to enforce its decision with arms."

As the situation continued to get worse in the Middle East, the biblically and prophetically minded fundamentalist-evangelicals were quite a contrast to most liberal Protestants or the

anti-Semitic right-wing extremists. While acknowledging imper-
fections in the Zionist movement, the bottom line for fundamentalist-evangelicals was the Jewish right to the land. While Harvard's William Ernest Hocking was becoming progressively and
viciously anti-Zionist (ridiculing those who would appeal to
"will of God" in the Palestine situation), fundamentalist-evangelicals appeared to concur with the early sentences of Blackstone's
Petition of 1891, that is, "According to God's distribution of
nations [Palestine] is their [the Jewish people's] home, an inalienable possession, from which they were expelled by force. . . . Let
us now restore them to the land of which they were so cruelly
despoiled by our Roman ancestors." When attacks on the British
and the assassination of Count Bernadotte were the final straws
in turning "enlightenment Christians" (such as *New York Herald
Tribune* columnist Dorothy Thompson) against the Jewish people
and the Jewish state, the fundamentalist Zionist appeared to
understand.

Gabriel Courier, for example, explained the assassination of
Count Bernadotte to the *Christian Herald* (November 1948) read-
ers with a sensitivity toward Jewish people and toward the anti-
Semitism that might surely develop. He wrote:

> So they shot Count Bernadotte. They shot at him before they got
> him. And when they murdered this man from the U.N., the Stern
> gang extremists did as much harm to their cause in Israel as they
> would have done by dropping an atomic bomb on New York. . . .
>
> Let's remember that "the Jews" did not do this thing; an irrespon-
> sible, lawless, barbarously ignorant Stern gang did it. And when
> they did it, they may have cut off from their cause the sympathy
> and resources of millions of friends around the world.[45]

"Completely innocent," Courier related, "the leaders of Israel
and their cause have suffered a tragic blow." Earlier, in June 1948,
Courier had ridiculed the United States for not backing the UN
Plan, concluding: "What then? Do we just hand Palestine over to
the Arabs?" Later, in 1949, he gloried in Israel's victory, asserting
that "Israel has made the Arab—and the U.N.—look foolish.
Egypt seems to have lost all stomach for the fight." Of England,

Courier questioned: "How can she deal with the Jew when she supported the Arabs?"

Gabriel Courier interpreted the news for the *Christian Herald* throughout the 1940s and 1950s. In his "Gabriel Courier Interprets the News" section in the 1950s he emphasized that the Arab world was in flux and was by no means unified. Violence threatened the Jewish state and world peace at every juncture. In April 1958, in "Furtive Crescent," Courier wrote of Egypt and Syria's merger to form the United Arab Republic "with Nasser, of course, as President." He believed that Nasser could not be satisfied with "one bite," expecting him to try to link by land Egypt and Syria. "No one felt the calculating gaze of the new Republic more than Jordan (unless it was Israel; Egypt already had ordered the name 'Israel' erased from all school maps and replaced by the name 'Arab Palestine')," Gabriel Courier reported, noting that King Hussein of Jordan and his second cousin King Faisal II of Iraq had agreed to merge economically, militarily, and diplomatically into an Arab Federation to protect themselves from Egypt and Syria. In coming months, Courier included reports on Lebanon's request to the United Nations to protect it from Nasser's United Arab Republic and also on the Israeli-Jordanian frictions.[46]

What is important to note about the attitudes of Gabriel Courier and Daniel A. Poling of the popular evangelical monthly *Christian Herald* is that there is every indication that their support of the Jewish state did not stop at the borders of Israel. It transcended Christian Zionism to be a genuine respect for Jewish people. As one reads through hundreds of their columns and comments, one gets the impression that they wanted every reader of their magazine to respect the Jewish people as well. Under the column "Good Man!" (November 1944), for example, Gabriel Courier related the story of Isaac Gilman, the beloved member of Temple Emanu-El in New York City and former resident of Fitzdale, Vermont. This Jewish man's life was a testimony to every Christian in Courier's estimation (and, in the meantime, broke several stereotypes about Jews in the telling). Courier's column stated:

Fifty years ago, the people of the town of Fitzdale, Vermont, saw a little Russian Jewish boy named Isaac Gilman peddling newspapers in the streets. At 19 years of age, he started that apprenticeship in journalism, and at 43 he became sole owner of the town's leading weekly. His business grew as Fitzdale's population grew, and as the years sped past, local respect and admiration for Isaac Gilman also grew—grew to the point where the town's name was changed from Fitzdale to Gilman. For Mr. Gilman, rich now, was beginning to make his influence felt in all directions. Wages in local mills went up; those mills never knew a strike. Mill-owner Gilman kept them running right through the Depression, called all his fellow workers by their first names, paid their medical and hospital bills; he would have cornered every vote in town (there would have been 1100 votes) had he run for governor.

One thing about his community bothered Isaac Gilman: it had no churches. So he built a Methodist Church for the Methodists, and it cost him $28,000. He built St. Theresa's for the Catholics; cost, $15,000. Last week Isaac Gilman died; he was 77, and well-beloved among his fellow-members of Temple Emanu-El, in New York City. A faithful Jew all the days of his life, he was honored in death as in life by men of many faiths. When Father William H. Cassidy of St. Theresa's, up in Gilman, heard that his friend Isaac was dead, he said sadly, "There was a good man!"[47]

Dr. Daniel A. Poling, the editor of *Christian Herald*, also took every opportunity to give his Christian readers a better feeling toward Jews and Judaism. To one reader who wrote in 1944, "I have heard many statements made concerning the low juvenile delinquency rate among Jews. What are the facts?" Dr. Poling responded:

I would not know all the facts nor all the reasons, but I do know that there is a strength of home training and child culture in the Jewish home not found generally in other homes. I have just received a statement from Judge Ellwood F. Melson, (a distinguished Methodist layman) of the Wilmington, Delaware, juvenile court. He tells me that since April 1, 1943, more than 1500 cases of juvenile delinquency have come before him. Of these, not one, not one has been a Jewish boy or girl. Let our Christian majority consider that![48]

Years later, Poling related the postwar statistics regarding religious instruction for a child. "A Jewish child receives 335 hours of religious training each year," he wrote: "a Roman Catholic child, 200 hours; and children of Protestant groups receive less than thirty hours a year."[49]

To the reader who was concerned that a church Sunday-school teacher had told her class that "statistics show the Jews control the wealth of the country and of the world," Dan Poling replied:

> The statement that the Jews control the wealth of the country and the world is part of the infamous anti-Semitic propaganda that first swept Europe and that repeatedly infiltrates our own life. It is utterly untrue. Those who make it, consciously or unwittingly, serve the cause of the enemies of freedom. It is un-American and un-Christian propaganda.[50]

For many years, Dr. Daniel A. Poling published the evangelical platform of the *Christian Herald* under his name and title as editor in chief in a box at the bottom of the editorial page. "OUR PLAT-FORM" declared: "Christian Herald is a family magazine for all denominations, dedicated to this platform: To advance the cause of Evangelical Christianity; to serve the needy at home and abroad; to achieve temperance through education; to champion religious, social and economic tolerance; to make Church unity a reality; to labor for a just and lasting peace; to work with all who seek a Christlike world."

### G. Douglas Young and Samuel Scheiner

When considering the attitudes of fundamentalist-evangelicals and Jews toward one another, a number of questions come to the fore. In spite of the apparent Zionism of the fundamentalist-evangelical, do the worldviews and attitudes toward religious belief within each community prohibit constructive interaction between these Christians and Jews? Is it possible for Jews and fundamentalists to develop sensitivity toward one another and cultivate an educated understanding that would overcome deep chasms of caricature and stereotype? Can fundamentalist-evangelicals and Jews become friends? Should, as some have suggested, traditional Jews only interact with fundamentalist-evangelicals, while liberal Jews interact only with liberal Christians? Is evangelism the major obstacle in Jewish-Christian relations today? Is the Christian evangelistic enterprise the major cause of anti-Semitism? Ironically, these questions permeated the postwar encounter between Sam Scheiner and G. Douglas Young.

The executive director of the Jewish Human Relations Council in Minneapolis, Minnesota, Sam Scheiner met Doug Young when Young was appointed dean of the seminary and professor of Old Testament at Northwestern Schools. After his graduation from Wheaton College, young evangelist Billy Graham had been the president of these schools prior to Dr. Young's arrival. As we have seen in previous chapters, the founder of Northwestern Schools, William Bell Riley, was a fundamentalist who was widely perceived within the Jewish community to be an anti-Semite. Needless to say, Scheiner and Young had two strikes against their eventual friendship when they first met in 1954. They progressively overcame their preconceptions, however, and developed a deep and abiding friendship.

Doug Young's early experiences prepared him for his later, intensive involvement in Christian-Jewish relations. The child of Nova Scotian Christian (Presbyterian) missionaries to Korea, Young later remembered that he had been "raised without any negative attitudes toward Jews whatsoever" in his fundamentalist-evangelical family. He could not recall "having heard anything negative about Jews, their religion, their politics, their going back to the land, or anything like that at all."[51] On the contrary, he remembered vividly an incident where his father excitedly called his attention to an article in the press reporting that the Jews were going back to Palestine. Magazines and newspapers arrived two months late in Ham Heung, Korea (now located in North Korea), but any mention of Jewish return to the Promised Land or to the "desert blossoming as a rose" in Palestine was pointed out to the children by their father. This fundamentalist-evangelical missionary family appeared to lack all animosity toward Jews.

When Young was in Acadia University, he came into contact with the only Jew in his class, Nathan, from St. John, New Brunswick. "Nate" and Doug "hit it off very well," and there was no feeling that "he is different." But contacts with Jewish people were infrequent. While studying for the ministry, he acquired a love for archaeology, history, and Hebrew. Young worked intensively in these fields with a professor at Westminster Theological Seminary in Philadelphia in the mid-1930s. This fundamentalist-evangelical professor, Dr. Alan MacRae, became involved in a debate with other professors at the conservative seminary over what the Bible taught about the future. Many of the professors held to the Reformed (Calvinist) theological position of amillennialism, a belief that there was no future for the Jewish people and that the church had taken over all the covenant promises. With the support of Doug Young and twenty-three other students, MacRae founded a new seminary, Faith Theological Seminary, which held to the premillennialist position. They preserved a sense of prophetic teaching that more closely related to the pro-Jewish beliefs of Douglas Young's missionary father. Current evangelical leaders Kenneth Kantzer and Vernon Grounds were part of the early student body at Faith Theological Seminary as well.

As we have seen, the chief theological controversy of the 1920s and 1930s, however, was the fundamentalist-modernist controversy. It was to affect Doug Young when he returned to Canada. The liberal Protestant leadership of the Presbyterian Church in Canada had had its fill of conservative evangelicals. When Doug Young applied for ordination in his father's church, the ordination committee spent nearly two and one-half hours debating how they could deny ordination to the son of one of their devoted missionaries. Stalling their decision, the committee recessed. Only two years later would Young find out that his application had been turned down.

Doug Young took a small storefront pastorate in North Philadelphia from 1938 to 1942. Because it was in a heavily Catholic neighborhood, he had little contact with Philadelphia's Jewish community. He continued to be drawn into the study of the Hebrew Bible when, in 1942, he was appointed principal of Kingston Academy in Nova Scotia. For the next two years he was required to teach Hebrew and Old Testament. By hindsight, Doug Young felt that ''what was developing all along was deeper integration into the Old Testament through teaching it." Two years later, Faith Theological Seminary in Wilmington, Delaware, called him back to be an instructor. Immediately, he became more intensely involved in ancient Near East studies and in the Hebrew language.

This led Doug Young into the Ph.D. program at Dropsie College in Philadelphia, to which he commuted daily. He decided to work with Cyrus Gordon, receiving his degree in Assyriology and Egyptology. Dropsie was a Jewish institution, and Young was quickly pulled into discussions with Jews on what had happened overseas during the war. "My embarrassment began to bother me as everyone asked, 'What were you doing during the war?,' 'Did you know what was going on?,' 'Didn't you know what was going on?'" Young realized, to his horror, that in Nova Scotia he had totally "missed" the Holocaust. "I've racked my brain many times [about the period, Hitler, any news about Jews]," Doug Young related, "and it is a total blank . . . just a total blank. You wonder how it is possible [to have missed the Holocaust] . . . There is no excuse."

In 1948 he went to New York, but again had little contact with the Jewish community. He preached occasionally at the request of the American Board of Missions to the Jews. Yet he was "forced" to teach the biblical books of Isaiah, Daniel, and Revelation by the president of the National Bible Institute (his teaching position in New York from 1948 to 1953). This institute would become Shelton College under the leadership of the controversial, ultraconservative, anticommunist fighter, Carl McIntire. For decades McIntire would speak to millions on the radio, railing against ecumenical and liberal movements, and criticizing fundamentalist-evangelicals who would not agree with all his positions. Doug Young learned two things from this experience: (1) he was drawn toward the promises to the Jewish people in the prophetic passages of the books he was forced to teach, and (2) he could not bear a situation where contention and strife ruled (as they had under chairman of the board Carl McIntire). With this background, he took the position at Northwestern Schools in Minneapolis.

Requested to take a weekly radio program over KTIS in Minneapolis, Dr. Young began interviewing Jewish leaders from America and Israel who were passing through the Twin Cities. In 1954, on the three-hundredth anniversary of the first Jews' coming to the shores of America, Young suggested to the new fundamentalist-evangelical president of Northwestern Schools that they have a large program celebrating the occasion and invite the Jewish community. A good crowd attended, hearing seminary students sing Israel's national anthem, "Hatikvah," and a conciliatory address by President Richard Elvee.

Sitting far back in the audience was Samuel Scheiner, the executive director of the Minneapolis Jewish Human Relations Council. Unprepared by his experiences for such a positive "fundamentalist" program, Sam had only come because he could not believe that a joint evangelical-Jewish program was being conducted at the institution founded by William Bell Riley. Suitably impressed but still wary, Sam and Doug began a tentative conversation. Soon, they had developed a real personal friendship. Together, they began learning about each other's religious tradition, and the barriers began falling down between their respective constituencies.

In a joint venture, Samuel Scheiner and G. Douglas Young developed a seminar on human relations at Northwestern Schools to acquaint students with minorities in the Twin Cities, including blacks and Jews. Involving a black clergyman, the program was so successful and helpful that President Elvee approved it as a requirement for all freshmen students. Also, a yearly kosher dinner was instituted at the Talmud Torah in Minneapolis, where an equal number of Jews and Christians enjoyed fellowship together. Dr. Young addressed the group as a Christian. The Jewish speaker was the famed W. Gunther Plaut, who was a rabbi in Minneapolis (1948–61) before his tenure in Toronto.

In the spring of 1979, Dr. G. Douglas Young reminisced about these relationships and the impact they made on his life:

> I had very few contacts [among the Jewish people]. . . . Then we moved to Minneapolis in 1953 . . . and there is where everything

began to take place. I met Sam Scheiner, now deceased . . . and Sam and a black clergyman and I started a human relations required course for all freshmen. And that was a great experience. I began to feel how a black feels. I began to feel how a Jew felt. When Sam would go home at night and say, "Excuse me, Doug, I'm in a hurry; I gotta go." I said, "What's the hurry?" He said, "My little girl is five years old, she's starting school this fall, and I've got to get her used to how to react when they start calling her a 'shee-nie,' a 'kike,' and so forth and so on." And so you see this Minneap-olis experience was a major turning point in my whole experience . . . and Sam was just such a nice person. We had a lot of good times together.

It was Samuel Scheiner who, together with Senator Hubert Hum-phrey, arranged for Doug Young to take his first trip to Israel in 1956. This led to an invitation from Yigael Yadin to join in an exca-vation the next summer.

G. Douglas Young's interest in prophecy was a powerful force in leading him to see Israel for himself, and he traveled there just after the Sinai Campaign of 1956. Totally enamored with what the Israelis had accomplished in spite of a worldwide campaign to annihilate the Jewish state, Dr. Young became a credible wit-ness with the Christian community in the United States and Can-ada to stem anti-Israel rhetoric. His fundamentalist-evangelical belief system and support for the Jewish people was important in an age of conservative Christian pastors and laypeople on the grass-roots level.

A 1958 survey conducted by Opinion Research Corporation showed that most Protestant clergymen in the United States considered themselves to be either "conservative" (39%), "fun-damentalist" (35%), or "neo-orthodox" (12%). Fundamentalist-evangelical Billy Graham had risen to prominence throughout the world, and fundamentalist-evangelical periodicals kept their readers informed on events taking place in the Middle East. For example, up to its merger with *Eternity* magazine in January 1958, *Our Hope* continued to run news about Israel and the Middle East in its "Current Events in the Light of the Bible" section. Through these news reports, Christians were made aware that the Israeli-Arab situation was even more complex and increasingly volatile as the weeks and months sped by. With the blessing of the Israeli government, Dr. G. Douglas Young founded the Institute of Holy Land Studies in Jerusalem in 1958, an educational institution where evangelical students and faculty (mainly from Christian colleges in the U.S.) could learn more about Israel.

In 1963 Doug Young and his wife, Georgina, moved to Israel. For almost two decades, he was actively involved in the everyday life of the Jerusalem community and in communicating a positive view of the Holy Land to Christians in America. Freda Keet, a prominent newscaster on Israel Radio's English-language program, summed up Young's accomplishments in 1978:

> For Israelis, and especially for Jerusalemites, Douglas Young represents the voice of Christianity, that part of Christianity which understands what Israel is, and what Israel does, and what Israel is trying to achieve. . . . For us he has truly been a builder of bridges. . . . And for this we owe him our eternal gratitude.[52]

During the Six-Day War in 1967, Dr. Young drove an ambulance through the bombed areas of Jerusalem, and his wife provided for as many neighbors and visiting soldiers as she could feed and shelter at the Institute of Holy Land Studies. The people of Israel reciprocated his love by appointing him to civic and municipal commissions, awarding him the Israel Pilgrim Medal and, later, Jerusalem's highest honor, the title "Worthy of Jerusalem." Young's "A Dispatch from Jerusalem" brought news from Israel to the American Christian community; and his organization, Bridges for Peace, an organization dedicated to interaction between Christians and Jews on the grass-roots level, still exists today. When he died of a heart attack while working with his new Bridges for Peace challenge in May 1980, he was mourned by the Jerusalem community and buried on the crest of Mount Zion after a stirring memorial service in the St. Andrew's Scottish church. Eight years later his wife, Georgina, was buried by his side. She had elected to stay in Israel—her (and his) "home."[53]

Dr. Young's love for Israel and for the Jewish people was evident in his numerous letters printed in the *Jerusalem Post* and in such articles as "The Feel for Jerusalem," which he wrote in 1969:

As a Christian I testify to the joys, privileges and freedom in Israel for me, my institution, my students and faculty, the other Christian people, churches and institutions in this dynamically exciting part of the world, where at long last once again, Jewish energy, creativity, and "follow-through" are making the wastes a garden, the desert to blossom, the crooked places straight.

I thrill to see so many of my own faith coming on pilgrimage to see and experience for themselves all that is taking place here. I could only wish that the pilgrim could find the way to stay a little longer to let the real Israel seep into his consciousness and expel the hate, the myths, the false reporting that seems to be getting through the mass media in other parts of the world, both in the secular and in the church press.[54]

In a published letter to the *Jerusalem Post* (October 31, 1975) entitled "Christian Zionists," Doug Young began: "I have been accused of being a Zionist—a Christian Zionist—by some of my coreligionists in Israel and in the administered areas. I would like to take this means of thanking them for this compliment."

To Dr. G. Douglas Young, Israel held the key to the welfare of the Jewish community as well as to that of the world. He felt that Bible-believing Christians had a stake in the continued existence of Israel and in Israel's meaning for all humankind. Refusing to buckle to world opinion, including that of eminent Christian church leaders, he continued to support the Jewish state and the Jewish people—the people of his Lord. Doug Young summed up his beliefs well in the conclusion of a speech at Cornell University in 1975:

And so this Christian's view of Israel is that in antiquity Israel has blessed this Christian by giving through the seed of Abraham one who loved me and redeemed me. But in addition to that, this Christian's view of Israel includes . . . the very deep-seated conviction that there are yet many cultural, educational and other ways in which these people can continue to bless the world as they did through the ancient Judeo-Christian tradition. . . . The Judeo part was not superseded by the Church. The Judeo part is alive and vital today, and we have a great deal in common.[55]

Samuel Scheiner would have been proud.

## APPROACHMENT

As national director for interreligious affairs of the American Jewish Committee, Rabbi Marc H. Tanenbaum was heavily involved in Jewish-Christian dialogue during the 1950s, especially among mainline Protestant churches and among Catholics. But already in the 1960s, Rabbi Tanenbaum had his eye on the evangelical community. He invited evangelical leader Russell T. Hitt, editor of *Eternity* magazine (which had absorbed Gaebelein's *Our Hope* magazine), to dinner in an effort to set up conversations between Jewish and Protestant leaders. In a correspondence dated November 25, 1963, Hitt was hopeful that the dialogue could begin and gave Tanenbaum a year's subscription to *Eternity* magazine.[56]

Contact continued, and the consultation between Jewish and Protestant leaders (mainly evangelicals) occurred in New York. On March 9, 1966, Russell Hitt thanked Rabbi Tanenbaum, stating: "I am sure reaction to our consultation was good on both sides. I personally was greatly helped although I am awed by Jewish scholarship."[57] At that time, actions were being taken to make connections with the Southern Baptist Convention, to have Rabbi Tanenbaum address the Evangelical Press Association at its annual convention, to organize another consultation, to hold local consultations in major cities, and to publish a special issue of *Eternity* devoted to Jews and evangelicals. They determined to write G. Douglas Young in Israel for an article.

This seminal issue of *Eternity* appeared in August 1967, during the crucial aftermath of the Six-Day War. In the editorial section of the magazine, under the heading of "Dialogue, Love and Witness," the editors of *Eternity* publicized for the first time their consultation of more than a year before with the American Jewish Committee. Emphasizing that a dozen evangelical leaders and a dozen Jewish leaders had been invited, the editorial commented:

> This unpublicized meeting was arranged to enable leaders of the two groups to share points of view and to understand one another better. Too often, we have long felt, does the Jewish community get the wrong idea of conservative Protestants. The only conservative Protestants that many Jews are aware of are anti-Semitic bigots.

One of the thorniest of problems in Jewish-evangelical relations is the problem of witnessing, or as Jews see it, the attempt to prose-lytize.

G. Douglas Young, author of "Lessons We Can Learn from Juda-ism," (page 22), shared with us the following quotation from a newsletter of the World Council of Churches' Committee on Juda-ism and the Jewish people. It is especially appropriate in discus-sion of the problem of witnessing.[58]

The six-paragraph statement from the World Council of Churches was printed in its entirety. The statement began by insisting that the "Christian brings to the dialogue with the Jew the hope that all men would acknowledge Jesus Christ as God, Savior, and Lord," but that "the Christian can do no more than witness. Con-version is a function of the Holy Spirit."

The editors of *Eternity* magazine attempted to present the pos-itive values of Jewish tradition to their readers in the interest of understanding, dialogue, and friendship. In huge letters on the cover, this issue was entitled: AND YOUR NEIGHBOR AS YOURSELF. The message was clear. If there was any doubt among readers, G. Douglas Young set the pace when he began his "Lessons We Can Learn from Judaism" with the words:

The very existence of modern Israel loudly proclaims that Judaism has survived two millennia in diaspora and thus it can neither be decadent nor of no interest to God. The existence of the new State of Israel should force every Christian back to St. Paul's mystery, back behind the sins of the early Church so long and so sadly per-petuated, back to the Bible itself where it is clear that God has a con-tinuing interest in Jews. There should come an awakening all over the world, a desire to see the values that God enabled Jews to per-petuate, the values He intends to keep on using.[59]

Insisting that "God still has something to teach us through the Jewish people," Dr. Young listed the qualities he had learned over the past decade from his interaction with Jews. These in-cluded caring for their own; religious values; living, working, and growing together in spite of differences in background and belief ("a message surely which God would have Christendom heed today," Young noted); a proper church-state relationship

and attitude; survival even under intense persecution; faithfulness; "loving our neighbors as ourselves"; helping others without
a conversion motive; the value of and need for education. Doug
Young maintained that "these values are biblical values" and that
"God is speaking to us today through them [the Jewish people]."

The article following Dr. Young's was "Our Subtle Anti-Semitism," by fundamentalist-evangelical Belden Menkus. Mr. Menkus pulled no punches when he told *Eternity*'s readers: "We
must honestly admit that far too many of us do not know the Jews
in our community as real persons." Strongly objecting to "the
high pressure salesmanship" that had dominated much of evangelical-Jewish relations to date, Menkus emphasized that "we are
'saved to tell others' – not called to convert them." Declaring that
the Holocaust is the evangelical's problem ("Jews died like ani-
mals because we did not care"), he sternly critized the "bigots
among us," both those who are in the open and those who are
polite and silent. "What is needed is a correction of perspective,"
Menkus stated. "Our Jewish friend or neighbor is not an imper-
sonal prospect. He or she is a vitally important person of worth
as an individual and of value in the context of his understanding
of his relation to God."[60]

The response to *Eternity*'s issue on evangelical-Jewish relations
was positive. One of the letters expressing appreciation was from
a famed evangelical educator, Dr. Frank E. Gaebelein. This youngest son of Arno C. Gaebelein still held to his fundamentalist-evangelical belief in the Bible and prophetic premillennial eschatology.
Living in Arlington, Virginia, Frank Gaebelein would forge a
solid friendship with Reform rabbi Joshua O. Haberman of the
prestigious Washington Hebrew Congregation in Washington,
D.C. Gaebelein would even lead a weekly Bible study at the congregation in the early 1980s, and Rabbi Haberman learned much
about the diversity of the Protestant movement (and the possibilities for dialogue with fundamentalist-evangelicals). In turn,
Frank Gaebelein would learn the sensitivity of the Jewish community to "Jewish" missions, "Hebrew" Christians, and "Messianic" Jews, and while not compromising his Christian witness,
cherished his friendship with the Jewish community.[61]

Rabbi Marc Tanenbaum and Russell Hitt's initial approachment would lead to national conferences between evangelicals and Jews in the 1970s and 1980s sponsored jointly by the American Jewish Committee and evangelical organizations. Fundamentalist-evangelicals and their premillennial view of the future would be key participants in these dialogues, and anti-Semitism would be discussed and repudiated. There was little doubt that 1967 found fundamentalist-evangelicals, their churches, and their organizations ablaze with eschatological fervor. The Six-Day War and Israel's victory had thrilled these Christian Zionists. The October 1967 issue of *Moody Monthly* featured a picture of the Wailing Wall on its front cover. This special issue on the Bible and prophecy was captioned: "The Amazing Rise of Israel." *Eternity* magazine's July cover had put it a bit more boldly a few months earlier with the headline: "Israel Is Here to Stay."

## DEBATE OVER ZIONISM

The featured article of *Eternity*'s July issue had been written a few months before the Six-Day War, but the editors explained that they found it "more timely than ever" in light of the "current violence." The article was by Raymond Cox and was entitled "Eyewitness: Israel." With the Arabs stockpiling armaments for an attack on Israel, Cox noted that "many wonder whether Israel can survive a united assault." He himself, however, believed that "this is more a prophetic question than a military question. . . . Israel will survive."[62]

Yet in the following issue, which was the issue on Christian-Jewish relationships discussed earlier in this section, Dr. William Sanford LaSor in "Have the 'Times of the Gentiles' Been Fulfilled?" questioned the prophetic scheme. A professor of Old Testament at the evangelical, missionary-oriented Fuller Theological Seminary in California, LaSor wrote that he was "not willing to concede that the State of Israel is to be identified as the Israel described in Holy Scripture," but he was "willing to admit that it seems quite likely that the regathering of the Jews to Palestine, the establishment of the State of Israel, and the almost incredible military successes of Israeli armies against what appeared to be overwhelming odds, are somehow to be related to God's promises." Admitting that "it is probably true that most Evangelical Christians are more sympathetic to the Israeli than to the Arab side of the continuing conflict," LaSor implored evangelicals not to forget "that a large number of Arabs are Christians" and "a vast number of Arabs are now wanderers on the face of the earth, and they, too, deserve a place to call home." Interacting and living in the Arab world as well as widely traveling the Middle East, LaSor explained to his evangelical community that "only one who has lived in the Arab world and has talked intimately with Arabs knows how deep are the wounds caused by the formation of the State of Israel." He related the extreme difficulty of using the "Old Testament" with its passages on "Zion" in a Christian service in the Arab world. "If you ask an Arab Christian what solution he has to offer to the present problem," LaSor noted with all candor, "you will get the same answer you get from a non-Christian Arab: Israel must be effaced, every Jew must be driven into the sea."[63]

Believing that Christians must devote themselves in larger numbers to missionary work among the Arabs, LaSor asserted:

It is my deep conviction that the Christian must be positively impartial in the present situation. By "positively impartial" I do not mean "neutral" or passive. We must have a positive approach and an impartial one. It is possible that the best peace-keeping force in the Middle East would be the State of Israel. The Arabs were unwilling and United Nations unable to keep the peace. If the nations involved would accept such a solution, and if Israel would rise to the occasion, this would result in tremendous benefit and blessing to Lebanon, to Jordan, even to Syria, and perhaps to Egypt. But such a decision is not ours to make.

He concluded by asking Christians to urge Arabs and Jews to "apply the principles of justice and mercy" and to urge "our own governments to act with the same principles, to remember that the safeguarding of human rights for both Arab and Jew is more

important than Jewish votes or Arab oil. . . . And, above all,"
LaSor ended, "to equip the nations of the Middle East with
instruments of peace instead of weapons of war."[64]

In *Moody Monthly's* October 1967 issue, President John F. Walvoord of dispensationalist Dallas Theological Seminary in Texas
was not as equivocal as LaSor. In "The Amazing Rise of Israel!"
Dr. Walvoord, a fundamentalist-evangelical, began his article
with these words:

> The recent dramatic victory of Israel over the Arab states electrified
> the entire world. The stunning impact of this war of only sixty
> hours on the political scene was not only a great setback for Rus-
> sian designs in the Middle East, but crushed Arab hopes of destroy-
> ing Israel. For students of the Bible the most significant aspect of
> the war lies in the fact that Israel, after almost 1900 years of exclu-
> sion from the capital city, Jerusalem, now possesses this holy place
> so rich in both history and prophecy.

Emphasizing that Israel had been attacked by Arab nations at its
inception, Walvoord related to his readers the great gains Israel
had made in reclamation of the land and progress in agriculture.[65]

Other articles on Israel as the depository of divine revelation
and Israel in prophecy followed in this *Moody Monthly* issue. In
"Why Did God Choose Israel?" Richard Wolff underscored his
belief that the Bible stresses that God's choice is the Jews and that
their covenant with God has not been nullified. Hal Lindsey, the
director of Campus Crusade for Christ at UCLA, who would
become a millionaire in the 1970s through his book *The Late Great
Planet Earth*, followed with the article "The Pieces Fall Together."
"For centuries Christians have pondered over the prophetic puz-
zle," the caption to his article asserts. "Now in this mid-twenti-
eth century they are seeing the pieces fall together." Lindsey
claimed in the 1980s that he was told by an Israeli that David Ben-
Gurion had *The Late Great Planet Earth* on the reading stand next
to his bed on the day he died in 1973.[66]

In spite of this fundamentalist-evangelical prophetic Zionism,
evangelicals were being bombarded from within and without by
anti-Israel rhetoric. Just like their liberal Christian colleagues,
evangelicals also could succumb easily to anti-Zionist rhetoric. It

took a strong dedication to the premillennial eschatology and prophetic interpretation of historic fundamentalist-evangelicalism to combat the incessant attacks on Israel from missionaries, academics, and antiprophetic clergypersons. In general, anti-Zionist evangelicals were swayed by many of the same arguments liberal Protestants had believed and used. In fact, the scholar who researches the attitudes of American Christians toward Israel is impressed by one striking reality: the same anti-Israel arguments are used decade after decade. Apart from new events and actions taken by Israel, the Arabs, the United Nations, and so on, reported in the media, the basic arguments in 1993 remain the arguments from 1967 (or even 1948!).[67] A good example of this can be found in the 1967 issues of *Christianity Today* magazine. Founded in 1956 with the support of evangelist Billy Graham and Sun Oil magnate J. Howard Pew to be an evangelical counterpart to *The Christian Century*, *Christianity Today* was going through an intense upheaval a decade later. Editor Carl F. H. Henry had embarked on gaining nationwide Christian respect for the magazine, which included more "balance" on the Middle East than Billy Graham had. During 1967, *Christianity Today* received most of its information on the Arab-Israeli situation from its correspondent, Dwight L. Baker, chairman of the Baptist Convention in Israel. The importance of the missionary movement (both liberal and conservative) and its anti-Israel rhetoric must not be underestimated, even in affecting the opinions and stance of evangelicals. Pastor Baker was concerned that the position of missionaries in Arab nations was becoming "more dangerous" because of the Israeli victory in the Six-Day War. The views of Harry W. Genet, assistant executive secretary of the Arabic Literature Mission in Beirut, were also included in the July 7, 1967, issue, as Genet related that the "slender missionary force in the Arab world" was experiencing "the hardening Arab attitude towards foreigners."[68]

The next issue of *Christianity Today* (July 21, 1967) contained a diatribe against Israel by James L. Kelso, a former Moderator of the United Presbyterian Church, which was so incendiary the editors labeled his remarks an "interpretive appraisal of the

Arab-Jewish conflict." Next to missionaries, Christian archaeologists (with notable exceptions, such as William Foxwell Albright) had been progenitors of the anti-Israel rhetoric, in both liberal and conservative circles. Kelso also worked with Arabs for forty-one years and had participated in a number of archaeological expeditions in Palestine. He began:

How did Israel respect church property in the fighting a few weeks ago? They shot up the Episcopal cathedral just as they had done in 1948. They smashed down the Episcopal school for boys so their tanks could get through to Arab Jerusalem. The Israelis wrecked and looted the YMCA upon which the Arab refugees had bestowed so much loving handcraft. They wrecked the big Lutheran hospital, even though this hospital was used by the United Nations. The hospital had just added a new children's center and a new research department. The Lutheran center for cripples also suffered. At Ramallah, a Christian city near Jerusalem, the Episcopal girl's school was shot up, and some of the girls were killed.

So significant was this third Jewish war against Arabs that one of the finest missionaries of the Near East called it "perhaps the most serious setback that Christendom has had since the fall of Constantinople in 1453."[69]

Dr. Kelso then went on to blame the Balfour Declaration as "the major cause of the three wars whereby the Jews have stolen so much of Palestine from the Arabs who have owned it for centuries." He expounded upon the Arab refugee problem, the mothers and babies that he saw suffering in the camps "in the bitterly cold winter of 1949–50," interjecting that "Mary and Christ received better treatment at Bethlehem than the Arab refugees did that winter."

Missionary and archaeologist came together in a duet of anti-Israel rhetoric in his following statements. The United Presbyterian pastor exclaimed:

A missionary who has worked constantly with Arab refugees through the long years since Israel became a state in 1948 speaks of them as "human sacrifices to political ruthlessness." It is the most accurate statement I know. Sometimes it was actual human sacrifice, as when 250 Arab men, women, and children were massacred at Deir Yassin. I know that massacre well, for one boy who was fortunate enough to escape that massacre later worked for me on my excavations. There is deep horror about all this history in the fact that great numbers of Christians in the United States applaud Israel's crimes against Arab Christians and Arab Muslims. How can a Christian applaud the murder of a brother Christian by Zionist Jews? The Arab church is as truly the body of Christ as the American church.[70]

This last question, unfortunately, came to dominate both liberal and conservative Christian propaganda against Israel. Either in blatant denouncement or a secretive whisper, the anti-Israel argument took the form of anti-Jewish thought, that is: how can you support the non-Christian Jew against your Arab Christian brother? More often than not, this was blatant anti-Semitism.

Some *Christianity Today* readers wrote that they were appalled at Dr. Kelso's interpretation. The shock and dismay in their edited letters published in the evangelical magazine is clearly evident. Elias Newman of Minneapolis wrote of his "chagrin and disillusionment," while Rev. Harold P. Warren of First Baptist Church in Oak Park, Michigan, emphasized that many of Kelso's statements "are contrary to the facts as I know them." Warren's church was attempting to build a good rapport with the Jewish community in its area, and he believed that "it is time for Christians to speak out on behalf of Israel and be identified as friends of Israel." In the September 29, 1967, issue, Benad Avital, first secretary of the embassy of Israel in Washington, D.C., responded to Kelso's "emotional charges."[71]

The following year, Dr. William Culbertson, president of the Moody Bible Institute in Chicago, wrote an article for *Christianity Today* that supported the Jewish restoration to the land of Israel by citing relevant biblical passages. A fundamentalist-evangelical, Dr. Culbertson was a former bishop of the New York and Philadelphia synod of the Reformed Episcopal Church. He mentioned the Arab refugee problem at the end of his article, declaring that his "heart" went out to them. But, in view of the fact that "Israel has incorporated hundreds of thousands of refugees" into its economic and social life, he asked: "Why have not Arab countries (especially those rich in oil) done more to help their own?'' Continuing with their special brand of ''balance,'' the editors of *Christianity Today* published a fifteen-point response by none other than James Kelso. Again, Kelso began by reminding *Christianity Today*'s readers that ''10 per cent of the Arab population is Christian.''[72]

*Christianity Today* had been striving since its inception not only to capture the entire spectrum of evangelicals, but also to affect Christians from all walks and of all theologies. Even the letters to the editor concerning Israel underscore the great diversity in the conservative Christian community regarding Israel. Among liberal Protestants, Dr. Henry P. Van Dusen, past president of Union Theological Seminary, deplored the Israeli victory in the Six-Day War as ''the most violent, ruthless (and successful!) aggression since Hitler's blitzkrieg across Western Europe.'' He argued that ''every square mile of Arab homeland appropriated by Israel, every additional Arab subjugated or driven into exile, will merely exacerbate the smoldering resolve for revenge.'' *The Christian Century* called for joint administration by Israeli and Jordanian forces, while the National Council of Churches favored an ''international presence'' to guarantee the holy sites and security.[73]

Reinhold Niebuhr, however, graced the pages of *Christianity and Crisis* (June 26, 1967) with his famous article ''David and Goliath.'' ''No simile better fits the war between Israel and the Arabs in lands of biblical memory,'' the respected theologian began, ''than the legend of David and Goliath. David, of course, is little Israel, numbering less than 2.5 million souls. . . . Goliath, of course, is the Arab world under Egyptian President Abdel Nasser's leadership, numbering a population of 20 to 40 million. This Goliath never accepted Israel's existence as a nation or granted it the right of survival.'' He approved of Jerusalem's administrative reunification, asserting that ''Judaism presupposes inextricable ties with the land of Israel and the city of David, without which Judaism cannot be truly herself.'' At times in the past, Reinhold Niebuhr had added editorial notes to correct false impressions made by others toward Israel in the journal. This time, the chairman of the editorial board, John C. Bennett, tried to counter

Niebuhr's pro-Zionism with his "Further Thoughts on the Middle East."[74] After Reinhold Niebuhr's death, the liberal Protestant magazine he founded was often unjustly critical of Israel, so much so that his widow, Ursula Niebuhr, requested *Christianity and Crisis* to withdraw her husband's name from the journal as "Founding Editor."

Liberal theologian Reinhold Niebuhr and world-renowned fundamentalist-evangelical evangelist Billy Graham seemed at least to agree on one thing: the miracle of modern Israel. In the fall of 1970, the Billy Graham Crusade film *His Land*, was released. It was widely shown in churches and on campuses, as well as on television and in synagogues (in a special Jewish edition without the evangelistic message at the end). In a standard premillennial prophetic format, the film narration begins: "Do you know what impresses me about Israel? It is that, well, God really has a long memory. I mean He just doesn't forget!" Biblical verses from Jeremiah, Isaiah, Zephaniah, Ezekiel, 1 Kings, and other books abound in the film to emphasize that "Yes, God promised it [to restore the Jewish people] and He is delivering on that promise in His Land," as Cliff Barrows of the Billy Graham Evangelistic Association puts it in his narration.[75]

The film relates how the Holy Land was a land stripped and starved by centuries of neglect, a rocky wilderness that awaited its people. The Jewish people, after centuries of trial and struggle, had turned the desolation into thousands of acres of fertile farmland, reclaimed the desert, and made Hebrew into a living language again. "Perhaps you have to be a Jew to really understand that work is a form of prayer when you are home," Barrows explains. The theme song reverberates:

> And as it blooms before our eyes,
> just like an Eden paradise,
> The world will understand,
> this is His Land.

In Jerusalem, "the stones seem to radiate it; it just seems to hang in the air." Jerusalem "has always been a promise of God's covenant that He is not through with man." Ultimately the blessing of the whole world will come through Israel, and everyone will understand that it is God who has done it. The theme song goes on:

> This is the Israel,
>     promised of old,
> This is the miracle happening now,
> by sages and prophets foretold.

With premillennial fundamentalist-evangelicalism permeating the greater evangelical movement and with one of the greatest evangelists of the era promoting the prophetic scenario, the majority of evangelicals had fond and positive feelings toward Israel. And yet, there was a growing segment within evangelicalism that could never share this vision and was quite antagonistic to it.

Such a view was formulated in a series of articles critical of the film by Bert De Vries, an evangelical professor of history at Calvin College, and a graduate of both Calvin Theological Seminary and Brandeis University. Writing in *The Reformed Journal* in 1971, De Vries disagreed emphatically with the film's premillennial eschatology and pro-Jewish stance. He insisted that the film's argument, "drawing a wrong conclusion from faulty premises, is false." He asserted:

> Nevertheless, it has served to convince many Americans that the founding of Israel on Arab land was justified. And the failure of "His Land" to see through this argument turns what is supposed to be a celebration of God's faithfulness into a piece of pro-Israel political propaganda.[76]

Reacting to Barrows's exclamation in the film, "There are just no words for that first glimpse of the Sea of Galilee!" De Vries notes dryly: "These sentimental and emotional speeches bolster the mistaken claim, based on out-of-context quotations of Old Testament references to the land, that modern Palestine is God's own special piece of real estate."[77]

By 1975, Professor De Vries had evolved a position that some other Calvinist amillennial evangelicals, who agreed with him earlier, could no longer tolerate. De Vries declared:

Why then the vehement Israeli reaction to Arafat and the PLO? The PLO call for an end to the state of Israel does not mean the destruction of its Jews, but the destruction of its Jewishness. Arafat proposes to replace Israel with a state in which Muslim, Jew, and Christian will live together in a "democratic, humanistic, and progressive society."[78]

A colleague of his at Calvin College, Ronald Wells, took issue with De Vries in an article in *The Reformed Journal*. Although he and De Vries agreed on many points of amillennial covenant theology and on Palestinians in general, Wells maintained that "Israel is a legitimate state and it has a right to existence."[79] While both men have problems seeing Israel as a "special place" and both believed the Christian church had taken over all the biblical promises to the Jewish people, Professor Wells's position is typical of those evangelicals who believe that some of their colleagues who oppose the premillennial view of the fundamentalist-evangelical can go too far in their hostility toward Israel. In other words, anti-Zionism could become anti-Semitism.

The paradox of evangelical anti-Zionism saddened Dr. G. Douglas Young. In an interview in 1979 he expressed deep concern for the ugly tentacles of anti-Israel teaching that was spreading through evangelical liberal arts colleges and seminaries by an ever-growing, hostile force of academicians. "It is tragic that some American evangelicals can't see it," he grieved. Then he remarked about some of his skeptical liberal Protestant coreligionists in Israel: "I don't see how one can live here for so long and not see the miracle of Israel."[80]

As moderate fundamentalist-evangelicals drew together with other conservative evangelicals, they were literally absorbed into the broad sea of evangelicalism. They called themselves "evangelicals" and drew more species of evangelicalism into their National Association of Evangelicals (an organization that at inception had a high percentage of premillennialists). To some, the premillennial view of the future and prophetic teaching was "too controversial" in their newfound evangelical ecumenism. They felt there were many evangelical causes to battle for other than Israel—other than the Jews. Among a growing number of evangelical academicians, missionaries, pastors and denominational leaders, dividing "God's people," God's "tools" to evangelize and teach the world, was too high a price to pay for Christian Zionism—at least the vocal kind. Christian Zionism was viewed as undisciplined, narrow, and unbalanced. Newfound liberal friends often frowned upon it.

But the word "fundamentalism" would reappear in a new form to haunt and challenge the premillennialist who was progressively being smothered by a theologically divergent ecumenical evangelicalism. It would reappear in the guise of "political fundamentalism"—a media term that added little light on the coalitions that were forming among basically conservative Christians and a few of their Jewish ideological supporters. In surveys and sociological studies, the prophetically minded historic fundamentalist-evangelical became only one segment (albeit a strong and important segment) of a larger evangelical voting contingent, while writers and newscasters categorized any right wing conservative as a "political fundamentalist." Confusion reigned in the midst of "approachment." Political, social, and theological dangers to both fundamentalist-evangelicals and the Jewish community were rampant on the American scene.[81]

# Conclusion

## TOWARD UNDERSTANDING

Throughout our study we have proved that current fundamental-ist-evangelical and Jewish attitudes toward each other trace back to at least the nineteenth century. Modern conflicts and concerns (such as Bible reading and prayer in public schools, "fanaticism," missionary activity and revivalism, church and state issues) are deeply embedded in the history of the past century. Most of these conflicts transcend the fundamentalist-evangelical movement, being rooted in the history of the Christian church. Evangelism is one such conflict, dating back to the early tenet of the Christian faith that the gospel message should be preached throughout the world.

In regard to anti-Semitism, the major focus of this study, it has been found that fundamentalist-evangelicals were generally more positive toward the Jewish community than were other Christians. Their premillennial view of the future and their regard for the place of Jewish peoplehood in the plan of God contradicted the triumphalism of much of Christendom. They disdained a liberal universalism that would annihilate Jewish peoplehood, and even their hope for Jewish belief in Jesus was predicated on the belief that a very Jewish Jesus would return to convince his people that he was their messiah. Fundamentalist-evangelical philo-Semitism also grew from their belief that the Jewish people continued to be in covenant with God and actually were the "chosen people," the "apple" of God's eye. This literal interpretation of the Bible, coupled with their view of God's plan, drove them to the conclusion that those who hurt "God's Jewish people" would be severely punished by God. God's very Word said so. To the fundamentalist-evangelical, anti-Semitism was anti-God.

Furthermore, it has been found that in the face of inexcusable ignorance about the Jewish people and in the face of lapses of sensitivity toward Jews, fundamentalist-evangelicals could, through interaction with Jews and education (from their own Bible!), become compassionate and loving neighbors. Our study of individuals such as Dr. G. Douglas Young have confirmed how great a gulf can be transcended between fundamentalist and Jew. Dr. Young never lost his evangelical zeal and prophetic faith, but he did become an understanding, respectful friend—a friend of the Jewish people worldwide and an unequivocal supporter of the State of Israel. Since, historically, communication between Jews and fundamentalist-evangelicals has been strained (rarely occurring until the "approachment" of the past twenty-five years), it is encouraging that such encounters are at least possible. We have found, however, that stereotype, prejudice, caricature, and misunderstanding abound throughout the history of fundamentalist-evangelical–Jewish relationships. Any change will be slow—much patience will be required.

In spite of scholarly perceptions to the contrary, the prophetically minded fundamentalist-evangelical has been (and currently is) a firm supporter of the Jewish state. And, in an age when anti-Zionism is often indistinguishable from anti-Semitism, this fact is crucial to our study. As we have seen throughout this study, the fundamentalist-evangelical was long a supporter of Jewish restoration to the Holy Land and, to this day, has received ridicule and scorn from other Christians for pro-Israel views. In spite of numerous liberal and conservative Christian cries to the contrary, this Christian Zionism has been a positive factor in combating any anti-Semitism within the fundamentalist-evangelical community. From sermons to lectures, from prophecy conferences to official leadership gatherings, fundamentalist-evangelicals have gone on record consistently to oppose anti-Semitism. And, just as consistently, scholars in the field of Christian-Jewish relations (including Jewish scholars) have often misinterpreted fundamentalist-evangelical theology and eschatology. Misperceptions abound. Nearly any abnormal analysis is readily believed. In our study, we have tried to present fundamentalist-evangelical views in context, spending a bit more time than usual on their own words and their own explanations of premillennial eschatology and "normative" biblical literalism. In addition, we have been made aware that fundamentalist-evangelicals are an independent breed, steeped in individualism and biblical piety at the grass-roots level—unafraid to argue with their religious leaders when they believe God's Word has been misinterpreted.

Our study of the primary materials of this complex movement has, nonetheless, uncovered flaws and dangers. Conspiracy theories built upon their very own theology could blossom into negative views of "radical Jews" and "secularist Jewish plots." The Antichrist was believed by some to be an apostate Jew. While their worst rhetoric sounds not unlike that of some Orthodox Jews toward their secularist brethren, it must be remembered that fundamentalist-evangelical missionary statesman Oswald J. Smith was convinced by German Christians that Nazi Germany was experiencing Christian "revival" and spiritual growth under Adolf Hitler. A man who wrote books on the Antichrist could not recognize evil when he came face to face with it. And his friend Gerald Winrod became an outright anti-Semite (one of the few dispensationalists in history to do so). Clearly evident in all of this, nevertheless, is the fact that the movement on the whole recognized at an early date that the Holocaust was impending and believed that six million Jews had been murdered at a time when more liberal Christians were labeling this Jewish "atrocity propaganda." The fundamentalist-evangelical watched for signs of the Great Tribulation and a corrupt world government.

As in the larger evangelical community as well as in Christendom itself, the biggest theological hurdle for the fundamentalist-evangelical is in stereotypes and caricatures of Pharisees and in misunderstanding of the Jewish faith. Although fundamentalist-evangelical theology clearly indicates that all men, women, and children are responsible for the death of Jesus, the Christ-killer theme still permeates sermons, theological training, and Sunday school classes. And yet, fundamentalist-evangelicals at the grass-roots level and in the pastorate seem to crave more accurate information on Jews and Judaism—seem, indeed, to be the first to abhor their old perceptions and trite misconceptions about Jews and Judaism when properly educated.

Our study has concluded as well that fundamentalist-evangelicals will not give up Christian "witness" and that their local pastors will continue to urge them to toss out the "life preserver" of the gospel to a "dying world, a world without Christ." And yet, it is false to assume that a fundamentalist-evangelical lurks around each corner, ready to pounce on a Jewish soul. It is also false to assume that sensitivity to Jewish feelings on this matter cannot be engendered on the grass-roots level as well as among some of the leadership. Missionary enterprises aimed solely at Jews (such as Jews for Jesus) are already complaining that dialogue between evangelicals and Jews is hurting their business.

While some in Christian-Jewish dialogue would assume that having a Christian give up the belief in the resurrection of Jesus would "solve" the problem of anti-Semitism, and others have proposed that denying that "Jesus is God" would solve the problem, the vast majority of Christians in this world hold to these beliefs. Conquering anti-Semitism in the individual without making that individual sacrifice his or her religious beliefs is a key to conquering anti-Semitism in a much larger religious grouping. Ironically, since prejudice and misunderstanding are learned behaviors, a human being can be changed by interaction and reasoning with those toward whom the prejudice is directed (with bolstering from those who have overcome the prejudice). The fundamentalist-evangelical can be approached from both the biblical imperative and the personal interaction aspects. Many crave Jewish friendships and, if not given the choice to be a Christian, would choose to be a Jew.

Which brings us to the crux of a tentative beginning at altering the path toward anti-Semitism, prejudice, scapegoating, and stereotyping that seems to lure the fundamentalist-evangelical at every turn. Building bridges of mutual respect, interaction, and dialogue between fundamentalist-evangelicals and Jews in this modern era is extremely important and necessary at the local and state levels. Fundamentalist-evangelical Sunday school curricula can be open to electives and seminars on Jews and Judaism. Rap-with-the-rabbi sessions and meet-your-Jewish-neighbor sessions would be helpful, as would be Christians willing to go into the churches and marketplaces with the message. For the Jewish community, such interaction is unwanted and, frankly, despised. For most Jews, any Christian would be taken as "friend" before the fundamentalist-evangelical. Part of this is Jewish bias against evangelicals, but it also relates to the large degree of vulnerability that such an interaction might impose on a Jewish person. Uncomfortable situations are bound to arise. Sometimes, there seems to be absolutely nothing in common—sometimes, Christians seem to lack sensitivity, compassion, and a decent common sense. Ignorance abounds. The unknown threatens.

Nevertheless, the ancient cry "Whom shall I send, and who will go for us?" is applicable in this situation. Because fundamentalist-evangelicalism permeates a growing global Evangelicalism, because the fastest-growing churches (even among mainline Protestant denominations) are related to this movement, and because the Third World is experiencing a phenomenal growth of "born again" religion, ignoring or ridiculing the fundamentalist-evangelical movement is not acceptable. In regard to Israel, a critical time has arisen when an embattled fundamentalist-evangelical Zionism, with a struggling philo-Semitism, is groping for answers. Misinformation abounds. In the United States a "crisis of identity" is facing American fundamentalist-evangelicals as they search for self-definition in the midst of their prophetic orientation, premillennial eschatology, and biblical literalism. A new generation of fundamentalist-evangelical young people need quality Jewish education in the midst of a society that encumbers its youth with millstones of bigotry and prejudice. The Jewish community itself understands well such an identity crisis.

In the meantime, Jews and fundamentalists—Jews and evangelicals—live in two different worlds most of the time. Perhaps the walls that have separated the respective communities need to be maintained. But it appears that gates—openings in those walls—must be inserted for interaction, understanding, and peace. Someone . . . some persons . . . some groups . . . need to respond: "Here am I. Send me!"

# Notes

## Introduction

1. See Franklin H. Littell, *American Protestantism and Antisemitism* (Jerusalem: Study Circle on World Jewry, 1985), 27, for his earlier analysis on provisional friendship, and page 40 for his later statement.

2. On the Moral Majority, note, for example, Peter Steinfels, "Moral Majority to Be Dissolved," *The New York Times*, June 12, 1989. Falwell's picture appeared on the front page of this issue. An editorial in the next issue asked: "Whose Morals? What Majority?" June 13, 1989.

3. Note Ari L. Goldman, "Baptists Elect a Conservative to Lead Denomination Again," *The New York Times*, June 14, 1989. Compare Ari L. Goldman, "Southern Baptists Meeting at Las Vegas After Revivals on Strip," *The New York Times*, June 13, 1989; and E. J. Dionne, Jr., "Politics: Taking Measure of the Impact that Moral Majority Has Left on America's Landscape," *The New York Times*, June 15, 1989.

4. Although Lutheranism in particular and Protestantism in general would at times be woefully intolerant toward those of other religious persuasions (even within their own religious community!), the principles of individual conscience and freedom of religious belief have been cherished by individual Protestants and groups throughout history. In fact, most Protestant groups have at one time or another appealed to these "God-given rights."

5. For a complete discussion of these movements within Protestantism, see David A. Rausch and Carl Hermann Voss, *Protestantism: Its Modern Meaning* (Philadelphia: Fortress Press, 1987).

6. The nine articles (1846) advocated by the Evangelical Alliance read as follows:

1. The Divine Inspiration, Authority, and Sufficiency of the Holy Scriptures.

2. The right and duty of private judgment in the interpretation of the Holy Scriptures.

3. The Unity of the Godhead, and the Trinity of Persons therein.

4. The utter depravity of human nature in consequence of the Fall.

5. The Incarnation of the Son of God, His work of Atonement for sinners of mankind, and His Mediatorial intercession and reign.

6. The Justification of the Sinner by Faith alone.

7. The work of the Holy Spirit in the Conversion and Sanctification of the Sinner.

8. The Immortality of the Soul, the Resurrection of the Body, the Judgment of the World by our Lord Jesus Christ, with eternal blessedness of the righteous and the eternal punishment of the wicked.

9. The Divine Institution of the Christian Ministry, and the obligation and perpetuity of the ordinances of Baptism and the Lord's Supper.

7. "New York News," *The Israelite* 21 (October 24, 1873): 5.

8. Isaac Mayer Wise, "What the Religion of America Will Be," *The Israelite* 21 (November 14, 1873): 4. Compare "The Free Religious Association: Opening of the Session—Addresses by Oliver Johnson, Charles Storrs, the Rev. O. B. Frothingham," *The Israelite* 21 (October 31, 1873): 4–5; "Free Religion (concluded)," *The Israelite* 21 (November 7, 1873): 4–5.

9. Isaac Mayer Wise, "The Religion of Future Generations: Part II," *The Israelite* 21 (December 5, 1873): 4. Compare Part I of this article in the November 28, 1873 issue, page 4.

10. Isaac Mayer Wise, "The Religion of Future Generations: Part I," *The Israelite* 21 (November 28, 1873): 4.

11. "Profane Passah Thoughts," *The Israelite* 22 (March 27, 1874): 4.

12. "An Outrage on the Jews," *The Israelite* 21 (November 7, 1873): 6.

13. Note Rev. C. W. Lane letter to the Congregation Children of Israel, Athens, Georgia, February 19, 1873, published in *The Israelite* 21 (July 18, 1873): 5.

## Chapter 1. The Rise of Fundamentalist-Evangelicalism

1. "Washington Letter," *The American Israelite* 25 (November 19, 1875): 5.

2. "Philadelphia Letter," *The American Israelite* 25 (December 10, 1875): 5.

3. "That Brooklyn, N.Y., Harangue," *The American Israelite* 25 (December 10, 1875): 2. In a later article in the same issue, "Great Excitement in the Drew Methodist Church at Port Jervis," Mrs. Lowrie, a converted actress, conducted a series of revivals, "attended by thousands of people, and over five hundred converts have been made," including a number of wealthy and prominent residents. The Peabody Literary Association was quoted as saying: "However, the self-elected apostles are not going to have it all their own way, and remarks objecting to the whole parade can be found in the Philadelphia papers, as the following extracts show: 'One objection, and a serious one, to Mr. Moody's preaching, is that he constantly cheapens the idea of God. His conception of the Deity appears to be essentially anthropomorphic. . . . This is a crude and primitive conception of the Almighty, and far behind the average enlightened Christian

idea. . . . ' A common objection to the revival among old-fashioned church members is, that it is advertised like a circus or theater. . . . But enough of this revival business for the present. The people of America will be ashamed of it before long, as they are of Know-Nothingism or any other spasmodic excitement'' (p.6). The article on Mrs. Lowrie did portray her as ''an eloquent speaker and an excellent vocalist.'' However, her discourses ''are full of extravagant and impassioned passages, interspersed with weird hymns and wild gestures.''

4. Note ''Mr. Moody's Passion Sermon,'' *The American Israelite* 26 (January 6, 1876): 4, and ''The Fruits of Revival,'' 6. Compare ''Christianity Disgraced: Moody's Latest and Most Villainous Performances'' (reprinted from the Philadelphia *Sunday Dispatch*), *The American Israelite* 26 (January 21, 1876): 5–6, and editorial blurb in ''Local and Domestic'' column at end; ''Moody and Sankey,'' *The American Israelite* 26 (January 28, 1876): 5; and ''Where Is Moody?'' *The American Israelite* 26 (February 4, 1876): 6. The last excerpt cajoled: ''Where is Moody? We would like to have a talk with him about that Crucifixion business, but can not find him anywhere. Did he go to heaven in advance of the Millenium? Any of our friends knowing his whereabouts are requested to report. We want to get the great Milleniumizer's autograph.'' Although Millennium is misspelled, the excerpt does show the Jewish community's familiarity with the term.

5. ''A Hoax and a Disclaimer,'' *The American Israelite* 26 (March 25, 1876): 7. Rabbi Isaac Mayer Wise did not believe this conversation took place, prefacing it with the words: ''A private conversation of Rev. Mr. Moody with a young Israelite is making the round in the papers, which, of course, never took place. It is one of the pious frauds sent forth by Mr. Moody in order to hitch on to it the following disclaimer . . .''

6. Charges of anti-Semitism against Dwight L. Moody did not pass. Note ''New York Letter, April 2, 1876,'' in *The American Israelite* 26 (April 7, 1876): 6, where Moody is reported ''in his Christian auction job'' to have ''lied again, and as lustily as ever.'' The New York correspondent reported that Moody ''has said again the Jews crucified Jesus, and asked pathetically, 'where are the Jews now?''' ''. . . He did repeatedly lie, abused the Jew, and upbraided the whole race.'' The Jewish correspondent noted, however, that Moody appeared to ''lie from ignorance,'' offering that he believed that Moody never ''ever read a book, except mission reports, tracts, and revival sermons.''

7. Dwight L. Moody, *To All People: Comprising Sermons, Bible Readings, Temperance Addresses, and Prayer-Meeting Talks* (Boston: Globe Publishing Company, 1877), 354.

8. Note his section on ''Clipping the Bible'' in D. L. Moody, *Pleasure and Profit in Bible Study* (Chicago: Bible Institute Colportage Association,

1895), 21–22. Moody uses the very same phrases about "figuring away" and "doubting" in this section that are quoted in the previous paragraph.

9. William R. Moody, *The Life of Dwight L. Moody* (New York: Fleming H. Revell, 1900), 392. Also note pages 386–91 for some of his experiences. Compare Richard K. Curtis, *They Called Him Mister Moody* (Garden City, N.Y.: Doubleday & Co., 1962), 229–30 for the insistence of Mr. and Mrs. Peter Mackinnon that Moody take a break and accompany them to Palestine.

10. L. Gaussen, *Theopneustia,* trans. David Scott, rev. ed. (Chicago: Bible Institute Colportage Association, n.d.), 351.

11. Charles Hodge, *Systematic Theology,* I (London: Thomas Nelson and Sons, 1875), 151.

12. While the terms "postmillennial" and "premillennial" may at first appear to be confusing, they concisely sum up two very different views of the future among evangelical Protestants. The prevalent postmillennialism of the 1800s believed that Jesus Christ would return only after the church "christianized" the world through evangelism and conversion. The fundamentalist-evangelical's premillennialism insisted that only the return of Jesus Christ before the millennium would convince the world that he was the Messiah and change the structures of world government. To the fundamentalist-evangelical, things would probably get worse until Jesus returned.

13. Nathaniel West, ed., *Premillennial Essays of the Prophetic Conference Held in the Church of the Holy Trinity, New York City* (New York: Fleming H. Revell, 1879), 11–14. Also compare Ernest R. Sandeen, *The Roots of Fundamentalism: British and American Millenarianism, 1800–1930* (Chicago: University of Chicago Press, 1970), 145–47 for the background of the British conference.

14. William P. Mackay, "The Return of Christ and Foreign Missions," in *Premillennial Essays,* 456. It must be noted that speakers at this conference constantly referred to European scholars who supported premillennial interpretation. See S. H. Kellogg, "Christ's Coming—Is it Pre-Millennial?" 74.

15. William P. Mackay, "The Three Days' Feast with David's Son," in *Premillennial Essays,* 475, 478. Although Mackay's topics did not deal specifically with the restoration of the Jewish people to Palestine, he brought his premillennial belief into view in these parenthetical remarks.

16. Charles K. Imbrie, "The Regeneration," in *Premillennial Essays,* 164. Rev. Imbrie ended: "Let us pray for Israel, that the Lord may pardon his iniquities and bring in the day of his deliverance" (p. 173). Imbrie defined "The Regeneration" as "'Restitution of All Things' Foretold in the Scripture" (p. 108).

17. Note Mackay, "The Return of Christ and Foreign Missions," 459. His premillennial view is quite a contrast to the postmillennial view that insisted on total conversion of the world (rather than just proclaiming the message to all). He stated: "We have failed simply because we have been aiming at universal conversion and not at universal evangelization. We have been trying to convert patches and not evangelize the whole. This is not the age of universal conversion; that is the age that is to come [when Jesus Christ returns and rules the earth]."

18. William R. Nicholson, "The Gathering of Israel," in *Premillennial Essays*, 223. On page 224 he noted of Ezekiel 37:15–22, "Reference to literal Israel could not be more demonstrated, nor the fact of their restoration to Palestine more positively stated."

19. Ibid. See especially pages 228, 231, and 235. Nicholson also noted that the spiritual blessings of millennial Israel will be the same as Christians have now, i.e., they will be sons of God, united to Christ, and with hope of resurrection (p. 236).

20. Ibid., 237.

21. Ibid., 239. Previous quote on England may be found on page 234.

22. Nathaniel West, "History of the Pre-Millennial Doctrine," in *Premillennial Essays*, 315. As others, West insisted that the millennium could come only through the literal return of Jesus Christ. "Thus does premillennialism become a protest," he asserted, "against the doctrine of the unbroken evolution of the Kingdom of God to absolute perfection on earth, apart from the visible and miraculous intervention of Christ. . . . The millennium is the transition-stage in this process of 'the Regeneration,' succeeded by the everlasting state."

23. Nathaniel West, *The Thousand Years in Both Testaments* (New York: Fleming H. Revell, 1889), vi.

24. Note George C. Needham, "Reasons for Holding the Prophetic Conference," in *Prophetic Studies of the International Prophetic Conference, Chicago, November 1886* (Chicago: Fleming H. Revell, 1886), 215. Other reasons he listed were "to emphasize the true principles of Scripture interpretation," "awakening of Christians from slumber," "motives for world-wide evangelism," to call "attention to the doctrine of 'last things' as a bulwark against the skepticism of modern theology," and "nearer fellowship one with another" (pp. 215–16). Dwight L. Moody's note of regret appears on page 41. Other great evangelists, preachers, and theologians from around the world sent their regards, support, and expository letters to the conference in absentia. For example, Rev. Archibald G. Brown of London, England, and Rev. Andrew A. Bonar of Glasgow, Scotland, sent letters of greeting, while Professor Franz Delitzsch of Leipzig, Germany, Canon A. R. Faucett of York, England, Professor F.

Godet of Neufchatel, Switzerland, Professor Volck of the University of Dorpat in Russia, and Professor A. Koch of Bardewisch, Oldenberg, Saxony, sent expository letters.

25. E. F. Stroeter, "Christ's Second Coming Premillennial," in *Prophetic Studies*, 17–18.

26. For above discussion, note Nathaniel West, "Prophecy and Israel," in *Prophetic Studies*, 122–25.

27. Ibid., 127.

28. Ibid., 133.

29. See Henry M. Parsons, "Judgments and Rewards," in *Prophetic Studies*, 81. For earlier quote, note W. J. Erdman, "Fullness of the Gentiles," in *Prophetic Studies*, 56–57.

30. Note *Catholic World* 25 (1877): 367. Ernest Sandeen mentioned in *The Roots of Fundamentalism* that an English reviewer [of premillennial thought] for the *Christian Observor* "seemed very much like Alice in Wonderland – stumbling around in an unfamiliar landscape, rather astounded at what he was finding and often quite cross" at the concept of the restoration of the Jews to Palestine (p. 23). Note page 93 for his synopsis of *The Princeton Review* and *Christian Intelligencer*.

31. "News Items," *The American Israelite* 38 (September 10, 1891): 4.

32. "Notes," *The American Israelite* 38 (November 19, 1891): 6. Compare "News Items," *The American Israelite* 39 (March 10, 1892): 4; and, in the same issue, "Rev. Dr. Mendes Shot," 6, when a vagrant shot and seriously wounded the rabbi. Here Rabbi Mendes is not called a "foreigner," but rather "the well beloved pastor of the Portuguese Congregation Sherith Israel" and "one of the most popular and best known Hebrew rabbis." In contrast to *The American Israelite*'s disdain for Mendes's Zionism, the fundamentalist-evangelical periodical *Our Hope* quoted him and held the rabbi in the highest regard. Cf. "Rabbi Mendes on Zionism," *Our Hope* 4 (September 1897): 98–102.

33. "Wm. E. Blackstone," *The Jewish Era* 47 (December 1937): 30. The U.S. Christian Commission was an organization like the YMCA or the Red Cross. Also compare Cutler B. Whitwell, "The Life Story of W.E.B.– and of 'Jesus Is Coming,'" *The Sunday School Times* (January 11, 1936): 19; and Beth M. Lindberg, *A God-Filled Life: The Story of William E. Blackstone* (Chicago: American Messianic Fellowship, n.d.), 3–5.

34. William E. Blackstone, *Jesus Is Coming* (New York: Fleming H. Revell, 1878.

35. Blackstone also had a role in the founding of Dwight L. Moody's Bible Institute. Note Bernard R. De Remer, *Moody Bible Institute: A Pictorial History* (Chicago: Moody Press, 1960), 25. Cf. Blackstone's letter to President James M. Gray of Moody Bible Institute dated September 24, 1915. When he moved to California to work with the Stewart Fund, he

had close connections with the Bible Institute of Los Angeles. The "Presentation Copy" of *Jesus Is Coming* was the Third Revised Edition (expanded to 252 pages) and was sent to ministers, missionaries, and theological students around the world. It contains laudatory endorsements from James M. Gray of Moody Bible Institute and Reuben A. Torrey, formerly of M.B.I and then Dean of the Bible Institute of Los Angeles.

36. For a Christian's view of this, note Lindberg, *A God-Filled Life*, 7–9. Beth M. Lindberg had access to all the Blackstone files and correspondence.

37. "Echoes from Washington," *The American Israelite* 37 (March 12, 1891): 1. This first report in the Reform periodical was forthright without much commentary. The presentation of the Blackstone Memorial and most of the contents were summarized, but the concluding portion was quoted. The correspondent related that Blackstone explained to the President "that the memorial was the result of a conference of Christians and Jews recently held in Chicago, and called especial attention to the fact that it did not antagonize Russia, but only sought in a peaceable way to give the Jews control of their homes in Palestine." The excerpt listed those in Washington, D.C., who signed the memorial. The Jewish correspondent concluded: "Many members of Congress have expressed to the writer the opinion that the Russian outrages would at no distant day become an international question, and favored calling a convention of representatives of all civilized countries to consider what should be done."

38. See "The Jews and Palestine," *The American Israelite* 37 (April 16, 1891): 4. The other "ridiculous" enterprise was a million-dollar hotel being erected in the Adirondacks by some of the members of the Society for the Prevention of Prejudice because Jews were refused accommodations at other hotels. The promoters had secured 10,000 acres of land, with a large frontage on Lower Saranac Lake in Franklin County.

39. Refer to "Zionism" section of William E. Blackstone's *Jesus Is Coming*, 3rd ed. (New York: Fleming H. Revell, 1908), 236–41. This quotation appears on page 238.

40. Lyman and Milton Stewart financed a number of important fundamentalist-evangelical projects, including *The Fundamentals*. Refer to "The Stewarts as Christian Stewards: The Story of Milton and Lyman Stewart," *Missionary Review of the World* 47 (August 1924): 595–602.

41. Note Whitwell, "The Life Story of W.E.B," 20.

42. For his correspondence, note Lindberg, *A God-Filled Life*, 12. Blackstone continued in his letter: "And now to think of the wonderful activity manifested by the Jews in the Zionist Movement, the cordial sympathy on the part of the officials and people of our country, the

remarkable kindness shown by the British Government, the triumphal entry of a British and Allied Army into Jerusalem itself, welcomed as deliverers by the people, and a Jewish Commission, authorized by the Allied governments already taking charge of the development of Jewish interests in Palestine—all of this does indeed thrill my heart with joy" (pp. 12–13).

43. Lindberg, *A God-Filled Life*, 16. The discussion of the three options mentioned above is found on pages 14–16.

44. Note Kemper Fullerton's statement in "Zionism," *Harvard Theological Review* 10 (October 1917): 334; and compare a similar attitude in *The Christian Century* 13 (December 1917): 718.

45. Shirley Jackson Case, *The Millennial Hope* (Chicago: University of Chicago Press, 1918), 231.

46. Refer to Shirley Jackson Case's "The Premillennial Menace," *Biblical World* 52 (July 1918): 16–23.

47. *Light on Prophecy: A Coordinated, Constructive Teaching Being the Proceedings and Addresses at the Philadelphia Prophetic Conference May 28–30, 1918* (New York: Christian Herald Bible House, 1918), 12.

48. William L. Pettingill, "The Coming Glory," in *Light on Prophecy*, 253. For the first statement, see "Did the Cross of Christ Fulfil All the Promises?" in *Light on Prophecy*, 105–6.

49. P. W. Philpott, "Coming Events Cast Their Shadows Before," in *Light on Prophecy*, 206–7.

50. A. E. Thompson, "The Capture of Jerusalem," in *Light on Prophecy*, 148.

51. Ibid., 144–45.

52. Ibid., 153.

53. James M. Gray, "The Regathering of Israel in Unbelief," in *Light on Prophecy*, 167, 171.

54. William B. Riley, "The Last Days; the Last War and the Last King," in Arno C. Gaebelein, ed., *Christ and Glory: Addresses Delivered at the New York Prophetic Conference Carnegie Hall, November 25–28, 1918* (New York: Publication Office of Our Hope, 1919), 175. Riley prefaced this statement by declaring: "Germany shall not have dominion; England shall not control, America shall not rule; but a nation [Israel] that is now weak, that is now scattered to the ends of the earth, without a land in which to dwell, a city to become her capitol, or even a flag floating for her protection, that nation will be the people of God."

## Chapter 2. Attitudes and Anti-Semitism

1. For example, note Yehuda Bauer, *Antisemitism Today: Myth and Reality* (Jerusalem: Study Circle on World Jewry, 1985). This is a translation of a lecture and discussion held on January 30, 1984, under the auspices of the president of Israel. Compare Robert Wistrich, *Anti-Zionism as an Expression of Antisemitism in Recent Years* (Jerusalem: Study Circle on World Jewry, 1985).

2. A. C. Gaebelein, *Hath God Cast Away His People?* (New York: Gospel Publishing House, 1905), 12–13.

3. Ibid., 13–14.

4. The premillennial eschatology of early fundamentalist-evangelicalism has been propagated throughout the twentieth century by the *Scofield Reference Bible* with its extensive notes and King James Version. Cyrus I. Scofield (1843–1921) was a lawyer who was converted in 1879 and who became a devout disciple of James H. Brookes and dispensationalism. Scofield was highly respected by D. L. Moody, speaking at Moody's Northfield Bible Conference and helping Moody to better understand prophecy. Begun in 1902, the *Scofield Reference Bible* incorporated suggestions from early fundamentalist-evangelical leaders such as James M. Gray and Arno C. Gaebelein. In fact, in a handwritten note concerning the *Scofield Reference Bible,* C. I. Scofield wrote to Gaebelein, ''I sit at your feet when it comes to prophecy.'' The first edition of the Bible was published in 1909 by Oxford University Press. By 1943, it had sold nearly two million copies. The *New Scofield Bible* was published by Oxford in 1967, the work of a new generation of fundamentalist-evangelicals, including Arno Gaebelein's son, Frank E. Gaebelein. Chaired by Dr. E. Schuyler English, all the members of the committee were dispensational premillennialists to varying degrees, but they adopted the rule that their ultimate criterion of editorial judgment must be the truth so far as they could determine it from scripture (not any system of biblical interpretation). Ernest R. Sandeen in *The Roots of Fundamentalism* (1970) assessed the *Scofield Reference Bible* to be ''perhaps the most influential single publication in millenarian and Fundamentalist historiography'' (p. 222).

5. Ibid., 14.

6. William E. Blackstone, *Jesus Is Coming* (Chicago: Fleming H. Revell, 1898), 11. Using Luke 1:31–33, Blackstone accused Christendom of taking literally the prophecy to Mary of Jesus' being conceived in the womb (v.31), but spiritualizing the next two verses, which refer to Jesus' gaining ''the throne of his father David'' and ''reign[ing] over the house of Jacob for ever.''

7. A. C. Tris, ''Is Israel a Nation? Or a Sect?,'' *The Truth* 5 (1879): 80.

8. Ibid., 83.

9. James H. Brookes, *Israel and the Church* (Chicago: Bible Institute Colportage Association, n.d.), 4.

10. James H. Brookes, *I Am Coming: A Setting Forth of Our Lord Jesus Christ as Personal-Private-Premillennial* (London: Pickering & Inglis, n.d.). This book was written in the early 1880s and was reprinted in at least seven editions.

11. A. C. Gaebelein, *The Jewish Question* (New York: Publication Office of Our Hope, 1912), 47.

12 E. F. Stroeter, "The Second Coming of Christ in Relation to Israel," *Addresses on the Second Coming of the Lord Delivered at the Prophetic Conference, Allegheny, Pa. December 3-6, 1895* (Pittsburgh: W. W. Waters, n.d.), 148, 150. Notice Stroeter's use of the term "elder brother" for the orthodox Jew.

13. Ibid., 138-39.

14. "Editorial Notes," *Our Hope* 2 (October 1895): 73. For additional details of this trip, note Arno C. Gaebelein, *Half a Century: The Autobiography of a Servant* (New York: Publication Office of Our Hope, 1930), 55-61.

15. "First Letter of Mr. Gaebelein," *Our Hope* 2 (October 1895): 78.

16. E. F. Stroeter, "Editorial Correspondence," *Our Hope* 4 (December 1897): 183-84. Sixteen of these letters were published in *Our Hope* from December 1897 to June 1899.

17. *Our Hope* reprinted an abridged edition of his letter. Note "Rabbi Mendes on Zionism," 4 (September 1897): 98-102. Rabbi Mendes, whom Rabbi Isaac Mayer Wise had criticized, was hazan of the Congregation Shearith Israel in New York City. A few Reform rabbis, such as Stephen S. Wise, would also work to turn the classical Reform movement back to Judaism's Zionist heritage.

18. Note David A. Rausch, *Zionism Within Early American Fundamentalism, 1878-1918: A Convergence of Two Traditions* (New York: The Edwin Mellen Press, 1979), for numerous examples in Brookes's *The Truth or Testimony for Christ*, *The* [Moody Bible] *Institute Tie*, Gaebelein's *Our Hope*, MBI's *The Christian Workers' Magazine*, Blackstone's *The Jewish Era*, and *Northfield Echoes*.

19. C. I. Scofield, "The Israel of God," *Our Hope* 8 (April 1902): 574. The quote that follows is on page 577.

20. William Martin, "Waiting for the End," *The Atlantic Monthly*, (June 1982), 35-36.

21. Note, for example, William G. Moorehead, the president of the United Presbyterian Theological Seminary in Xenia, Ohio, as he used this illustration in his lecture "The Conversion of Israel and the Conversion of the World," in *Addresses of the International Prophetic Conference Held December 10-15, 1901 in the Clarendon Street Baptist Church, Boston,*

*Mass.* (Boston: Watchword and Truth, n.d.), 38. Compare Arno C. Gaebelein's use of the account in "Fulfilled Prophecy a Potent Argument for the Bible," in *The Fundamentals,* vol. 11 (Chicago: Testimony Publishing Company, n.d.), 60. Published from 1910 to 1915, the twelve small volumes of *The Fundamentals* contained articles by leaders in the earliest phase of the fundamentalist-evangelical movement and were distributed throughout the world. By 1915 over three million copies had been distributed, and the mailing list of Christian workers receiving the volumes had expanded to 100,000.

22. See William E. Blackstone, *Jesus Is Coming* (Chicago: Moody Bible Institute, 1916), 72–93, for an outline of events and an overview. Many other passages of the Bible and proof texts are cited throughout the book. The following discussion of this dispensational fundamentalist-evangelical scenario will be based on this same "Presentation Copy" volume.

23. On the Antichrist, note *Jesus Is Coming,* chap. 12, 107–12.

24. See the chart devised by Nathaniel West in 1879 which compares verses in the book of Daniel with verses in the book of Revelation to prove the premillennial scenario in "History of the Pre-Millennial Doctrine," in *Premillennial Essays,* 320–321.

25. Blackstone's *Jesus Is Coming,* 79. "This accords with the great tribulation described in Matthew 24:21," William Blackstone emphasized, quoting Jesus' words in the verse: "Tribulation, such as was not since the beginning of the world . . . nor ever shall be."

26. For example, note Blackstone's *Jesus Is Coming,* 65–66. William Blackstone continues: "Therefore we have need of patience that we may receive the promise [of the Rapture]. . . . Wait until you have realized a few of the mighty cycles of eternity, and then these eighteen centuries will indeed appear to be 'a very, very little while.' O! let us fix our eyes upon Jesus. Let us watch and wait for the King Eternal."

27. Nineteenth- and twentieth-century Christian missionary enterprises aimed at Jews and the Jewish response to them present a complex and enigmatic history. Refer to David A. Rausch, *Messianic Judaism: Its History, Theology, and Polity* vol. 14 of *Texts and Studies in Religion* (Lewiston, N.Y.: Edwin Mellen Press, 1982). For an individual Jewish convert to Christianity and his subsequent missionary effort for William Blackstone's mission, compare David Rausch's introductory essay (pages ix–xxxi) in his edited volume of Louis Meyer's *Eminent Hebrew Christians of the Nineteenth Century: Brief Biographical Sketches* vol. 17 of *Texts and Studies in Religion* (Lewiston, N.Y.: Edwin Mellen Press, 1983).

28. *Jesus Is Coming,* 84.

29. "A Word of Caution to Our Readers," *Our Hope* 1 (August 1894): 27.

30. William L. Pettingill, "Prophecy–Why Study It?" *God Hath Spoken:*

*Twenty-five Addresses Delivered at the World Conference on Christian Fundamentals, Philadelphia, Pennsylvania, May 25–June 1, 1919* (Philadelphia: Bible Conference Committee, 1919), 355.

## Chapter 3. From War to War

1. Theodore Graebner, *War in the Light of Prophecy — "Was It Foretold?":
A Reply to Modern Chiliasm* (St. Louis: Concordia Publishing House, 1941), 129.

2. Note Theodore Graebner, *Prophecy and the War — Was It Foretold?: An Answer for Questioning Christians*, 2nd ed. (St. Louis, Concordia Publishing House, 1918), 3. This edition is (in the author's words) "a reprint, virtually without change, of the first [eight weeks earlier edition]." Professor Graebner added another paragraph of introduction in the second edition, stating in part: "Meanwhile the chiliastic [premillennial] propaganda has been active in the distribution of pamphlets now mounting, in the aggregate, high into the millions. One of these tracts has had a circulation of 365,000, another has now run through 35 editions [perhaps William Blackstone's *Jesus Is Coming*]. *Prophecy and the War* was written to offset the effects of this delusion so far as the Great War is made the pivotal point of millenarian perversions of Scripture. The author has heard from many readers who have been benefited by the perusal of these chapters, and his prayer is that many others may be strengthened in their hold on saving truth by the argument presented in these pages. February 12, 1918" (p. 3).

3. Ibid., pp. iii–iv.

4. Note Graebner's *War in the Light of Prophecy*, 138–40. Italics are added. Compare pages 50–51 on his criticism of the dispensationalists. Professor Graebner continued about his view of future Armageddon: "This [present time] is but a season of waiting for the return of Christ in glory. Then the enemies, the spiritual (Antichrist) and the carnal (Gog and Magog and his unclean tribe), will be slain in a universal crash not only of empires, but also of visible nature and of the very elements. After that great Armageddon, when all things will be put under the feet of Christ, there will be — eternity" (p. 139). While the papacy as the Antichrist had been conquered by the Protestant Reformation in this amillennial view, the "spirit of the Antichrist" would be conquered once and for all by the return of Jesus Christ.

5. Ibid., 140. Professor Graebner explained earlier: "In the first World War [the Church] was a horrified spectator, but not a participant, except as an agent of mercy; nor was Christian truth at stake" (p. 140).

6. Even the liberal Protestant journal *The Christian Century* used the

term from time to time during World War I. For example, an editorial in the April 4, 1918, issue began: "Religion has suffered because of its lack of fundamental thinking. Christians have laid themselves open to the cultivation of the most outlandish cults" (p. 5). Near the end, this *Christian Century* editorial stated: "The great ministers of the Bible were ripened for their work by years of spiritual preparation. . . . Even our Lord sought out the lonely places at times. When we secure a more spiritual and a more thoroughly prepared ministry, we shall have a more religious church" (p. 6). Such statements prove that in spite of modernism, some University of Chicago Divinity School liberals could be very religious.

7. Shirley Jackson Case seems to have been very fortunate that these fundamentalist-evangelicals did not believe in lawsuits. In "Unprincipled Methods of Post-Millennialists," *Our Hope* 24 (May, 1918): 679–81, Reuben A. Torrey quoted from a slanderous interview Case gave the *Chicago Daily News* (January 21, 1918). Professor Case stated: "Two thousand dollars a week is being spent to spread the doctrine [of premillennialism]. Where the money comes from is unknown, but there is a strong suspicion that it emanates from German sources. In my belief the fund would be a profitable field for government investigation." Using war scare tactics, this postmillennial professor of early church history and New Testament interpretation at the University of Chicago Divinity School tried to label premillennialists as secret subversives to the war effort, paid with "German gold." For a modernist theologian, this tactic conveyed a less than liberal attitude and action.

8. "The Millennial Hallucination," *The Christian Century* 35 (January 31, 1918): 8. This editorial was only one of many preparatory editorials for Willett's series. It praised professor Shirley Jackson Case's recently released diatribe against premillennialists, *The Millennial Hope*, calling the book a "constructive discussion" and a "sane and convincing antidote to this hallucination." Herbert L. Willett was a contributing editor of *The Christian Century* (Charles Clayton Morrison was the editor), and his name appeared after Morrison's on the masthead. Professor Willett's series began a month later than scheduled on March 14, 1918 with the article "Millennial Hope and the War" (pp. 3–5).

9. All the quotes above may be found on pages 216 and 217 of Chester Charlton McCown's *The Promise of His Coming: A Historical Interpretation and Revaluation of the Idea of the Second Advent* (New York: Macmillan Co., 1921). Professor McCown urged his fellow theologians to turn the "other-worldly" premillennial zeal into a "this-worldly" social action "through faith in a living Christ" (p. 232). He called this the social-spiritual view.

10. "The Most Dangerous Infidelity," *Our Hope* 26 (December 1919): 267. Compare other articles in *Our Hope*, including "The Conflict Is On,"

23 (July 1916): 12–13; "Dean Shailer Mathews and the Moody Bible Institute," 24 (August 1917): 108–10; and "Who Is the Menace?" 25 (March 1919): 521–24. Also note "Attacking Moses," 26 (April 1920): 570 on the liberal higher critical approach to the Jewish scriptures.

11. Ibid., 269. Gaebelein wrote that "Canon Driver is just as bad and even worse, and Hastings' Bible Dictionary and Encyclopedia Biblica are compilations of these statements." He also quoted Sir Robert Anderson, who for a time questioned biblical inerrancy, as stating: "It was S. R. Driver's Introduction to the Literature of the Old Testament which first shook my faith in the Bible." Cf. Sir Robert Anderson's twelfth edition of *The Coming Prince: The Marvelous Prophecy of Daniel's Seventy Weeks Concerning the Antichrist* (London: Pickering & Inglis, 1929), where he uses a dispensational premillennial approach and takes the higher critics to task. In this twelfth edition, Anderson's responses to Canon Driver are in the introductions (the fifth and tenth edition introductions are included) and it is apparent that Sir Robert Anderson and Canon Driver had correspondence over these issues. Anderson takes to task many of the respected higher critical scholars of the past throughout his treatise, which was a standard in the fundamentalist-evangelical movement.

12. "The Scopes Trial," *The American Israelite* 72 (July 16, 1925): 4.

13. Is Fanaticism in Last Ditch?" *The American Israelite* 72 (July 2, 1925): 1.

14. Ibid. Bainbridge Colby was a former Secretary of State and associate counsel for the defense in the evolution trial of John T. Scopes. Colby often insisted that the issues involved in the Scopes trial were "grave in character" and embodied "principles at the base of our security of happiness and American citizenship." Dudley Field Malone, along with Dr. John R. Neal and Clarence Darrow, were the other defense attorneys.

15. Ibid. The article ended as it began with a quote from Charles Mackay:

> "But the sunshine aye shall light the sky,
> As round and round we run;
> And the Truth shall ever come uppermost
> And Justice shall be done."

Asmodeus was an evil spirit of Hebrew demonology mentioned in the apocryphal Book of Tobit. Later, he was used as the king of demons.

16. For an analysis of American Protestantism between the world wars, refer to David A. Rausch and Carl Hermann Voss, *Protestantism—Its Modern Meaning* (Philadelphia: Fortress Press, 1987), chaps. 7 and 8.

17. See "The Church Should Act," *The American Israelite* 72 (July 16, 1925): 4.

18. Untitled editorial note on page 4 of the July 30, 1925, issue.

19. "In Re Evolution," *The American Israelite* 72 (July 23, 1925): 4. Actually, fundamentalist-evangelicals were in a constant fight with the Roman Catholics. Compare "The Tragi-Comedy at Dayton," on the same page, where editorial opinion from the *New York World* is viewed by the Jewish editors as "terse" and "succinct" in "characterizing the role of Mr. Bryan in the anti-science movement in Tennessee." The *New York World* editorial stated: "A national politician has started a religious crusade among the ignorant and illiterate which aims to arm fundamentalism with the police power of the State."

20. Rabbi Jerome Mark, "Sidelights on the Evolution Trial," *The American Israelite* 72 (July 30, 1925): 7.

21. I. M. Haldeman, *Why I Preach the Second Coming* (New York: Fleming H. Revell, 1919). Chapter 5 is on pages 94 through 111.

22. Ibid. Note pages 94–99 for his discussion on these points.

23. Ibid. Refer to chap. 6, "Only at the Second Coming of the Christ of God Will a Government of Everlasting Righteousness and Peace Be Established Upon the Earth," 112–132.

24. Ibid., 100–101.

25. Ibid., 100, 102.

26. Ibid., 103–4.

27. Ibid., 106–7.

28. Ibid., 110–11.

29. "The Beast Lifts the Head in Our Land," *Our Hope* 26 (July 1919): 50–51.

30. Jews Facing New Massacres in Russia," *Our Hope* 26 (August 1919): 105–6.

31. "The Increasing Suffering of the Jews," *Our Hope* 26 (February 1920): 481.

32. *Our Hope* 33 (October 1926): 202–3.

33. *Our Hope,* 34 (June 1928): 750.

34. "Adolf Hitler—Will He Be Germany's Dictator?" *Our Hope* 37 (December 1930): 363–64.

35. "The Shadows of Jacob's Trouble," *Our Hope* 39 (August 1932): 102.

36. Arthur I. Brown, M.D., F.R.C.S.E., *Into the Clouds* (Findley, Ohio: Fundamental Truth Publishers, 1938), 78–79.

37. Ibid., 80.

38. H. A. Ironside, *The Lamp of Prophecy or Signs of the Times* (Grand Rapids: Zondervan Publishing House, 1940), 112. The following quotations are from pages 112–13.

39. Ibid., 114.

40. John W. Bradbury, ed., *The Sure Word of Prophecy: Report of the New York Congress on Prophecy Assembled in the Calvary Baptist Church, New York*

*City, November 1–8, 1942* (New York: Fleming H. Revell, 1943), 13. Dr. Bradbury was the editor of the national Baptist weekly, *The Watchman-Examiner*. The pastor of the Calvary Baptist Church of New York was Dr. William Ward Ayer. He delivered the message "What It Has Cost the Church to Neglect the Bible's Prophetic Message." Dr. Bradbury delivered the messages "Have the Gentiles Failed?" and "God's New Testament Ecclesia." Dr. Harry A. Ironside also delivered two messages, "Why the Church Will Not Go Through the Great Tribulation" and "The Seventy Weeks of Daniel Nine." Other speakers included W. H. Rogers, Charles H. Stevens, I. L. Yearby, Lewis Sperry Chafer, L. Sale-Harrison, B. B. Sutcliffe, C. Gordon Brownville, Albert G. Johnson, Howard W. Ferrin, Louis S. Bauman, John F. Walvoord, Henry E. Burke, Joseph Hoffman Cohn, J. Palmer Muntz, Charles Lee Feinberg, W. M. Robertson, W. E. Pietsch, Albert Lindsey, Harris H. Gregg, A. B. Machlin, Dean S. Bedford, R. L. Powell, Adam B. Hunter, and Donald James MacKay. These represented an important sector of fundamentalist-evangelical leadership. The affair was quite spectacular. In the words of John Bradbury: "For eight glorious days great audiences assembled from ten o'clock in the morning to ten o'clock at night, with interim periods only for meals. While much of the attendance was drawn from the Metropolitan Area [of New York City], a great number came from all parts of the United States and Canada. The attenders truly represented a broad cross-section of the Christian Church."

## Chapter 4. Conspiracy Theories, Anti-Semitism, and the Holocaust Years

1. Charles Lee Feinberg, "What Israel Means to God," in John W. Bradbury, ed., *The Sure Word of Prophecy: Report of the New York Congress on Prophecy Assembled in the Calvary Baptist Church, New York City, November 1–8, 1942* (New York: Fleming H. Revell, 1943), 255.

2. Ibid., 251. The Hebrew Christian, Dr. Charles Lee Feinberg, prefaced that "to this day, these specific [biblical] injunctions are kept. [Jewish] Parents are diligent in teaching their children the sacred Scriptures that have been handed down to them. In other ways also Israel has preserved the sacred text, so that today scholars still marvel at the wonderful preservation of the Hebrew text. . . . Throughout the centuries, moreover, Israel has shown to the world the sustaining power of the Scriptures. We do not argue that Israel has always been obedient to the Word, but even during the times of her disobedience, she has manifested how capable the Scriptures are of sustaining" (pp. 250–51).

3. These are John W. Bradbury's words in the Foreword of *The Sure Word of Prophecy,* p. 5.

4. R. A. Torrey, "Passages of Scripture to Use in Dealing with Various Classes of Men," *The Institute Tie* 1 (May 10, 1892): 99. In "Jesus Christ— Notes on lectures delivered by R. A. Torrey," 2 (February 15, 1893): 48–49, Torrey told students that some of the purposes of Christ's second coming related to the Jewish nation, including "coming again to deliver Israel," and "coming again to gather the outcasts of Israel . . . into Jerusalem." He lectured: "Because of the Coming again of Jesus Christ, Israel shall be gathered together from the four corners of the earth and brought into their own land. . . . Israel shall be pardoned from all their sins; a new heart given them. . . . Israel shall be wondrously multiplied, the waste and desolate and ruined cities be rebuilded and the desolate land made like the garden of Eden. Jerusalem shall be called 'the city of truth' and shall be filled with peace, prosperity and gladness. . . . Because of the coming again of Jesus Christ, Israel shall be greatly exalted above the nations."

5. Samuel H. Wilkinson, "The Jewish Question" (New Series), *The Institute Tie* 5 (October 1904): 75–77; and "The Jewish Question: Second Article," 5 (November 1904): 126–27. Because the large majority of these fundamentalist-evangelicals believed in the imminent rapture of true Christian believers (to meet Jesus Christ in the air before the seven-year tribulation period), they did not believe that the Bible dictated the conversion of all Jews to Christianity before they entered and established a nation in Palestine. Wilkinson's eschatology is definitely premillennial and corresponds to that which we have seen was prevalent in the early fundamentalist-evangelical movement.

6. Note "The Jewish Problem and Its Solution: Synopsis of Address by Rev. Louis Meyer" (New Series), *The Institute Tie: The Christian Workers' Magazine* 10 (September 1909): 23–24.

7. "The Capture of Jerusalem," *The Christian Workers' Magazine* 18 (January 1918): 396. This editorial emphasized that "many Jews do not favor Zionism" and therefore all Jews would not return to Palestine. This again was in line with the fundamentalist-evangelical's premillennial eschatology. The editorial also claimed that while these events suggested "the end of this age, and the dawning of a better one for the world," they "would set no dates, but labor on with the seriousness and joy of men who wait for their Lord."

8. Wilbur M. Smith, "With the Bible in the Land of the Book," *Moody Monthly* 39 (October 1938): 69.

9. Ibid. In his footnote, Wilbur M. Smith stated: "Among the passages predicting great suffering for Israel in the last days are Deuteronomy

4:26–31; 28:63–68; Jeremiah 4–9; 10:18–25; 11:1–12:14; Joel 2:1–17; Amos 8:1–11; Micah 3; Zephaniah 2. On the subject of anti-Semitism, one might consult a very exhaustive work published in 1936, *Anti-Semitism Historically and Critically Examined* by H. M. Valentin; an interesting and informative booklet of seventy pages, that has just been issued, *The Time of Jacob's Trouble,* by Louis S. Bauman; and some relevant pages in *The Jews and the Passion for Palestine in the Light of Prophecy,* by Keith L. Brooks."

10. Ibid.

11. Ibid., 69–70. In a footnote on page 69, Smith stated: "'Predictions of Israel's turning to her Redeemer in her great trouble are found in Isaiah 63:17–64:12; Jeremiah 14:7–9; 19–22; 29:12, 13; Lamentations 1:20–22; 2:20–22; 5; Hosea 8:3. There seem to be indications in Zechariah 13:8, 9 of what proportion of those who have returned to Palestine, will be slain during the time of Jacob's great trouble."

12. Note Wilbur M. Smith, "The Bible and Palestine," *Moody Monthly,* 39 (November 1938): 127. With a letter of introduction from Dr. William F. Albright, Dr. Smith met with Dr. Joseph Klausner in Talpiot, a small Jewish village south of Jerusalem. He also visited Protestant missions, one sponsored by the Southern Baptists which worked with Jewish children in Jerusalem. To his delight, the director of the mission, Miss Elsie B. Clor, was a former student at the Moody Bible Institute of Chicago, where Wilbur Smith taught.

13. "Jewish Notes," *Moody Monthly* 40 (May 1940): 494.

14. "It's Suicide or Christ," *Moody Monthly* 40 (May 1940): 491. The article/advertisement was provided by the Million Testaments Campaign, 1505 Race St., Philadelphia, Pa.

15. "Evangelizing the Jews" in Grant Stroh's "Practical and Perplexing Questions," *Moody Monthly* 40 (August 1940): 682. On page 680, a reader asked if Hitler would win the war, and if so, "is he the Antichrist?" Stroh answered that they did not personally believe that Hitler was the Antichrist. "The Antichrist will rise out of the Roman empire," the columnist noted, "but we are inclined to believe that the Antichrist will be a Jew."

16. Joseph Taylor Britan, "Comfort Ye My People," *Moody Monthly* 41 (November 1940): 120. Britan also mentioned that Palestine had been bombed and over 400,000 Jews there "are menaced." He also related that the racist ideology of the Nazis had threatened the very life of the Christian church. "A growing sense of fear possesses the hearts of millions of fine Christian people of Europe," he related, "who have the misfortune to have a small fraction of Jewish blood in their veins."

17. Rev. Jacob Peltz, "The Agony of Israel in War Torn Lands: A Report of the Appalling Sufferings of Jews and Jewish Christians," *Moody Monthly* 41 (November 1940): 145.

18. Note "Editorial Notes," *Moody Monthly* 41 (November 1940): 123–24. In this same issue compare Clarence H. Benson's "Bitter Present Persecution of the Jews" and "The Return of the Jews to Palestine" on pages 147–48; George F. Held, "Meeting the Jew on God's Ground" (pp. 125–26, 166–67); Morris Gordin, "Of Whom Moses in the Law, and the Prophets, Did Write" (pp. 127–29, 182); Rev. E. H. Moseley, "Origin of Israel" (pp. 130–31); E. Adams, "Christ and the Jewish Law" (p. 131); B.A.M. Schapiro, "Without HIM We Can Do Nothing" (pp. 132, 141); Helen Schafer, "The Jews and Israel, Are They the Same?" (pp. 133, 161); Lewis Sperry Chafer, "The Future of the Gentiles" (pp. 134–35, 155–57); and Rev. Paul Stewart, "The Gospel for Such a Time as This" (pp. 133–37).

19. "New Prophets," *Our Hope* 40 (September 1933): 143.

20. Arno Clemens Gaebelein, *The Conflict of the Ages: The Mystery of Lawlessness—Its Origin, Historic Development and Coming Defeat* (New York: Publication Office of Our Hope, 1933), 147.

21. Ibid., pp. 147–48. Gaebelein reminded his readers that according to the prophetic scriptures the Antichrist would not demand worship in a "church," but rather in a Jewish temple in Jerusalem.

22. Ibid., 97–98. For my research on Gaebelein's attitudes and his views on the Protocols and conspiracy theory, refer to David A. Rausch, *Arno C. Gaebelein, 1861–1945* (Lewiston, N.Y.: Edwin Mellen Press, 1983).

23. See "Misrepresenting 'Our Hope,'" *Our Hope* 46 (December 1939): 379–82. The small booklet, *We Hold These Truths,* was published by an organization called the League of American Writers, and it had concluded with "a partial list of anti-Semitic publishers, organizations and individuals in America." Gaebelein noticed that among those responsible for the booklet was Earl Browder, head of the Communist Party in America. While legally able to sue these individuals, Gaebelein chose to let God be his "defender," noting that "such attacks and slanders show how the enemies of the truth of God and the enemies of the Cross of Christ are getting ready for the final Struggle."

24. Billy Graham's statement appears in *Oswald J. Smith, The Peoples Church and Its Founder* (Toronto: The Peoples Press, 1961), ii.

25. Oswald J. Smith, *Antichrist and the Future* (Toronto: Toronto Tabernacle Publishers, 1932), preface. The preface was written in May of 1932, and this book is the fifth in a series of books dealing with the events that are predicted to enter into the end of the present age. In the words of Gerald B. Winrod, *Is the Antichrist at Hand?* and *When Antichrist Reigns* "have had enormous sales" (see pp. 5–6 for Winrod's Foreword).

26. Ibid., 14.

27. Ibid., 17. On page 22, Smith questions: "Christian people, why don't we awaken to these momentous facts? We would not waste our

time then. Look at these moneyed men, these influential men, who are giving their time and money to peace conferences, trying to stop war, usher in the millennium and establish world peace. If they would stop long enough to read their Bibles, they would know perfectly well that their efforts are fruitless and ineffective, and they would get to the business of preaching the Gospel and making Christ known, and leave the establishment of worldwide peace to the Prince of Peace, for He alone can do that, and no one else can possibly undertake what He Himself will do by His own power."

28. Ibid., 23.

29. Ibid., 62.

30. Ibid., 14.

31. "James G. McDonald Calls Upon Jews and Christians to Succor the Stricken," *The American Israelite* 84 (December 2, 1937): 1, 11. The page-1 story began about McDonald: "The Christian who has come to have an almost unique understanding of the quality and quantity of the Jews' present-day heartaches challenged some thousand men and women Sunday evening to enlist in a financial and cultural program so that they might 'rise to the greatness of their own past.' The speaker was James G. McDonald, now of the editorial staff of *The New York Times*. He was founder and for 14 years (1919–1933) national chairman of the Foreign Policy Association. His intimate knowledge of the Jewish situation springs from his 1933–1935 labors as League of Nations high commissioner for German Refugees — a period in which some 60,000 of a total of 80,000 exiles were placed in new homes and $10,000,000 was raised for their rehabilitation."

32. Refer to *Oswald J. Smith, The Peoples Church and Its Founder* (Toronto: The Peoples Press, 1961), 95, for his travels in 1936.

33. Oswald J. Smith, "My Visit to Germany," *The Defender Magazine* 11 (September 1936): 15.

34. Ibid. This would correspond to Rev. Helmut Thielicke's testimony that German Christians continued, even when the worst occurred, to believe that the Führer would do nothing wrong and that he was a good Christian. Note Helmut Thielicke, *Between Heaven and Earth*, trans. and ed. John W. Doberstein (New York: Harper & Row, 1965), pp. 151–52.

35. Ibid. A list of books and tracts by Gerald Winrod were advertised on the same page as Oswald J. Smith's remarks, including such conspiracy titles as *The Jewish Assault on Christianity; The Truth About the Protocols; World Trends Toward Antichrist; Mussolini's Place in Prophecy; Communism and Roosevelt's Brain Trust; Is America Seeing Red?; Liberalism, Socialism and Communism;* and *Jewish-Communism, the International Foe of Christianity.*

36. Ibid., 16. Smith's analysis contended: "And now, what has happened? Well, to begin with, there are today only a little more than one

million still unemployed. That is an achievement in itself. To travel through Germany is to realize that everybody is busy. Families are being placed on the land. Old street cars have been set down here and there in which they live during the summer months. We saw them everywhere. They are most picturesque. Flowers are grown around them. Beautiful gardens, filled with vegetables, are to be seen on every side. The people are contented and happy. I listened, spellbound, as the workers told me of the joy experienced because of work. The crops in Germany are simply wonderful. If nothing happens there will be an abundant harvest. I have not seen such grain for years. The smile of heaven seems to be on the land. Unemployed and relief had almost ruined the morale of the country. Young men and women, because of idleness, became a prey and a menace, but work has changed all that. For now everyone has to work. No young woman can go to the University until she has spent six months taking care of a poor family. She is sent to a home. There she washes and cooks. Only then may she pursue her education. She must know how to keep house, and that from practical experience. With the young men it is the same. For six months they must do manual labor, helping somewhere, either in road construction or on the farm, or reclaiming the land. Thousands of them work in the homes of the poor, scrubbing floors, washing dishes, cooking food, in order that they may know the meaning of toil. Only then are they allowed to enter the University. Thus idleness is a thing of the past. All must work. There is no time for dissipation" (pp. 15–16).

37. Note page 16. Smith related: "I asked my German friends about the recent Nazi 'purging' that had horrified the world. And to my amazement I was told something that never got into our newspapers at all. The reason Hitler suddenly executed one in high authority, was not only because he was found guilty of treason. That in itself would have been sufficient cause in most countries. And, by the way, had he not acted as he did, many thousands would have been slain in the rebellion that had been planned. But the real reason was because he had discovered much to his grief, that his friend was a Sodomite. And that he had degraded many of the young soldiers under his command. When Hitler heard that, he was furious. He could scarcely believe it, and did not at first. But it was proven by witnesses. 'The army must be a safe place,' he said, 'for any mother to send her son.' No wonder the women of Germany almost worship their leader. . . .

"Before Hitler came into power, Germany's asylums were full. Multitudes of imbecile children were being cared for in institutions. These had to be kept by those able to work and pay taxes. One mother had nine such children and each by a different man. A father brought his fifth imbecile child to be taken in. These in turn were becoming parents and

bearing the same kind of children. Thus Germany was fast going insane. Then came the new laws. Sterilization was enforced, and now no
longer can weak-minded, imbecile parents bring such children into the
world. Hence Germany is destined to become a strong and healthy
nation. . . .

"Before the days of Hitler the papers and magazines were filled with
advertisements of preventatives of all kinds. Young people travelling
together read and discussed them freely, both sexes. They were the common topics of conversation on the street cars, in the parks, and everywhere. Now they are gone. Laws have been enacted against their use.
Anyone caught advocating them is severely punished. Before they can
be used even in medical circles or an abortion performed, the verdict of
three doctors must be obtained."

38. Ibid., 17.
39. Ibid. Compare Rev. Helmut Thielicke's description in *Between
Heaven and Earth: Conversations with American Christians,* 152–53, where
he related how a daily diet of Nazi propaganda affected the spirit and
intellect of good, decent, religious citizens of Germany. He remembered: "Good care was taken that one should not see this [massive injus-
tice] happening to others. It either did not appear in the newspapers at
all or in such a way that the readers (or those who listened to the
speeches) were subjected by means of inflammatory accounts to the sug-
gestion that the terrorist measures were simply retaliatory justice. When
day after day for years nothing but fictitious 'documentary' accounts of
Jewish owners of houses of prostitution, mass profiteering, exploita-
tions, wars, and the multiplication of armaments, when the image of the
Jews was obtained almost solely from caricatures and pornographic
political newspapers, it required a very considerable inner substance,
insight, and objectivity to arm oneself against it. Perhaps, then, one can
understand that naive people (and how many such there are all around
us!) would say what I heard said any number of times: 'I know a decent
Jew, for whom I feel sorry, but the others must be horrible!'"

40. Ibid. Rev. Oswald J. Smith quoted a "leading Zionist" as saying:
"Palestine is grateful today for Hitler and the splendid type of German
Jews he has sent. We do not want Jews from southern Europe. We want
Jews from Germany and America. If a Hitler were to arise in America it
would be a God-send to Palestine."

41. Ibid., 18. In his last section on the revival of spirituality in Germany, Rev. Smith wrote: "And now I want to mention the most favorable
sign of all. I refer to the spiritual awakening that is coming to the German people. Rev. M. Billester and I visited the Dom Cathedral in Berlin,
the former Kaiser's church. It is Lutheran, a magnificent edifice. It seats

well over 2000, and every Sunday now it is packed to the doors. In fact,
it is necessary to get there a full half hour ahead of time in order to get
a seat. And the minister preaches the old-fashioned Gospel. He spares
no one. And none interferes with him. He deals openly with sin and salvation. . . . "At the time of the election he called for a prayer meeting, and my Berlin friends attended. Not only was the vast auditorium packed; crowds
on the outside were unable to get in. And it was on a week day and in
the afternoon. But most amazing of all—one of the pastors, without a
prayer book (a thing unknown) breaking out in a prayer of humiliation
and confession, confessed the sins of the nation and called upon God to
be merciful. And the people burst out sobbing, as a mighty tide of intercession swept over the entire audience. 'As long as such preaching and
praying as that continues, Germany is safe,' exclaimed the Christian
leaders who told me the story" (pp. 17–18).

  42. Note, in the same issue that Oswald J. Smith's article appeared,
the article by Gerald B. Winrod, "Spain in Bible Prophecy," pages 9–12.
Of Trotsky's Jewish background and public deception that he is no
longer a conspirator, Winrod wrote in part: "Had newspaper editors
published the truth about him being a Jew, who was sent to Russia from
the United States, financed by a Jewish banking concern in Wall Street,
to set fire to the Czar's government—THEY WOULD HAVE BEEN CHARGED
WITH ANTI-SEMITISM AND ACCUSED OF TRYING TO START A POGROM. Bernard J. Brown, a Jew, says in his book 'From Pharaoh to Hitler': 'Jews
have muzzled the non-Jew press to the extent that American newspapers abstain from pointing out that any person unfavorably referred to
is a Jew.' Two horrible spectres have risen over Europe—JEWISH COMMU-
NISM AND ROMAN FASCISM" (p. 11).

  43. Gerald B. Winrod, D.D., "Christians, Stir Yourselves!" *The
Defender Magazine* 11 (February 1937): 3. Winrod continued about Olgin's
front-page editorial "Time For the Jews to Get Busy" in *Freiheit* (December 10, 1936): "After stating his reason for supporting Roosevelt in the
last election, he said: 'The anti-Semitic issue was not raised in the election campaign directly by any party, except the Communist Party.' There-
upon he devoted a full column to an explanation of how Jews should
proceed in silencing certain publications which are exposing the true
Jewish facts behind Communism and the present program of world revolution. He concluded his vicious attack with the following significant
phrase: 'This is the time for action, not words.'" Winrod told readers
that the next day after this editorial was published, another Jewish newspaper in Los Angeles, California, announced that a campaign was being
"inaugurated to bar from the United States Mail literature tending to

create racial or religious hatred" [Winrod's quote of the exact wording].
Winrod interpreted this as an attempt to deny "Christian Patriots" the
right of dealing with "the cause behind the menace of Communism!"
44. Ibid. In subsequent articles in the same February 1937 issue, an
immigrant from Russia, John Jacob of Chicago, Illinois, wrote an "eyewitness" account of the martyrdom of Russian Christians by "the Jewish
rulers of the nation" who were "trying to wipe out all religious, patriotic
and racial traits which are distinctly Russian. They aim to destroy every
characteristic at variance with their international program. This broad
plan has already meant the extermination of millions of human beings
from all walks of life" (p. 6). In a rhetorical question he asked whether
or not one can "deny that Jewish Atheists rule Russia—and France?"
Quoting from "Jewish author Isaak Bluemchen" in his book *The Right of
the Superior Race* (1935), he concluded his article: "The victory of the Jews
is so complete that the subjugated French people do not show the slightest opposition, but obediently carry out every order issued by Israel.
Every attempt to rebel would be insane, for the fate of France is sealed.
We, the Jews, rule France, and we wish the whole world to understand
this. The superior race rules the inferior race; that is a law of Nature" (p.
8). Rev. John F. Harvey of Sierra Madre, California, followed with a prophetic piece, "Is the Gentile Age Closing?" He wrote that God was not
"through with the Jew" and that Israel is not "cast off forever." But he
contended that "Apostate Jews today, still cherish a deep feeling of ego-
ism that they are superior to other races and think they have the right to
overthrow Gentile governments and take to themselves the rulership of
the world. They are trying to realize this goal through international
Communism. . . . Atheistic, Communistic Jews, who persist in their rebellion against God, and engage in the persecution of Christians, will
perish the same as Atheistic, Gentile Communists, in the awful slaughter
of Armageddon" (p. 9).
	45. Refer to Leo P. Rebuffo, "Gerald B. Winrod: Prophet in Politics,"
chap. 3 in his *The Old Christian Right: The Protestant Far Right from the
Great Depression to the Cold War* (Philadelphia: Temple University Press,
1983), 80–127.
	46. Elmer A. Josephson, *Israel, God's Key to World Redemption* (Hills-
boro, Kansas: Bible Light Publications, 1974), 15–16. Professor David
Flusser of Hebrew University in Jerusalem wrote the Introduction to this
book (pp. 5–13).
	47. Ibid., 16. Josephson continued: "Since the Roman Catholic Church
at that time was the only united voice taking a strong stand against communism, Dr. Winrod suggested that I see the archbishop of the Leavenworth diocese, Father Hoolihan, about securing the Catholic High
School auditorium for the meeting. This attempt also failed. We finally

moved the rally to Atchison, Kansas, twenty-five miles north, which I chairmaned."

48. Refer to *Prophecy* (October 1939): 17–18. Compare "Our Manifesto," *Prophecy* (January 1940): 35–36.

49. See "New Manifesto," *Prophecy* (May 1940): 29. The American Prophetic League bragged that the "number of signers has been increased to 67 and the names represent practically every outstanding Fundamentalist organization in the country."

50. "European Jewish Conditions," *Our Hope* 39 (February 1933), 486.

51. "Hitler Successful in Germany," *Our Hope* 39 (March 1933): 550–51.

52. "King Feisal Is Dead," *Our Hope* 40 (November 1933): 305.

53. Note "The Different Colored Shirts," *Our Hope* 40 (November 1933): 301–2.

54. Refer to the following articles in *Our Hope*: "Significant Political Developments" (April 1934): 606; "Hitlerism Gone to Seed" (August 1934): 98; "The Dreadful Training of the Young for War" (December 1934); 359–60; "Noble German Confessors of the Faith" (January 1935): 432; "Put in Jail for Praying for the Jews" (May 1936): 760; "The New Paganism in Germany" (May 1935): 671–72; "The Unbalanced Aryomaniacs of Germany" (December 1935): 401–2; and "Jewish Notes of Interest and the Latest from Palestine" (June 1936): 838–39.

55. "The Devil Marches On in Germany," *Our Hope* 42 (February 1936): 539.

56. "The Shadow of That Tribulation," *Our Hope* 43 (July 1936): 37–38.

57. "The Lying Blood-Accusation Appears Again," *Our Hope* 43 (October 1936): 261–62.

58. "David Lloyd George on Germany," *Our Hope* 43 (December 1936): 404.

59. "What Will Happen in 1937?" *Our Hope* 43 (January 1937): 477. For the chart and previous quote, refer to "Military Christendom," *Our Hope* 43 (November 1936): 335.

60. "Observations and Experiences," *Our Hope* 44 (April 1938): 676. Compare "Observations and Experiences," 44 (May 1938): 750.

61. "Observations and Experiences," *Our Hope* 44 (January 1938): 461–62.

62. Ibid., 463–65. Gaebelein insisted that "this anti-Christian clique" had and would turn against the Christian church, and therefore "believers everywhere should pray earnestly for our tested brethren and for their continued loyalty to the faith delivered unto the saints" (p. 465). In "The Announcement of the Black Squadron," *Our Hope* 44 (April 1938): 686, Gaebelein detailed the Nazis' new program for the German church, declaring it to be "viciously anti-Semitic and therefore anti-Christian."

63. "The Plight of the Austrian Jews," *Our Hope* 44 (June 1938):
825–26. Compare "The Increasing Anti-Semitism" (April 1938): 687;
"Happenings in Romania," (April 1938): 552; "Anti-Semitism Rising
Higher and Higher" (June 1938): 822–23. In this last article, "Jewish liqui-
dations" in Soviet Russia are scrutinized and the Communist program
in the United States against the "owning class" Jew is mentioned.

64. "Another Modern Haman Speaks," *Our Hope* 45 (November
1938): 332. The following excerpt, on pages 332–33, is entitled "Refugees
Arriving in America."

65. Refer to "The Anti-Semitic Situation in Germany," *Our Hope* 45
(December 1938): 385–86.

66. "A Church Report from Germany," *Our Hope* 45 (March 1939):
605. Compare "New Troubles for Jewry in Eastern Europe," page 604 in
the same issue, and "The Dissection of Czechoslovakia" (December
1938): 386.

67. "Alfred Rosenberg, the German Anti-Christian Leader Speaks
Again," *Our Hope* 45 (April 1939): 689.

68. Note "The Palestine Situation," *Our Hope* 43 (September 1936):
190–91. Compare "The Jewish Population of Palestine," *Our Hope* 43 (February 1937): 552. In "Interesting Palestine Conditions" (May 1937):
764–65, Gaebelein gloried in the fact that friction between two major
Arab families (Husseini and Nashashibi) might destroy the Arab unity
against the Jewish people in Palestine.

69. See "Editorial Notes," *Our Hope* 50 (December 1943): 377. Dr.
English wrote: "We cannot close this lengthy paragraph without calling
attention once more to Amillennialism, which we might rightly term
'unbiblical Postmillennialism gone to seed.' According to this perversion
the Jew has no future whatever. We quote from a letter from a certain professor who has been fighting for many years the literal fulfillment of the
promises made to Israel, 'God is through with the Jews.' If this were true
we might just as well close our Bibles. And here is another one who
wants us to believe, to quote his words, 'that the Jews have no more place
in God's plan for the world than have the Japanese.' What a Bible- and
God-dishonoring assertion!"

70. "Will Britain's White Paper Keep the Jews out of Palestine?" *Our
Hope* 46 (September 1939): 179.

71. "Anti-Semitism in the U.S.A.," *Our Hope* 46 (February 1940):
543–44.

72. "Ghetto in Warsaw," *Our Hope* 47 (January 1941): 489. Compare
"The Poor Jews," *Our Hope* 46 (March 1940): 625; "Christian or Gentile?"
*Our Hope* 47 (December 1940): 413; "Armbands in Antwerp," *Our Hope*
47 (January 1941): 489; and "Anti-Semitic Tentacles Spread," *Our Hope*

47 (October 1940): 263. The following account and quote are from this last article.

73. "Jewish Problems," *Our Hope* 48 (June 1942): 839. Compare "Two Attitudes Toward the Jews in Britain," *Our Hope* 49 (September 1942): 192–93.

74. Arno C. Gaebelein, "The New Great World Crisis: XV," *Our Hope* 49 (October 1942): 240.

75. Refer to Arno C. Gaebelein, "The New Great World Crisis: XXIII," *Our Hope* 49 (June 1943): 815–16.

76. "Biggest Atrocity Story Breaks in Poland," *The Christian Century* 61 (September 13, 1944): 1045. The liberal Protestant editors rationalized: "There may or may not be a relation between the fact that the Lublin account came out immediately after it was charged by London Poles that the Russians had stopped their advance within artillery range of Warsaw and waited until the Germans had killed 250,000 Poles within the city who had risen to fight for their freedom in response to the call of the Polish government-in-exile."

77. Arno C. Gaebelein, "The New Great World Crisis: XXIV," *Our Hope* 50 (July 1943): 22.

78. "The Jewish Problem," *Our Hope* 50 (October 1943): 250.

79. "A Handful of Testimonials," *Our Hope,* 50 (November 1943): 324–30.

80. E. Schuyler English, "The Judgment of the Nations," *Our Hope* 51 (February 1945): 565. Note especially the "Editorial Note" on page 514. For the following quote, refer to "Zionist Demand to Atlee," *Our Hope* 52 (September 1945): 189.

81. "Better and Better?" *Our Hope* 51 (June 1945): 851.

## Chapter 5. The Cold War

1. See Robert J. Wells, ed., *Prophetic Messages for Modern Times* (Dallas, Tex.: Texas Printing House, n.d.). Each of the speakers mentioned was nationally known and traveled to conferences across the United States. Louis S. Bauman was pastor of First Brethren Church in Long Beach, California; Charles L. Feinberg was a professor at Dallas Theological Seminary in Dallas, Texas; Howard W. Ferrin was president of Providence Bible Institute in Providence, Rhode Island; Dan Gilbert was an evangelist, author, and journalist based in Washington, D.C.; Vance Havner was a Bible teacher and author from Greensboro, North Carolina; J. Palmer Muntz was director of the Winona Lake Bible Conference; W. H. Rogers was pastor of the First Baptist Church in El Paso,

Texas; and Robert J. Wells was the founder of Dallas Bible Institute in
Dallas, Texas.

2. Charles L. Feinberg, "The Right of the Jews to Palestine," in *Prophetic Messages*, 191.

3. Ibid., 198–99.

4. J. Palmer Muntz, "The Jew in History and Destiny," in *Prophetic Messages for Modern Times*, 47–48.

5. Ibid., 48.

6. Ibid., 48–49.

7. Ibid., 49.

8. Ibid., 50.

9. Louis S. Bauman, "World War Number Three," in *Prophetic Messages*, 173–74. Compare his previous lecture, "What Will Be the Outcome of the Present War?" 161–69.

10. "The Spirit of Hitler," *Moody Monthly* 44 (January 1944): 255.

11. "The Election," *Moody Monthly* 45 (November 1944): 121.

12. "Israel Becomes a Nation Again," *Our Hope* 55 (July 1948): 26–27. The editorial also stated: "Ten days later (as we write), it is evident that this small state has been launched in stormy waters. Regular military units of the Arab states are attacking on many sides, crying out: 'We are ready to die for Allah!' while well-equipped Jewish forces, called 'Haganah,' are defending their strongholds with steadfast zeal and this word on their lips: 'We are ready on every front.'" Of Russia, it continues: "The U.S.S.R. has recognized Israel as a sovereign state, thus performing another of her enigmatic operations—for on the one hand, Communist-controlled Czechoslovakia, through the firm of Skoda, has accepted orders from Syria for arms, totalling $24,000,000, while on the other, Russia is financing the Stern Gang in Palestine. In backing both sides the Kremlin, no doubt, expects to create chaos upon chaos."

13. "Have Jews a Jewish Citizenship?" *The Christian Century* 62 (January 3, 1945): 4–5.

14. Ibid., 5. The editorial concluded: "When a Jewish body asks that special representatives be seated, as Jews, in the councils of nations it is by implication maintaining that Jewry is a separate nationality, and that Jews should be treated, not as Americans or Englishmen or Frenchmen or Germans or Palestinians, but as something else—as persons with an allegiance which differs from that of all other citizens of their countries. Pointing this out may not be welcomed in certain Jewish quarters. But we believe that there are millions of thoughtful Jews who, when they ponder the implications of the Pittsburgh resolutions, will agree that a mistake has been made."

15. Note "Sources of Jewish Insecurity," *The Christian Century* 62 (January 17, 1945): 83. Compare "Jerusalem, Not Geneva" on pages 82–83,

which contains a letter from Vida D. Scudder of Wellesley, Massachusetts, and a rabbi's response to her idea of Palestine bearing the same
relation to the future United Nations which the District of Columbia
bears to the United States, and Jerusalem as the Geneva of the future
center of international control. Scudder began: "Queer things happen
during wakeful nights. Recently, my troubled thoughts were centered
on the distressful cleavages among idealistic Jews. Suddenly, an idea! I
had been a Zionist, I had withdrawn my allegiance; today with our growing consciousness of the perils of nationalism, the plan for another small
nation to be the prey of power politics had ceased to entice."

16. "Germany's Regeneration," *The Christian Century* 62 (June 13,
1945): 702. Compare the editorial, "Are the Arabs Ready for a Palestine
Compromise?" (March 28, 1945): 389, which stated: "With Arab readi-
ness to bargain thus established, it would be tragic if the Jews continued
to insist on an all-or-nothing solution."

17. "The Statement Should Be Read Again," *The Christian Century* 62
(June 27, 1945): 761. At this time, Charles Clayton Morrison was editor,
Paul Hutchinson was managing editor, Harold E. Fey was associate editor, and Winfred Ernest Garrison was literary editor of *The Christian Century*.

18. See "A Post-War Program for Jews," *The Christian Century* 61
(November 8, 1944): 1274-75. Compare "American Council Sets $300,000
Goal, Reports 11,000 Membership" in *The American Israelite* 92 (January
24, 1946): 1, where announcement of the second annual convention of
the American Council for Judaism is made, at which Lessing J. Rosenwald was reelected as president of the ACJ at this two-day (January
19-20) meeting. Some 130 delegates were present from various sections
of the country, and the Council announced that it had doubled its membership to 11,000.

19. Note Henry C. Segal, "'Neutrality' Resolution on Political Zionism Is Ratified Unanimously by UAHC Convention," *The American Israelite* 92 (March 7, 1946): 1.

20. "Significance of UAHC Vote," *The American Israelite* 92 (March 14,
1946): 4. A debate, however, had taken place in a Sunday evening "town
hall" session of the UAHC biennial council between two Zionists and
two anti-Zionists. All 2,200 seats in Emery Auditorium were filled, with
scores of listeners standing. Robert P. Goldman, Cincinnati UAHC past
president, was moderator. Monday morning the debate continued by
throwing it open to all delegates at the convention.

21. Morris S. Lazaron, "Palestine and the Jew: A Study of the Future
of the Holy Land and of Judaism," *The Christian Century* 64 (November
19, 1947): 1410-11. The entire Lazaron "Special Section" may be found
on pages 1401-22.

22. Ibid., 1413–15.

23. Ibid., 1414. The Christian friend of Morris Lazaron continued in his letter: "Rightly or wrongly, I think they believe that in a city like New York the Zionist reaction would be unbelievably nasty in expression and, if possible, would show itself in various forms of reprisal, including the economic. The result is, of course, what might be expected. There is a deep resentment, suppressed for the moment as a matter of individual discretion, but growing. Many Christians, from whose lips and in whose manner I have never detected the slightest indication of anti-Semitism, are today, very privately to be sure, expressing not merely anti-Zionist but anti-Jewish sentiments."

24. Ibid., 1422.

25. "U.N. Assembly Votes for Palestine Partition," *The Christian Century* 64 (December 10, 1947): 1509. The editorial began: "Palestine is to be divided, like Gaul, into three parts. There are to be a Jewish state, an Arab state and an international state." Although wishing the situation to have at least a week to clear up before commenting at length, the editors noted: "It can be said at once, however, that few more momentous decisions have been made in modern times." To *The Christian Century*'s liberal Protestant editors, the UN decision was definitely wrong. Compare the much longer editorial in the next issue, "The Partition Gamble," *The Christian Century* 64 (December 17, 1947): 1541–43. In the December 31, 1947, issue on page 1621, *The Christian Century* offered a 24-page reprint of the Lazaron article for 25 cents, insisting: "Discussion groups are forming all over the country. Why not start one among your friends? This handy pamphlet is excellent basic material." The only reader response quoted stated: "This magnificent article will long out-last the tragic mistake of the U.N. because it has stated a great truth in a classic form while the politicians have done a false thing in a weak manner."

26. Note "Lazaron on 'Palestine and the Jew,'" *The Christian Century* 64 (December 17, 1947): 1555. The entire section of letters (including those quoted in the text below) may be found on pages 1555–57.

27. "The Palestine Tragedy (Continued)," *The Christian Century* 65 (May 26, 1948): 500. Compare "Do the World's Jews Want to be Feared?" (June 16, 1948), where the editors quote Lessing Rosenwald's speech at the University of Virginia that Adolf Hitler is more responsible than anyone else for the ultranationalistic character of the present-day Zionist movement, and citing Rabbi Uri Miller's statement hailing the "heroic underground fighter." This *Christian Century* editorial ended: "It is not difficult to understand this shout of joy at Jewish 'toughness' after what so many Jews suffered from nazi toughness. But how long will Judaism, with its message of peace, continue to find satisfaction in believing that Israel is feared?"

28. Note "Letters from Our Readers," *The American Israelite* 92 (August 9, 1945): 6. Compare Alfred Segal, "More About $2," *The American Israelite* 92 (July 12, 1945): 1.

29. Carl Hermann Voss, "The American Christian Palestine Committee," in *Essays in American Zionism, 1917–1948*, ed. Melvin I. Urofsky, *Herzl Year Book*, vol. 8 (1978), 261–62. Compare "Hadassah Announces Gain of 100 Members; Will Aid JNF Collection," *The American Israelite* 94 (October 16, 1947): 4, where Carl Hermann Voss, "executive chairman of the American Christian Committee for Palestine," is listed as one of the speakers at Hadassah's 33rd annual convention, to be held in Atlantic City on October 24–28. The beloved Mayor Teddy Kollek of Jerusalem told Dr. David Rausch in 1988 about Dr. Carl Hermann Voss and his work: "What I can say about Carl Voss is that he was here with us at the beginning."

30. Alfred Segal, "I Am Unsaved," *The American Israelite* 95 (November 3, 1949). The following quotations are from this column, found on pages 1 and 9.

31. Alfred Segal, "Jesus and Jews," *The American Israelite* 92 (April 25, 1946): 4. This "Plain Talk" column began on page 1.

32. Alfred Segal, "Christmas and Jews," *The American Israelite* 95 (November 24, 1949): 8. Segal continued, "We spend hundreds of thousands of dollars annually to make ourselves better understood to the world. Anti-Defamation League, American Jewish Committee, Jewish Congress . . ." He believed gestures like this would foster better Jewish-Christian relations. This column of "Plain Talk" began on page 1.

33. John C. Bennett, "Evangelism," *Christianity and Crisis* 7 (February 3, 1947): 1.

34. Ibid., 1–2.

35. "America for Christ!" *The Christian Century* 66 (October 19, 1949): 1222.

36. Ibid., 1223.

37. Note Francis J. Bloodgood, "Palestine's Christian Remnant," *The Christian Century* 66 (October 19, 1949): 1226–28. "And what is the general situation in Israel now?" Bloodgood wrote. "The Zionists are exclusive; the Arabs are bitter; the Christians, humanly speaking, are helpless in the midst of a new state which shows small concern at what happens to them" (p. 1227). He charged the Israelis with threatening religious liberty.

On attitudes toward Billy Graham, refer to Cecil Northcott, "Billy Graham in Britain," *The Christian Century* 71 (June 2, 1954): 669–70; the editorial, "Why Not Export Billy Graham?" *The Christian Century* 66 (March 24, 1954): 356–57; "Special Reports I & II: Billy Graham in New York," *Christianity and Crisis* 17: 71–72, 119–20.

On Carl McIntire's American Council of Christian Churches, see the *Christian Century* editorials "Legion Misled by Fundamentalists," 71 (March 24, 1954): 356; "Threaten Baptist Student Leaders," 71 (March 31, 1954): pp. 388–89; "Baptist Fat in North Carolina Fire," 71 (April 21, 1954): 484; "Discord's Apostle Hard at Work," 71 (April 28, 1954): 507–8; and "Blueprint for Discord," 71 (June 30, 1954): 782–83. The liberal Protestant journal recognized that there was a difference between "fundamentalists." The latter editorial, for example, stated: "Responsible fundamentalists are having no part in this attempt to smear and cripple the World Council. Such a body, for example, as the National Association of Evangelicals does not support the World Council, and sometimes expresses fears that it may be headed toward formation of a 'superchurch.' But it will have no part in the McIntire assault—and consequently is violently attacked by McIntire. The Southern Baptists, conservative ministers such as Harold J. Ockenga, Paul S. Rees and J. Elwin Wright, such a conservative but ecumenically minded evangelist as Billy Graham—all will have nothing to do with the McIntire hate campaigns, and as a result are subjected to the same vituperation. Without any backing in responsible fundamentalist quarters, how does McIntire hope to fool the American people into a belief that the Evanston assembly is a communist-run affair?" Compare earlier *Christian Century* editorials "The Baptist Dilemma," 61 (July 5, 1944): 798–800; "Sister Aimee," 61 (October 11, 1944): 1159–60; "Churches in the Postwar World," 64 (March 26, 1947): 391–93; "Confusion in the Colleges," 64 (June 18, 1947): 762–64 [note especially 763]; and "Fundamentalists Fly to Bangkok," 66 (November 30, 1949): 1412 (on McIntire's other group, International Council of Christian Churches).

In its editorial "Disciples Set an Example," *The Christian Century* 63 (September 18, 1946) emphasized that "all, or nearly all, of the major Protestant denominations are deeply disturbed by theological tensions." Defining fundamentalism in this postwar world, the editors wrote: "It is among Presbyterians, Baptists and Disciples [of Christ] that the strain occasioned by the emergence of the new knowledge of the Bible, the mandatory obligation of the social gospel and the new consciousness of ecumenical Christianity is most pronounced. In these three bodies reversionary movements have assumed organized and militant forms. This reversion goes generally by the name of fundamentalism. It distinguishes itself from conservative orthodoxy by its militancy. The late Curtis Lee Laws, Baptist editor, who coined the word, said it meant 'militant orthodoxy.' The adjective is of the essence. It is orthodoxy or conservatism aggressively organized to capture the leadership of the denomination from a leadership which, it alleges, is reorienting the denomination sympathetically toward the modern knowledge of the Bible, toward the social gospel and toward ecumenical Christianity—in a word, toward what it calls 'liberalism'" (pp. 1109–10). "The spirit of cooperation is foreign to fundamentalism," the editorial added.

38. Note "Dr. Poling Answers Your Questions," *Christian Herald* 70 (October 1947): 4. Compare Poling's columns in the July 1947 issue (p. 4) and the June 1948 issue (p. 5). In this latter issue, Poling expounds: "CHRISTIAN HERALD is inter-denominational and undenominational. Its managing editor is a Methodist, its publisher a Presbyterian. Practically every Protestant Evangelical denomination is represented on its roster, and all races and colors as well."

39. See Joyce Van Patten and Richard Tyler, "Children's Memorial Forest in Palestine," *Christian Herald* 70 (August 1947): 32.

40. Gabriel Courier, ed., "Palestine," *Christian Herald* 67 (May 1944): p. 7.

41. Gabriel Courier, ed., "League," *Christian Herald* 69 (January 1946): 8–9.

42. Gabriel Courier, ed., "Palestine," *Christian Herald* 69 (April 1946): 9.

43. Gabriel Courier, ed., "Palestine," *Christian Herald* 69 (August 1946): 8.

44. Gabriel Courier, ed., "Without Hamlet," *Christian Herald* 69 (November 1946): 10.

45. "Gabriel Courier Interprets the News," *Christian Herald* 71 (November 1948): 13.

46. Note "Furtive Crescent" in "Gabriel Courier Interprets the News," *Christian Herald* 81 (April 1958): 11. Compare "Lebanon" in his July 1958 column (p. 14), and the excerpt "Scopus" in the same column which explains the "tension point" between Israel and Jordan over the Mount Scopus "enclave" and the intervention of the Israel-Jordan Armistice Commission of the United Nations.

47. Gabriel Courier, ed., "Good Man!" *Christian Herald* 67 (November 1944): 10.

48. "Doctor Poling Answers," *Christian Herald* 67 (June 1944): 4.

49. "Doctor Poling Answers," *Christian Herald* 69 (December 1946): 4.

50. "Doctor Poling Answers," *Christian Herald* 69 (November 1946): 4.

51. The following quotes and account are taken from a series of taped interviews with Dr. G. Douglas Young by David A. Rausch. The interviews were conducted in Israel in March 1979, one year before Dr. Young's unexpected death by heart attack. Compare Calvin B. Hanson's *A Gentile, with the Heart of a Jew: G. Douglas Young* (Nyack, N.Y.: Parson Publishing, 1979).

52. Freda Keet was speaking at a banquet in Chicago, and her words are transcribed from a tape of that session. Two years earlier, at the time

of the raid on Entebbe and the successful rescue of the passengers of the hijacked Air France plane, Keet was on writing assignment in London. The news of the daring Israeli mission brought forth a flood of emotion and relief built up during a tense week. Freda's London hosts insisted that she call Israel and share her joy with her family. To their surprise, the "family" she called was Dr. G. Douglas Young and his wife, not her Jewish relatives. It was with this Christian couple that she first shared the triumph, the exhilaration, and the relief all of them felt.

53. In 1979, when the host of a Minneapolis television program, "The Henry Wolf Show," asked Dr. G. Douglas Young, "When do you expect to go back to Jerusalem?" Dr. Young's immediate response was, "I'll be home on the second of November." See tape of television interview, September 16, 1979.

54. This article appeared in a special supplement to the *Jerusalem Post* (December 24, 1969). Some of his letters to the editor of the *Jerusalem Post* include the following: "Al Aksa—A Christian Accuses the Churches" (August 27, 1969); "Fulbright and M.E. Realities" (December 11, 1973, Overseas Edition); "Murdering of Jews" (May 17, 1974); "Misconceptions About the Refugee Problem" (September 22, 1970); "The Church and Terror" (January 21, 1973); "Arab Riots" (June 9, 1976).

55. G. Douglas Young, "A Christian View of Israel," speech at Cornell University, November 2, 1975.

56. Letter from Russell T. Hitt to Rabbi Marc H. Tanenbaum, November 23, 1963. Hitt wrote: "I hope our paths cross again soon and often."

57. Letter from Russell T. Hitt to Rabbi Marc H. Tanenbaum, March 9, 1966. Hitt noted: "Also I want you to know it would be a great privilege to bring our families together. We both are busy but we'll fit in with your plans in New York. I'd love to entertain you and your wife in our home in Merion. No doubt AJC business brings you this way often."

58. "Dialogue, Love and Witness," *Eternity* 18 (August 1967): 6–7.

59. G. Douglas Young, "Lessons We Can Learn from Judaism," *Eternity* 18 (August 1967): 6–7.

60. Belden Menkus, "Our Subtle Anti-Semitism," *Eternity* 18 (August 1967): 23–24. Menkus tried to alert evangelicals to differences between Orthodox, Conservative, and Reform Jews.

61. Note the hundred pages of edited conversations with Frank E. Gaebelein in David A. Rausch, *Arno C. Gaebelein, 1861–1945* (Lewiston, N.Y.: Edwin Mellen Press, 1983). Frank E. Gaebelein's letter appeared in the October 1967 issue of *Eternity*, on page 4.

62. Note Raymond Cox, "Eyewitness: Israel," *Eternity* 18 (July 1967): 6–8.

63. William Sanfor LaSor, "Have the 'Times of the Gentiles' Been Fulfilled?" *Eternity* 18 (August 1967): 32. Compare the editorial "Pro-

phetic Overtones in the Middle East," pages 6 and 7 in the same issue.

64. Ibid., 34.

65. John F. Walvoord, "The Amazing Rise of Israel!" *Moody Monthly* 68 (October 1967): 22–25.

66. Ibid. See Richard Wolff's article on pages 24–25. It is actually inserted as a lower sidebar to Walvoord's article noted above. Hal Lindsey's article is found on pages 26–28.

67. For an analysis of this phenomenon, refer to Carl Hermann Voss and David A. Rausch, "American Christians and Israel, 1948–1988," *American Jewish Archives* 40 (April 1988): 41–81.

68. Note "Mideast: Weighing the Effects," *Christianity Today* 11 (July 7, 1967): 31. Compare "Middle East Crisis: A Biblical Backdrop," *Christianity Today* 11 (June 9, 1967): 38–40; and "Jews in Old Jerusalem!—A Historic Re-Entry," *Christianity Today* 11 (June 23, 1967): 37–38. On the magazine's history and turmoil, see Carl F. H. Henry, *Confessions of a Theologian: An Autobiography* (Waco, Tex.: Word Books, 1986).

69 Rev. James L. Kelso's "interpretive appraisal of the Arab-Jewish conflict" follows the special news report of Dr. Dwight L. Baker, "Jerusalem: A Third Temple?" *Christianity Today* 11 (July 21, 1967): 34. The quotation from Kelso is on page 35.

70. Ibid., 35–36.

71. Refer to "Letters to the Editor," *Christianity Today* 11 (August 18, 1967): 24. Benad Avital's letter appears in the September 29, 1967, issue on pages 18–19.

72. See "Perspectives on Arab-Israeli Tensions," *Christianity Today* 12 (June 7, 1968): 6–8.

73. *Christianity Today* even reports these views. Note its editorial "Casting Lots for Jerusalem," 11 (August 18, 1967): 29–30.

74. Note Reinhold Niebuhr's "David and Goliath," *Christianity and Crisis* 27 (June 26, 1967): 141–42. For one of Niebuhr's early notes correcting an anti-Zionist article, see Reinhold Niebuhr, "Editor's Note," *Christianity and Crisis* 8 (March 15, 1948): 30. In this note he attempts to neutralize comments given by Bayard Dodge, president of Beirut University, in his article "Peace or War in Palestine." Niebuhr's three-paragraph editorial note followed Dodge's article.

75. All of the material quoted here and below on *His Land* is from a tape of the television presentation. I have viewed the film several times in a variety of settings: in a synagogue, in a church, and on college campuses.

76. Bert De Vries, "'His Land' and History," *The Reformed Journal* 21 (April 1971): 10–11.

77. Bert De Vries, "*His Land* and Prophecy," *The Reformed Journal* 21 (November 1971): 13.

78. Bert De Vries, ''The Palestinian Issue,'' *The Reformed Journal* 25 (January 1975): 4.

79. Ronald Wells, ''More About the Palestinians,'' *The Reformed Journal* 25 (March 1975): 7.

80. Taped interview, March 1979.

81. Refer to David A. Rausch, *Communities in Conflict: Evangelicals and Jews* (Philadelphia: Trinity Press International, 1991) for information on this broader evangelical movement. Note especially chapter 5, ''Political Agendas,'' pp. 141–170.

# INDEX

WITHDRAWN

WITHDRAWN